FIVE
VIEWS
OF

CHRIST IN THE
OLD TESTAMENT

T0308509

Books in the Counterpoints Series

Church Life

Bible and Theology

FIVE VIEWS OF CHRIST IN THE OLD TESTAMENT

GENRE, AUTHORIAL INTENT, AND THE NATURE OF SCRIPTURE

John Goldingay

Tremper Longman III

Havilah Dharamraj

Jason S. DeRouchie

Craig A. Carter

Brian J. Tabb and Andrew M. King, general editors
Stanley N. Gundry, series editor

COUNTERPOINTS
▶ BIBLE & THEOLOGY ◀

ZONDERVAN
ACADEMIC

ZONDERVAN ACADEMIC

Five Views of Christ in the Old Testament
Copyright © 2022 by Brian J. Tabb, Andrew M. King, John Goldingay, Tremper Longman III, Jason S. DeRouchie, Havilah Dharamraj, and Craig A. Carter

Requests for information should be addressed to:
Zondervan, *3900 Sparks Dr. SE, Grand Rapids, Michigan 49546*

Zondervan titles may be purchased in bulk for educational, business, fundraising, or sales promotional use. For information, please email SpecialMarkets@Zondervan.com.

ISBN 978-0-310-12553-2 (audio)

Library of Congress Cataloging-in-Publication Data

Names: Goldingay, John, author. | Tabb, Brian J., editor.
Title: Five views of Christ in the Old Testament : genre, authorial intent, and the nature of Scripture / John Goldingay, Tremper Longman III, Havilah Dharamraj, Jason S. DeRouchie, Craig A. Carter ; Brian J. Tabb, Andrew M. King, general editors.
Other titles: 5 views of Christ in the Old Textament | Counterpoints. Bible and theology.
Description: Grand Rapids, Michigan : Zondervan Academic, 2022. | Series: Counterpoints: Bible and theology | Includes bibliographical references and index.
Identifiers: LCCN 2022009711 (print) | LCCN 2022009712 (ebook) | ISBN 9780310125518 (paperback) | ISBN 9780310125525 (ebook)
Subjects: LCSH: Typology (Theology) | Jesus Christ--Biblical teaching. | Bible. Old Testament--Criticism, interpretation, etc. | BISAC: RELIGION / Biblical Criticism & Interpretation / Old Testament | RELIGION / Biblical Studies / Old Testament / General
Classification: LCC BT225 .F58 2022 (print) | LCC BT225 (ebook) | DDC 220.6/4--dc23/eng/20220512
LC record available at https://lccn.loc.gov/2022009711
LC ebook record available at https://lccn.loc.gov/2022009712

Cover design: Tammy Johnson; Cover photo: ©Masterfile; Interior typesetting: Kait Lamphere

Printed in the United States of America

22 23 24 25 26 27 28 29 30 31 32 /TRM/ 15 14 13 12 11 10 9 8 7 6 5 4 3 2 1

CONTENTS

ABOUT THE EDITORS AND CONTRIBUTORS ▮▮▮▮▮

Editors

Brian J. Tabb (PhD, London School of Theology) is academic dean and professor of biblical studies at Bethlehem College & Seminary in Minneapolis, Minnesota, and general editor of *Themelios*.

Andrew M. King (PhD, The Southern Baptist Theological Seminary) is assistant professor of biblical studies at Midwestern Seminary and Spurgeon College in Kansas City, Missouri.

Contributors

John Goldingay (PhD, University of Nottingham; DD, Archbishop of Canterbury at Lambeth) is senior professor of Old Testament and David Allan Hubbard Professor Emeritus of Old Testament at Fuller Theological Seminary in Pasadena, California.

Tremper Longman III (PhD, Yale University) is the distinguished scholar and professor emeritus of biblical studies at Westmont College in Santa Barbara, California.

Havilah Dharamraj (PhD, University of Durham) is head of the department of biblical studies at South Asia Institute of Advanced Christian Studies in Bangalore, India.

Jason S. DeRouchie (PhD, The Southern Baptist Theological Seminary) is research professor of Old Testament and biblical theology at Midwestern Seminary and Spurgeon College in Kansas City, Missouri.

Craig A. Carter (PhD, University of St. Michael's College) is research professor of theology at Tyndale University and theologian in residence at Westney Heights Baptist Church in Ajax, Ontario.

ABBREVIATIONS

AB	Anchor Bible
ACCSOT	Ancient Christian Commentary on Scripture, Old Testament
ANET	James B. Pritchard, *Ancient Near Eastern Texts Relating to the Old Testament*. Princeton, NJ: Princeton University Press, 1955
BAR	*Biblical Archaeology Review*
BCOTWP	Baker Commentary on the Old Testament Wisdom and Psalms
BECNT	Baker Exegetical Commentary on the New Testament
BibInt	*Biblical Interpretation*
BibInt	Biblical Interpretation Series
BSac	*Bibliotheca Sacra*
CP	*Classical Philology*
EBC	Expositor's Bible Commentary
Gk.	Greek
HBT	*Horizons in Biblical Theology*
Heb.	Hebrew
ICC	International Critical Commentary
JBL	*Journal of Biblical Literature*
JETS	*Journal of the Evangelical Theological Society*
JSNT	*Journal for the Study of the New Testament*
JSOT	*Journal for the Study of the Old Testament*
JSSEA	*Journal of the Society for the Study of Egyptian Antiquities*
LHBOTS	The Library of Hebrew Bible/Old Testament Studies
NICNT	New International Commentary on the New Testament
NICOT	New International Commentary on the Old Testament
NovT	*Novum Testamentum*
NTS	*New Testament Studies*
OTL	Old Testament Library
PNTC	Pillar New Testament Commentary
SBJT	*Southern Baptist Journal of Theology*
StBibLit	Studies in Biblical Literature

STI	Studies in Theological Interpretation
Them	*Themelios*
TJ	*Trinity Journal*
TNTC	Tyndale New Testament Commentaries
TOTC	Tyndale Old Testament Commentaries
TSAJ	Texte und Studien zum antiken Judentum
TynBul	*Tyndale Bulletin*
VT	*Vetus Testamentum*
VTSup	Supplements to Vetus Testamentum
WBC	Word Biblical Commentary
WTJ	*Westminster Theological Journal*
ZIBBCOT	Zondervan Illustrated Bible Backgrounds Commentary: Old Testament

INTRODUCTION

BRIAN J. TABB AND ANDREW M. KING

O n the Emmaus road, the risen Lord "beginning with Moses and all the Prophets . . . explained to them what was said in all the Scriptures concerning himself" (Luke 24:27). He opened the Scriptures and also opened the disciples' minds to grasp what was written about him (vv. 31–32, 45). This famous scene moves us to reverent wonder and also prompts hermeneutical and biblical-theological questions: Why were the disciples "slow to believe" what the prophets had said (v. 25)? Should faithful Israelites in the centuries before Christ have grasped that these ancient texts spoke in some way about the Messiah? In what sense did Christ "fulfill" what is written in the Scriptures?

Early Christian preachers followed their Lord's example by arguing from the Scriptures that "the Messiah had to suffer and rise from the dead" (Acts 17:3). Peter proclaimed Christ's resurrection and enthronement from Psalms 16 and 110 (Acts 2:25–35), Philip shared the good news of Jesus's suffering and death from Isaiah 53 (Acts 8:30–35), and Paul explained that he testified only to "what the prophets and Moses said would happen" (Acts 26:22). Klyne Snodgrass writes, "At every point early Christians attempted to understand their Scriptures in the new light of the ministry, death, and resurrection of Jesus Christ. They used the Old Testament to prove their Christian theology and to solve Christian problems. The Old Testament provided the substructure of the New Testament theology."[1]

---

1. Klyne Snodgrass, "The Use of the Old Testament in the New," in *The Right Doctrine from the Wrong Texts? Essays on the Use of the Old Testament in the New*, ed. G. K. Beale (Grand Rapids: Baker Academic, 1994), 29. The last line of this quotation alludes to the subtitle of C. H. Dodd's seminal study *According to the Scriptures: The Sub-Structure of New Testament Theology* (London: Nisbet, 1952).

Does Every Road Lead to Christ?

If the apostles read the Old Testament Scriptures in light of Christ, we may ask whether Christians today should follow their example. Some scholars are hesitant, citing the apostles' unique revelatory stance and hermeneutical context. The apostles' methods were steeped in Jewish exegetical practices that were appropriate to contextualize the gospel for their first-century audience but not for contemporary readers. Thus, Richard Longenecker contends that "unless we are 'restorationists' in our attitude toward hermeneutics, Christians today are committed to the apostolic faith and doctrine of the NT, but not necessarily to the apostolic exegetical practices as detailed for us in the NT."[2] Others insist that we should follow not only the apostles' doctrinal conclusions but also their hermeneutical and theological presuppositions about the unity of the Scriptures and the centrality of Christ in redemptive history. G. K. Beale, for instance, explains that while we cannot replicate the biblical authors' "inspired *certainty*," their interpretive practices (such as typology) remain "viable . . . for all saints to employ today."[3]

The famed Baptist preacher C. H. Spurgeon once remarked that as every English town and village has a road going to London, "so from every text in Scripture, there is a road to the metropolis of the Scriptures, that is Christ." He added, "I have never yet found a text that had not got a road to Christ in it, and if I ever do find one that has not a road to Christ in it, I will make one."[4] Many pastors and scholars concur that every Old Testament passage relates ultimately in some way to the gospel of Jesus Christ.[5] Others would say, "Not so fast," citing what they believe are examples of creative yet forced attempts to find Christ in the Old Testament, such as Justin's claim that Rahab's scarlet

---

2. Richard N. Longenecker, "'Who Is the Prophet Talking About?' Some Reflections on the New Testament's Use of the Old," *Them* 13 (1987): 8.

3. G. K. Beale, *Handbook on the New Testament Use of the Old Testament: Exegesis and Interpretation* (Grand Rapids: Baker Academic, 2012), 25, emphasis original.

4. C. H. Spurgeon, "Christ Precious to Believers," in *The New Park Street Pulpit Sermons* (London: Passmore & Alabaster, 1859), 5:140 (sermon 242).

5. See the nuanced treatments by G. K. Beale, "Finding Christ in the Old Testament," *JETS* 63 (2020): 25–50; Graeme Goldsworthy, *Preaching the Whole Bible as Christian Scripture: The Application of Biblical Theology to Expository Preaching* (Grand Rapids: Eerdmans, 2000).

thread signifies Jesus's blood[6] or various allegorical readings of the Song of Songs from Hippolytus to Bernard.[7]

How should Christians today understand the relationship of the Old Testament to Christ? Some studies of "Christ in the Old Testament" adopt a forward-looking approach to the development of messianic expectation within the Law, Prophets, and Writings. Along these lines, you may examine the thirty-nine uses of the Hebrew word *meshiah* ("anointed" or "anointed one") in the Old Testament with particular focus on texts such as Psalm 2:2 (the earth's kings rise up "against the Lord and against his anointed") and the enigmatic reference to "the Anointed One" in Daniel 9:25–26. For example, Andrew Abernethy and Greg Goswell thoroughly explore the Old Testament hopes of a coming king to carry out God's kingdom purposes, considering various texts that prefigure, predict, or depict a royal messianic figure.[8]

Scholars also examine the historical development of Jewish messianic expectation during the Second Temple period. For example, Joseph Fitzmyer detects few traces of messianism in the Old Testament Scriptures but explores the widespread and diverse messianic hopes among Jews during the Second Temple period.[9] Well-known examples include the Dead Sea Scrolls' discussion of the coming "prophet . . . and the Messiahs of Aaron and Israel" (1QS 9:11), and Psalms of Solomon 17:21–18:9, which speaks of "the Lord's Messiah," the Davidic Son who will one day rule righteously over Israel and destroy their enemies, drawing on Old Testament texts like Psalm 2 and Isaiah 11.[10]

Others adopt a backward-looking approach to "Christ in the Old Testament," examining the Old Testament in light of the New Testament's testimony about "Jesus the Messiah the son of David, the

6. Justin Martyr, *Dialogue with Trypho* 111.

7. See the overview by Tremper Longman III, *Song of Songs*, NICOT (Grand Rapids: Eerdmans, 2001), 28–35. Also see Mitchell L. Chase, *40 Questions about Typology and Allegory* (Grand Rapids: Kregel, 2020), 207–45.

8. Andrew T. Abernethy and Gregory Goswell, *God's Messiah in the Old Testament: Expectations of a Coming King* (Grand Rapids: Baker Academic, 2020), 1.

9. Joseph A. Fitzmyer, *The One Who Is to Come* (Grand Rapids: Eerdmans, 2007), 82–133. See also John J. Collins, *The Scepter and the Star: Messianism in Light of the Dead Sea Scrolls*, 2nd ed. (Grand Rapids: Eerdmans, 2010).

10. Translations of the Dead Sea Scrolls come from Florentino Garcia Martinez and Eibert J. C. Tigchelaar, eds., *The Dead Sea Scrolls Study Edition* (Grand Rapids: Eerdmans, 2000). Translations of the Pseudepigrapha follow James H. Charlesworth, ed., *The Old Testament Pseudepigrapha*, 2 vols. (Garden City, NY: Doubleday, 1983, 1985).

son of Abraham" (Matt 1:1). For example, Richard Hays explains that the evangelists "reread" the Scriptures following Christ's resurrection and proposes, "We learn to read the OT by reading backwards from the Gospels, and—at the same time—we learn how to read the Gospels by reading forwards from the OT."[11]

Key Questions for the Debate

With these differing approaches to the question, how should Christians today read the Old Testament in light of Christ? This book, *Five Views on Christ in the Old Testament*, takes as a given that Jesus Christ is, in some sense, the one who fulfills the Old Testament Scriptures. What this means in practice, however, is what this book is all about. The contributors and editors are Christian biblical scholars and theologians from North America, the United Kingdom, and India who write for Christian readers. They wrestle with a number of hermeneutical and biblical-theological questions, such as the following:

- How do you understand the nature, unity, and progression of the Scriptures, and what role does the New Testament play in your interpretation of Old Testament texts?
- What is the relationship between the intentions of the human authors and editors of the Old Testament and the divine author?
- What criteria are necessary for identifying connections to Christ in the Old Testament?
- What specific steps should Christian readers take to responsibly study the Old Testament in light of Christ?
- How does your approach to Christ in the Old Testament benefit readers?

Each of these questions uncovers the presuppositions and methodology of the contributors and provides crucial context for the interpretive moves that follow. To help readers see the similarities and differences of these views on Christ in the Old Testament, the contributors engage the same three case studies: Genesis 22, Proverbs 8, and Isaiah 42—one

---

11. Richard B. Hays, *Reading Backwards: Figural Christology and the Fourfold Gospel Witness* (Waco, TX: Baylor University Press, 2014), x, 4.

text from each of the major divisions of the Hebrew canon. Readers are invited to evaluate the strength and consistency of each view on its own terms. Does this approach make best sense of each passage? Does it "work" for texts in different genres? Does it help us put the two Testaments together as Christian Scripture? The responses from other contributors will draw out some of these questions. Our hope is that readers will be able to apply the method they find most compelling to their own reading of the Old Testament.

Introducing the Five Views

The first contributor, John Goldingay, is senior professor of Old Testament and David Allan Hubbard professor emeritus of Old Testament at Fuller Theological Seminary. He is author of numerous commentaries and books, including *Do We Need the New Testament? Letting the Old Testament Speak for Itself*.[12] In his "First Testament Priority Approach," Goldingay urges readers to take seriously the First Testament (his preferred term for the Old Testament) on its own terms rather than immediately looking for the nearest road to Christ. He provocatively asserts, "The prophets were not telling the ancestors about Jesus" (28). It is essential to distinguish the Scriptures' meaning—what the biblical authors sought to communicate to the original hearers—from the Scriptures' significance or application, which may or may not be connected to the authors' original message. So the New Testament does not determine or alter the meaning of the First Testament or offer its "fuller sense," although it may influence the ancient text's significance for us.

Next, Tremper Longman III presents a "Christotelic Approach" to Christ in the Old Testament. Longman is the distinguished scholar and professor emeritus of biblical studies at Westmont College. He has authored or edited numerous books, including *An Introduction to the Old Testament* (with Raymond Dillard).[13] Longman acknowledges that Old

---

12. See, for example, John E. Goldingay, *Do We Need the New Testament? Letting the Old Testament Speak for Itself* (Downers Grove, IL: InterVarsity Press, 2015); *Genesis*, Baker Commentary on the Old Testament Pentateuch (Grand Rapids: Baker Academic, 2020).

13. See, for example, Tremper Longman III and Raymond B. Dillard, *An Introduction to the Old Testament* (Grand Rapids: Zondervan, 1994); Tremper Longman III, *Psalms: An Introduction and Commentary*, TOTC 15–16 (Downers Grove, IL: InterVarsity Press, 2014).

Testament authors would have been surprised by how their writings prepare for the suffering and resurrection of Christ, who is revealed as the goal (*telos*) of the Scriptures. Christian interpreters must "read an Old Testament text twice" to properly grasp an Old Testament passage's "discrete voice" in its original context as well as the ancient text's fuller meaning in light of Christ's coming (74).

Third, Havilah Dharamraj adopts a "Reception-Centered, Intertextual Approach" to Christ in the Old Testament. Dharamraj is head of the department of biblical studies at South Asia Institute of Advanced Christian Studies in Bangalore, India. Among other books, she is the author of an intertextual study of the Song of Songs and a commentary on Ruth.[14] While other contributors emphasize the intention of biblical authors, Dharamraj offers a "reception-centered, intertextual method" that focuses on the effect of texts on readers (128–29). She begins by proposing a "Common Reader," who is familiar with the Old Testament and seeks to connect it with Christ. This Common Reader is acquainted with the Bible's "public meaning"—associations developed through sermons, songs, church liturgy, the arts, and more—and he or she reads an Old Testament text with "christological resonance," identifies the text's dominant theme or "icon," and puts this text in conversation with another text that features the same icon (132). By studying both intertexts in their historical context and attending to their literary and theological resonances, readers may make christological sense of the Old Testament.

Jason S. DeRouchie, research professor of Old Testament and biblical theology at Midwestern Seminary and Spurgeon College, is the book's fourth contributor. DeRouchie is the author or editor of many books, including *What the Old Testament Authors Really Cared About: A Survey of Jesus' Bible*.[15] In his "Redemptive-Historical, Christocentric Approach," DeRouchie asserts, "Christ Jesus stands as both the climax and center of God's saving purposes" (182). He explains that readers should attend

---

14. Havilah Dharamraj, *Altogether Lovely: A Thematic and Intertextual Reading of the Song of Songs* (Minneapolis: Fortress, 2018); *Ruth*, Asia Bible Commentary (Cumbria, UK: Langham Global Library, 2019).

15. See, for example, Jason S. DeRouchie, ed., *What the Old Testament Authors Really Cared About: A Survey of Jesus' Bible* (Grand Rapids: Kregel, 2013); *How to Understand and Apply the Old Testament: Twelve Steps from Exegesis to Theology* (Phillipsburg, NJ: P&R, 2017).

to an Old Testament passage's literary and biblical-theological context to discern God's intended meaning of the text. DeRouchie proposes seven principles for reading the Old Testament "through Christ and for Christ": (1) messianic predictions, (2) the salvation-historical story line, (3) similarities and differences between the old and new covenants, (4) typology, (5) Yahweh's identity and activity, (6) ethical standards, and (7) the law's guidance in a life of love.

The final contributor is Craig A. Carter, who is research professor of theology at Tyndale University and theologian in residence at Westney Heights Baptist Church in Ajax, Ontario. Carter's many publications include *Interpreting Scripture with the Great Tradition* and *Contemplating God with the Great Tradition*.[16] Carter advocates a "Premodern Approach" to Christ in the Old Testament, which is more of a "spiritual discipline" than a singular "method" (242). This approach employs various interpretive techniques to discern and rightly respond to God's message in the Scriptures, including messianic prophecy, typology, allegory, prosopological exegesis, and other theological readings common throughout church history. Carter sharply criticizes the methods and results of historical criticism and sets forth four principles to guide Christian readers of the Old Testament: (1) the unity of the Scriptures; (2) the priority of the text's literal sense; (3) the reality of the text's spiritual sense; and (4) the christological control on the text's meaning, which "enables a coherent system of doctrine to emerge from exegesis" (255). Carter insists that "the true interpretation of Scripture depends on recognizing it as a unified book centered on Jesus Christ" (265).

The views of Goldingay, Longman, Dharamraj, DeRouchie, and Carter are representative but by no means exhaustive of Christian approaches to the relationship of Christ to the Old Testament Scriptures. The contributors in their main chapters and counterpoint responses debate theological, hermeneutical, and exegetical principles, as well as their specific application to Genesis 22, Proverbs 8, and Isaiah 42. Do these texts directly predict or typologically anticipate Christ's coming as the greater son of Abraham, incarnate Wisdom, and Yahweh's chosen servant? Or do such claims go beyond what is written and obscure God's

---

16. Craig A. Carter, *Interpreting Scripture with the Great Tradition: Recovering the Genius of Premodern Exegesis* (Grand Rapids: Baker Academic, 2018); *Contemplating God with the Great Tradition: Recovering Trinitarian Classical Theism* (Grand Rapids: Baker Academic, 2021).

rich message to our ancestors through the prophets? Readers must weigh the authors' arguments and search the Scriptures for themselves. Our hope is that this volume will better equip readers to read all Scripture more faithfully for the upbuilding of the church.

Now, to the teaching and the testimony . . .

FIRST TESTAMENT APPROACH

JOHN GOLDINGAY

Introduction to the Approach

In the New Testament, the works we call "the Old Testament" are simply "the Scriptures." The rather sad title "Old Testament" was devised later. I like to call these writings the First Testament rather than imply that they are old, antiquated, and out-of-date. These Scriptures issued from the real relationship between God and Israel, as testimony to God's acts with Israel and documentation of his speaking to Israel. The New Testament encourages us to let these Scriptures illumine Jesus for us, but my argument in this chapter is that we are unwise to read Jesus back into them and thus miss what they have to say. On the other hand, we are wise to read the New Testament in light of them and to read the two Testaments in light of each other, as both comprise the Christian Scriptures.[1]

God has always been Father, Son, and Holy Spirit; and Father, Son, and Holy Spirit were all involved in God's relationship with Israel. But it was only through the incarnation and through Pentecost that this threefold aspect to God emerged, as it became actual in people's lives. Whenever the First Testament refers to God, one may assume that

---

1. I presuppose here arguments and convictions developed in John Goldingay, *Do We Need the New Testament? Letting the Old Testament Speak for Itself* (Downers Grove, IL: InterVarsity Press, 2015); and Goldingay, *Biblical Theology: The God of the Christian Scriptures* (Downers Grove, IL: InterVarsity Press, 2016).

Father and Son are included and that the Holy Spirit was also engaged in inspiring these references. But God's speaking in the First Testament did not make Christ part of the content of the communication. Christ is everywhere in the First Testament story, involved in the events, but he is not "in the First Testament" as someone whom the text mentions. Its message to God's people does not invite them to think in terms of him. It simply invites them to relate to God. In reading the First Testament, we are wise to look at what it tells us about God and to allow it to draw us into a fuller relationship with the God to whom Jesus wants to introduce people (John 14:6).

Part 1: The Nature of Scripture

In the study that follows, we will first consider the God-breathed nature of the Scriptures and the difference between ascertaining their meaning and discerning their significance for us. We will go on to the unity of the Scriptures in their theology, ethic, and spirituality, and the sense in which Jesus is indeed the climax to the scriptural story. Third, we will consider three approaches to the relationship between the Testaments that might encourage the idea that Christ is in the First Testament: God's acts and typology, God's use of language, and God's promises and threats.

Two passages that come conveniently near each other in the New Testament encapsulate some assumptions about the First Testament that provide illuminating insight on reading the First Testament in light of Jesus.

> The sacred writings . . . are able to make you smart with a view to salvation through faith in Anointed Jesus. Every Scripture is God-breathed and useful for teaching, for testing, for correcting, for training in right living. (2 Tim 3:15–16)[2]

> Having spoken in many varying ways long ago to our ancestors through the prophets, at the end of this time God spoke to us through a Son. (Heb 1:1–2)

---

2. All Scripture translations are my own.

"The prophets" would cover anyone through whom God spoke to Israel whose words appear in the First Testament. The comment in Hebrews implies that the prophets were wholly reliable messengers for God. When Samuel told Saul to "devote" Amalek by eliminating them (1 Sam 15:3) and Jeremiah promised there would always be Levites to offer sacrifices in Jerusalem (Jer 33:18), they spoke as God's reliable messengers to Israel. The same was true when prophets spoke of a girl who would soon have a baby and would have reason to call him "God-is-with-us," or of God's servant as crushed but destined to be exalted (Isa 7:14; 52:13–53:12). God spoke to Israel through them, and the meaning of the prophecies resides in what God was saying to those ancestors. The Holy Spirit did inspire prophets to speak to Israel about events to happen in a time to come (Isa 2:2; cf. 1 Pet 1:12). But Isaiah 7 and 52:13–53:12 do not indicate that these passages are referring to events that will happen in some centuries' time. They point rather to events in the prophet's own day. The passages' spiritual meaning, the divine author's meaning, lies in the message the Holy Spirit was giving to these ancestors for their lives with God. And we access the divine author's meaning via the human author. What the human author meant is what the divine author meant.

On the other hand, Paul's description of the Scriptures as "God-breathed" has a complementary implication. The implication of the Scriptures being God-breathed does not simply mean that the prophecies are infallible and inerrant (though they are). Other New Testament references to the Holy Spirit's involvement with the Scriptures relate this involvement to their extraordinary capacity to say further things to people other than the audience that they originally addressed (e.g., Acts 1:16; 4:25–26; 28:25–28). The Scriptures being God-breathed provides the conceptual background or foreground to these extraordinary and surprising references. While the spiritual meaning of the prophets' messages was the Holy Spirit's message to their own people, everything the First Testament says is also instructive beyond its original context. Being God-breathed underlies the Scriptures' capacity to inform people about salvation through Jesus and be useful for teaching, testing, correcting, and training in right living. They have this capacity whether or not the authors were aware of saying things that would benefit people who would eventually believe in Jesus. That's why Matthew, for instance, when seeking to understand Jesus's virgin birth, could find illumination in Isaiah.

The Meaning and Significance of the Scriptures

We thus need to distinguish the meaning of the Scriptures from their significance or application. The meaning of something is inherent in it; a message's meaning is what the giver of the message was seeking to communicate to the recipient. The significance of something is the illumination the message might bring to someone else, which may have little to do with that original act of communication. Matthew's linking of Isaiah 7:14 to the virgin birth does not involve finding a new meaning in Isaiah or finding a "fuller sense" there; the full sense is the passage's meaning for Israel's ancestors. Nor does Matthew find the "spiritual" meaning as opposed to the "literal" meaning. Matthew finds significance in Isaiah that the Holy Spirit can produce when the Scriptures are read in a new context, and especially in the context of Jesus. The dynamic is similar when an African diplomat asks if Isaiah 53 is about the prophet or about someone else. Philip, "beginning from this Scripture, told him the good news about Jesus" (Acts 8:35). There is a suggestive gap between the question and the answer. Philip does not say that Isaiah 53 is about the prophet or the Jewish people or King Jehoiachin or any of the other people who have been suggested.[3] But he also does not say, "It's about Jesus." He wisely sidesteps the question about the passage's meaning and goes on to explain its significance in connection with his own concern, which is to talk about Jesus. Elsewhere, the New Testament takes up Isaiah 53 to communicate its significance in a different direction: the chapter has implications for the way believers respond to abuse (1 Pet 2:22). The passage's meaning belongs to the Holy Spirit's speaking to the ancestors (about the prophet, in my view).[4] But it can also have application to Jesus and to believers.

One might reframe this point in terms of two approaches to interpretation that emerged a few decades ago. It is possible to speak of there

---

3. See, for example, John Goldingay, "Servant of Yahweh," in *Dictionary of the Old Testament Prophets*, ed. M. J. Boda and J. G. McConville (Downers Grove, IL: InterVarsity Press, 2012), 700–707.

4. See, for example, John Goldingay, *The Message of Isaiah 40–55: A Literary-Theological Commentary* (London: T&T Clark, 2005), 473–77.

being an "intertextual" relationship between what God said through the prophets and the writings in the New Testament. Now the word *intertextuality* can be used in various senses; here I refer to the way the New Testament can be alluding to the First Testament and reflecting its words even when it is not quoting from it.[5] Jesus speaks in this way when he takes up phrases from Isaiah 35 and 61 in describing what he has been doing (Luke 7:22). John 1 does so in describing the message (the "word") that was a reality from the beginning. Considering the meaning of a text that is taken up by a later writer can aid our understanding of the later writer, but there is no presumption that the later writer works with the meaning of the original text. More likely, the original text becomes the vehicle whereby the later writer makes a new point and uses the text to this end.

To put it another way, the New Testament's linking Jesus with promises that God made through the prophets is an aspect of how the prophets have been "received" over the centuries, as other works from Second Temple Judaism interacted with them, and as did Christian and Jewish, agnostic and atheist, ordinary and critical readers over subsequent centuries. Studying the "reception" of the First Testament is unfailingly interesting and illuminating, but it does not imply that the interpreters of texts see themselves as defining the actual meaning of the texts.

God spoke "by" or "through" the prophets. The prophets emphasize God's initiative in connection with speaking, and they describe God as the source of their words. One sometimes gets the impression that God dictated these words (cf. 1 Sam 3:1–14). The prophets are then simply God's scribes. Yet the variety in the prophets' forms of expression indicates that dictation is not the only model for this speaking. The First Testament also suggests the model of king and messenger. When Sennacherib sends a message to Hezekiah (Isa 36–37), Sennacherib prescribes its content, but his lieutenant frames the words; the message loses none of its authority. Analogously, God may determine the burden of a message and the prophet may devise the words, but it is still God's message with his authority, and it loses nothing of its truth. It still results

---

5. See, classically, Richard B. Hays, *Echoes of Scripture in the Letters of Paul* (New Haven, CT: Yale University Press, 1989); Hays, *Echoes of Scripture in the Gospels* (Waco, TX: Baylor University Press, 2016).

from the prophet being carried along by the Holy Spirit and speaking from God (2 Pet 1:21). It is both God's message and the prophet's words.

Different arrangements hold with other forms of speech. With narrative, Luke indicates that he takes the initiative (Luke 1:1–4). With most psalms, worshipers take the initiative and say what they want to say by way of praise or prayer. Human authors did their work, and Israel recognized that they told the truth about God and us or about us and God in important ways. The New Testament's finding that they help believers understand Jesus then confirms that God had been involved in their origin, even if the human author didn't know it. The human authors turn out to be God's instruments—a positive counterpart to the negative way whereby an Assyrian emperor could be God's instrument. Their words were wholly theirs, but they were also wholly God's.

There is variety in the relationship of human author and divine author, but for interpreters it makes no difference. The Scriptures issue from a combined effort involving the Holy Spirit and human authors, and we discover what the Holy Spirit was saying by attending to what the human author was saying. It's the same whichever Testament we are reading.

One God through the Two Testaments

Whereas God spoke in varying ways through the prophets, he has now spoken through his Son. There is no difference between the content of what he said through the prophets and through his Son. The difference lies in his varying ways of speaking through different prophets and the unified embodiment of this teaching in Jesus. Neither Jesus's followers nor his enemies saw him as saying anything new about God; what was new and scandalous was his presenting himself as an embodiment of God. The Jewish people knew that God was loving and merciful but also rigorous and capable of being threatening; so was Jesus. The Jewish people knew that God had power over the natural world and had supernatural knowledge; so did Jesus. Everything the First Testament says about God is true in Jesus and about Jesus. The way the New Testament speaks of Jesus and of the Holy Spirit meant that believers in Jesus indwelt by the Holy Spirit needed to think in new ways about God's oneness, and this process of thinking eventually issued in the doctrine of the Trinity. But the New Testament tells us nothing new about God's character; nor does it suggest that there was anything about God that the Torah, the Prophets, and the Writings lacked. The gift it reflects on is the embodiment of this God in Jesus.

"In the beginning was the word" (John 1:1). The "word" is the gospel message, the message that Jesus and the apostles proclaimed (e.g., John 5:24; 8:31; Acts 4:31; 8:4). John begins, then, by asserting that this message was not novel; it went back to the beginning. But it is then embodied in Jesus, and he is therefore full of grace and truthfulness. Torah came through Moses; grace and truthfulness came through Jesus (John 1:14, 17). John hardly implies that grace and truthfulness were not proclaimed or present in the Torah. The words "gracious" and "abounding in truthfulness" come together in God's description of himself in the Torah (Exod 34:6), and "grace" and "truthfulness" recur many times elsewhere in the Torah. John's point parallels the one in Hebrews 1 about the prophets. In many different ways, the Torah and the Prophets declare God's grace and truthfulness; in Jesus they "came" embodied in a person.

The view that the First Testament God is a God of wrath and the New Testament God a God of love doesn't survive a reading of either Testament. There is no difference between God as he appears in the First Testament and Jesus as he appears in the New. And there is nothing about Jesus in the New Testament that was not present in God as he appears in the First Testament. While God often threatens to abandon Israel for its faithlessness, he never finally does so. He declines to go back on his commitment to them. "If we are faithless, he remains faithful, because he cannot deny himself" (2 Tim 2:13). The grace and truthfulness that God shows in many different ways through Israel's story and that are embodied in Jesus come to a most spectacular expression in his letting himself be killed. Being faithless is what characterized Israel over centuries, and being faithful to the end is what characterized God. Being faithless is what characterized Israel when confronted by Jesus, and being faithful to the end is what characterized Jesus. Because Jesus is God, he is the embodiment of what God has always shown himself to be. Whatever Jesus is, God is. And as the theology of the First Testament and that of the New are similar, so are their spirituality and their ethics. They have a similar understanding of worship, praise, prayer, and thanksgiving. Both combine challenges about God's ultimate standards with allowance for human hardness of heart. Moses did it (Matt 19:3–12), and Paul did it, for instance, in accepting slavery (e.g., Col 3:22).

Whatever Jesus is, God is. Conversely, whatever God is and has been also applies to Jesus. Whatever God has been doing, Jesus also has been doing. The story of God's involvement with Israel is the story of Jesus's involvement with Israel. "Before Abraham was, I am" (John 8:58). The rock from which the Israelites drank "was Christ" (1 Cor 10:4). When Isaiah saw God, he saw Jesus's glory (John 12:41). But Isaiah didn't know that. Jesus is not the subject of the revelation Isaiah gave to his people. The prophets were not telling the ancestors about Jesus.

Jesus as the Climax to the Story

The Scriptures are an account of God's activity in creating the world and placing humanity in his garden to serve it and enjoy it, and of his taking humanity to its destiny in a new world and placing humanity in his city to enjoy it as his servants. In the unfolding of this story, God attached himself to Israel and then came to Israel and to the world in Jesus. Intermingled with this story is teaching about its meaning and its implications for people's lives, about God's person and his intentions, and about their identity and his expectations of them, along with examples of the way people can talk to him. The story is one story, a metanarrative in the narrow sense, a big overall story, inferred from the many smaller-scale narratives in the Scriptures. The teaching is one body of teaching, a metanarrative in the looser sense of a coherent understanding of God, life, and humanity.

Jesus is the climax to the story. He came to restore and free the Jewish people, to announce that God was starting to reign. He came as the embodiment of God's grace and truthfulness, allowing the world and his own people to do their worst to him, and causing their action to be the means of sealing his relationship with them. His ministry to the Jewish people also issued in another way that he brought the scriptural story to a climax. It did it in a paradoxical fashion, in that the Jewish people's not being convinced about Jesus led to an emphasis on a proclamation of him to the gentile world, in fulfillment of the vision of the Psalms. And he opened up the possibility of resurrection

(1 Cor 15). To put it another way, he opened the door into the inner sanctuary for his people (Heb 9–10). In the terms of yet another image, he opened the gates of the new Jerusalem (Rev 21–22). His opening the way into God's eternal presence does not imply that Jewish people previously lacked access to God's presence. God met with them when they came to the temple and met with them elsewhere in their praise and prayer. It meant that both Jews and gentiles could now look forward to resurrection life.

This last result of Jesus's coming meant that he brought something that one might call progress in revelation. In the First Testament, people didn't know about resurrection life; now they do. Yet the model of "progress" for understanding diversity and change within the Scriptures is misleading. In outline, all the truth we need about God and us, and about the world and life, is present in the creation story. Even the gift of resurrection life links with the presence of the tree of life at the beginning of creation (cf. Rev 22:14). What happens over the centuries is a filling out of the detail. No radically new truths need to emerge. New things happen, actions such as God's summons to Abraham, his rescue of Israel from Egypt, and eventually Jesus's coming. These events put more flesh on the bones of the truth, but they do not bring radically new truths. If anything, indeed, rather than progressive revelation, humanity's rebellion against God means that there is regressive de-revelation (see Rom 1–3).

In light of the progression in the story, however, like any story its beginning can be understood more fully in light of its end and its end must be understood in light of its beginning. In the Scriptures' teaching, there is accumulation rather than progress, and each part of the whole must be understood in light of the rest. Songs of Songs, for instance, needs to be understood in light of 1 Corinthians 7, and vice versa. Each Testament contributes to an understanding of the other, not so much in the understanding of specific texts as in seeing their implications in the context of the whole. We can treat all the Scriptures in a similar way as a resource for a knowledge of God, and thus of Jesus. Earlier Scriptures do not need to be corrected by later parts. If anything, Jesus's comment about hardness of hearts implies that later parts need to be corrected by earlier parts.

The Relationship between the Testaments

The New Testament begins by giving us the Scriptures' basic story line as its own starting point. It runs not from creation to fall, to redemption, to new creation, but from Abraham to David, from David to the exile, and from the exile to Jesus (Matt 1:1–17). We could broaden and spell out that scriptural story line by saying that it runs from creation to rebellion, to Abraham, to the exodus, to Sinai, to Canaan, to David, to the fall of Jerusalem, to the rebuilding of the temple, to Antiochus Epiphanes, to Jesus, to the pouring out of the Holy Spirit, to the proclamation of the gospel around the Mediterranean, to the fall of Jerusalem, to the new Jerusalem. How can one see interrelationships between the episodes in the story as the two Testaments tell it? Thinking about this question can help readers understand the sense in which they may make a link between Jesus and a First Testament text. It can help readers see how to understand Jesus in light of the First Testament and vice versa.

God's Acts: Typology

First, there are consistencies and recurrences in God's patterns of action. Jesus's coming constitutes the definitive expression of the patterns, while the expressions in Israel form smaller scale versions. In other words, the story has typological aspects.

Typology has three elements.[6] First, we see resemblances in God's actions. Rescuing the Israelites from Egypt was an exodus, a deliverance (Exod 1–13); rescuing them from Babylon was another exodus, another deliverance (e.g., Isa 43:14–21); rescuing them from sin was yet another exodus, another deliverance (cf. Col 1:13–14; in Luke 9:31 Jesus speaks of his *exodos*). Second, when God repeats the pattern, it is enhanced, not simply repeated. The rescue from Babylon was to be better than the rescue from Egypt: people won't have to rush this time (Isa 52:11–12). The rescue from sin is better still (Col 1:13–14). Third, the original

---

6. See further John Goldingay, *Approaches to Old Testament Interpretation*, updated ed. (Leicester: Apollos, 1990), 97–115, with references to works such as D. L. Baker, *Two Testaments, One Bible* (Leicester: Inter-Varsity, 1976); Patrick Fairbairn, *The Typology of Scripture*, repr. ed. (Grand Rapids: Zondervan, 1952); Leonhard Goppelt, *Typos: The Typological Interpretation of the Old Testament in the New*, trans. Donald H. Madvig (Grand Rapids: Eerdmans, 1982).

expression of the pattern is literal, in the sense that it refers to something material; the subsequent expression(s) may be figurative. The exoduses from Egypt and from Babylon meant geographical movement; for the exodus from sin, geographical rescue is a figure of speech. Hebrews looks back to literal priests offering sacrifices in a literal sanctuary; it then sees Jesus as a priest in a figurative sense when it speaks of him offering a sacrifice that opens the way to a sanctuary that stands for being in the eternal presence of God.

In the First Testament, the priests, the sacrifices, and the sanctuary are not shadows of something else. They are the real thing. The sanctuary is where God really meets with people as they bring their worship and their prayers and know that God is present, listening, and answering there. They don't think of it as a shadow of another sanctuary to which people will have access later. But in Hebrews, the earthly sanctuary and its offerings help people understand that future sanctuary. While Hebrews is the chief body of typological thinking in the Scriptures, Paul also sees Adam as a type of Christ: Christ's action (potentially) affects the whole world, as Adam's did; Christ's action was obviously better (!); and whereas we are related to Adam in the body, we are related to Christ in the Spirit. Isaiah 52:13–53:12 is not a prophecy of a servant to come, but the servant who is described there did provide a type in light of which Jesus can be understood.

One cannot tell from the form of something or from the words describing it that it has a typological reference—that it prefigures something else or that it points to something else. Only *a posteriori* does one know that. No texts were designed to be typological of something in the future for the people to whom God spoke through the prophets. It is when one looks back from Jesus that one can say that Adam or the high priest or the servant in Isaiah was a type of Christ. The value of doing so is then that it enables one to understand Jesus. It does not affect the meaning of the First Testament passage. The sanctuary, the priesthood, the sacrifices, or the servant's suffering do not point forward to Jesus. They point in the present to God as one to whom people could relate in the present. As readers, we then pay attention to them in that connection, not in connection to what they (don't) point to. And we have to be wary of losing the possible significances of the text by focusing too much on its typological significance.

God's Use of Language

Matthew's use of the First Testament can be seen as implying a typological way of thinking,[7] though Matthew doesn't give any direct clues of this approach, as Hebrews and Paul do. It may rather be verbal links that stimulate Matthew's insights. He knows that Jesus embodied the presence of God and that he was conceived through the Holy Spirit's direct action on a girl who was not married, and he is stunned by Isaiah's talk about a girl being pregnant and having a baby who will embody the amazing fact that God is with us. Verbal parallels of this kind may also lie behind the connections he makes with other passages in Matthew 1:18–2:23.

Links in language thus suggest links of substance, an aspect of the verbal inspiration of the Scriptures, of the words being God-breathed. This principle may underlie allegorical interpretation, which starts from scriptural words and lets them suggest something different from the meaning they had as an act of communication between God and their human audience.[8] The classic example is the interpretation of the love songs in the Song of Songs. They give no hint that they concern the love relationship between God and his people. Indeed, the Scriptures as a whole give no hint that the relationship between God and his people or Christ and the church is anything like the egalitarian relationship of the man and woman in the Song (they do indicate that it's like a patriarchal relationship, in a positive sense).

Paul uses the verb *allēgoreō* to describe his interpretation of Sarah and Hagar (Gal 4:24). He may not mean quite what we mean in English by allegory, but his interpretation of the story uses the words of Genesis to throw light on salvation in Christ in a way that looks unrelated to their inherent meaning.[9] Like Matthew, Paul shows that the Holy Spirit can use interpretation that ignores the text's meaning, and on two important

---

7. See, for example, the introduction and the commentary on 1:18–2:23 in R. T. France, *The Gospel of Matthew*, NICNT (Grand Rapids: Eerdmans, 2007).

8. See, for example, Goldingay, *Approaches to Old Testament Interpretation*, 102–15, with references to works such as James Barr, *Old and New in Interpretation: A Study of the Two Testaments* (London: SCM, 1966); also Andrew Louth, *Discerning the Mystery: An Essay on the Nature of Theology* (Oxford: Clarendon, 1983); Leroy A. Huizenga, "The Old Testament in the New, Intertextuality and Allegory," *JSNT* 38 (2015): 17–35.

9. On the Galatians passage, see David I. Starling, "Justifying Allegory: Scripture, Rhetoric, and Reason in Gal. 4:21–5:1," *JTI* 9 (2015): 227–45, with his references.

occasions I have had God bless me through such allegorical interpretation. Still, I'd rather not take the risk of undertaking allegorical interpretation on my own initiative. It is in this connection that the difference between meaning and significance is worth preserving, because letting Genesis or Isaiah and Galatians or Matthew have their separate meanings gives us two texts to learn from. If we assimilate Genesis and Isaiah to Galatians and Matthew, we have only one meaning.

God's Promises (and Threats)

A more intrinsic link between episodes in the scriptural story as a whole is seen when God makes promises and keeps them (or restates them).

For example, in Genesis 41 and Acts 11:28, God reveals to Joseph and Agabus that there is to be a famine, and it happens. They make predictions that are fulfilled. But the general run of God's statements about the future in the Scriptures are not predictions. The word *prediction* hardly comes up in the Scriptures (not at all in the KJV). God doesn't really predict things. What God does is promise and threaten things. A person predicts things that someone else will do, but that the person doesn't control. We do not predict what we ourselves will do. We declare intentions. And God in the First Testament (and in the New Testament) declares intentions. Whether he fulfills his intentions depends on the response he receives (as Jer 18:1–11 makes most explicit) or on whether he finds reason to change his mind. And the intentions God announces in the First Testament rarely resemble an advance video of an event, as one might expect if they were predictions (I suspect that the same applies to intentions God declares in the New Testament about Jesus's final appearing). God declares the intention to cause the fall of Jerusalem, Babylon, and Egypt, but their fall doesn't correspond to the nature of the warning. God announces the intention to send a son of David to rule in Israel, but the son of David who came does not correspond to the promise: God speaks of someone sitting on David's throne and establishing proper exercise of authority, but makes no reference to him preaching, healing, expelling demons, raising dead people, cleansing people, engaging in controversy, calling disciples, or being crucified. It's hardly surprising that John the Baptizer wonders if Jesus is really the one who was to come (Luke 7:18–19).

To illustrate the point another way, 1 Kings 13:1–2 makes a declaration about Josiah, who would be born in several centuries' time. There could have been passages in the First Testament that refer to Jesus in a parallel way, but there are none. Isaiah 7:14 tests and proves the point; the name of the child to whom it refers will be Immanuel, not Jesus. Isaiah 9:6 speaks of a child who has been born for us and gives him a name, but neither the name Jesus nor the designation "Anointed" or "Messiah" is part of the name. Conversely, the New Testament never says that Christ himself is "in" the First Testament.

Jesus does say that there are "things about him" there (Luke 24:27). If we ask what they are, two earlier passages in Luke are illuminating. When John the Baptizer had his disciples ask Jesus if he was the one who was to come, he drew attention to his having healed people, expelled bad spirits, cleansed people, enabled deaf people to hear, and preached good news to the poor (Luke 7:22). He did not refer to any messianic prophecies, and I have noted that several actions he describes have no scriptural parallels. Some recall Isaiah 35, which is a prophecy but not a messianic one. Some recall Isaiah 61, which are the words of someone anointed, but words in a testimony, not a prophecy. Jesus quotes it earlier (Luke 4:16–21) and comments that this Scripture has been "filled" or "filled out" or "filled up" in his hearers' ears. The traditional translation "fulfilled" makes this comment sound as if the testimony was a prediction, but *plēroō* is a more ordinary (yet interesting) word than that, and one may set the occurrence of the verb here alongside the occurrence of it in Matthew 5:17 in connection with the Torah and the Prophets.[10]

Christian interest in First Testament prophecies also has to keep in mind that only a few passages there could count as messianic prophecies. God's main purpose in speaking through the prophets was not to give them promises about the Messiah. There are no First Testament passages that use the Hebrew word *meshiah* to refer to the Messiah. The word occurs only to describe a present priest or king. The clearest "messianic prophecy" appears in Micah 5:2, which Matthew 2:1–12 quotes, and it does not use the word *meshiah*, though it is a promise of a ruler to come, and it can help people who believe in Jesus to understand him.

---

10. Cf. John Goldingay, *Reading Jesus's Bible: How the New Testament Helps Us Understand the Old Testament* (Grand Rapids: Eerdmans, 2017), 209–11.

The importance of such prophecies is the way they help us understand Jesus, but there are no promises of Jesus that parallel the promise or threat about Josiah. Thus, one cannot prove from the First Testament that Jesus is the Messiah. Jesus's response when John the Baptizer asks his question fits that conclusion. And rabbinic teachers seeking to counter the arguments of modern evangelists have no difficulty in demonstrating that the "messianic prophecies" to which the evangelists appeal are not messianic prophecies at all. The First Testament's significance in relation to Jesus as Messiah is to help us see what his messiahship means, not to prove anything. And we don't have to ask whether the scriptural author saw a passage as messianic, because all the Scriptures help us understand who Jesus is.

All God's promises find their "Yes" in Jesus (2 Cor 1:20). He hasn't "fulfilled" them all; there are key aspects to the way the First Testament talks about the "son of David" that he has not yet "fulfilled." But he has confirmed them all, guaranteed that God's promises will be fulfilled.

Part 2: Interpretive Steps for Readers

So how do we go about interpreting the First Testament—or for that matter the New Testament? Discovering a passage's meaning involves discerning what act of communication was happening or was designed to happen between the human author in the service of the Holy Spirit and the human audience.

Questions and Steps

One might then think of a series of steps in reading the Scriptures. Here are some of them.

1. What sort of passage is it—for instance, narrative, exhortation, prayer, something else?
2. What was the question to which the passage was the answer?
3. How does it fit into the book in which it comes—how is it illumined by its context in this book?
4. If we know the book's historical or social context, how does it illumine the question?
5. How does who I am, and the context in which I live, help and hinder my understanding the question and the passage?

6. What was the passage's broad answer to the question it presupposes —in other words, what was it saying to the ancestors?
7. How do the different parts of the passage or the different characters in the narrative contribute to this answer?
8. When I set the passage in the context of the rest of the Scriptures, how does it illumine them, and how do they illumine it?
9. When I set the passage in the context of my life, how does its being God-breathed prove itself?
10. And given our concern in this book, we can ask of any text, what light does it throw on Jesus?

Discovering a passage's meaning happens as we ask the kinds of questions we can ask as the people we are in our context, and as we listen for the answers from the text in light of what we can know about its context. We then seek to formulate new questions if there seems to be more in the text than our first questions have unlocked. Other Scriptures may help us to formulate questions and guess at answers, and this dynamic includes the two Testaments in relation to each other.

For instance, I interpret the Scriptures as a free, modern, Western, urban, white male, who is old enough to be retired, an academic, a married man, an Anglican priest, belonging to a post-Christian society and a powerful nation. I have a home, food to eat, and health care. The Scriptures were exercises in communication between people who were few of those things. So I will be helped to understand the Scriptures if I seek to look at them through the eyes of people in a traditional society, of people who farm, of women and people in need—and of readers from the past, such as Jews in Second Temple times, the Jews who wrote most of the New Testament, and the Jewish, Christian, agnostic, and atheist scholars who have studied the Scriptures over two millennia. This reading helps me perceive aspects of the text's meaning that I might otherwise miss. It also enables me to understand how these readers were seeing the text's significance for themselves. This may also be its significance for me, or it may model the way I go about seeking to see its significance for me. None of these readings of the text determines the text's meaning or its significance. What they do is offer pointers or suggestions for my understanding of the Scriptures themselves.

We will be keen to understand the text's inherent meaning, because that is what God was actually saying through the prophets, and we will want to listen in on that conversation because of what we may learn and because it may be directly important for us. In other words, the text's meaning may also be its significance for us. Yet it is not always so. We would have to think and pray about the significance for us of Jesus's command, "If you want to be perfect, sell your possessions and give to the poor" (Matt 19:21). Conversely, sometimes God may speak to us through a text in a way that has little to do with its original meaning. I have mentioned how there have been times when that has happened to me. The validity of someone's use of a text requires that it broadly fits with the Scriptures but not necessarily that this use corresponds to the particular text's meaning.

The New Testament's Example

This consideration fits with the New Testament's use of the First Testament. Sometimes the New Testament uses a First Testament text in a way that ignores its inherent meaning. Its use of that text does not then determine its meaning. Allowing it to do so would dishonor the work of the Holy Spirit and the Scriptures' human author in speaking to "our ancestors." For instance, Paul's references to the Torah as suggesting that we get right with God by doing as it says (Rom 10:5–8; cf. Gal 3:10–14) do not override the Torah's own perspective, that we are right with God by his grace and through trust in him, and that we respond to that grace by doing as the Torah says. Paul himself elsewhere draws attention to that dynamic; the comments just noted were counteracting the possibility that people might read statements in the Torah to make the opposite point. They counter a way in which people might see the text's significance; they do not define its meaning. Conversely, the meaning of a First Testament text in its context does not determine its significance as the New Testament uses it. At Sinai, God declares that he will be gracious and merciful to all the people he decides to be gracious and merciful to; he will not have his grace and mercy constrained (Exod 33:19). Paul quotes his words to indicate that God is free to withhold grace and mercy (Rom 9:15).

The different implications that those two statements have in the context of the Torah and of Romans draw attention to a different matter. In addition to understanding the meaning of a text as an exercise in communication between a divine and a human author on one hand

and a human audience on the other, it is important to set this text in the context of the rest of the Scriptures. As the opening sentence in Hebrews notes, there is rich diversity in the Scriptures. They need to manifest this diversity because most questions are complex and their answers need to be nuanced differently in different contexts. But the nuancing for one context may then not be the nuancing for another. And bringing texts into interrelationship is one safeguard against preaching yesterday's message in today's context. Interpretation involves holding together the point about the importance of obeying God and the point about God's grace being the reality that puts us in touch with God in the first place. The same applies to the Torah's point about God's generosity with his mercy and Paul's point about God's sovereignty over his mercy. Whereas God had declared that Israel was not his people, he will declare once again that they are his people (Hos 1:10; 2:23), but Paul quoted this promise with reference to God making gentiles his people (Rom 9:25–26). Hosea's meaning does not determine the new significance that Paul saw in God's words, and Paul's quotation does not determine the meaning of Hosea. Both statements (about grace and mercy to God's people and about grace and mercy to the gentile world) are important aspects of scriptural theology. An interpreter needs intelligence and the gift of the Holy Spirit to see whether one of these pieces of good news is the message for now. Reading the First Testament after Jesus and thus in light of the New Testament does not change the text's meaning, though it may make a difference to its significance for us.

In inspiring the First Testament, the Holy Spirit presupposes that the God who was at work in its entire story is the God and Father of our Lord Jesus Christ. But we will be wise not to remind ourselves of this fact too often. If we do so, we will risk missing what the Holy Spirit wanted us to see. Christ is not in the First Testament in the way Josiah is in 1 Kings 13 or the way Antiochus is in Daniel 11.

Part 3: Case Studies

Here is how I approach three sample passages in light of the principles outlined so far.[11]

---

11. See further John Goldingay, *Genesis*, Baker Commentary on the Old Testament Pentateuch (Grand Rapids: Baker Academic, 2020); Goldingay, *Proverbs, Ecclesiastes and the*

Genesis 22:1–19

The key motif in the story of Abraham and Sarah is God's promise that they would become the parents of a big nation. It was an implausible promise, because Sarah could not have children; it is almost as if God likes to make things difficult for himself. The story continually underlines what a hazardous promise it was. Isaac's birth made the promise more plausible, but one chapter later God himself radically imperils it.

"God tested Abraham" (Gen 22:1). The Scriptures often refer to God testing people, usually by putting pressure on them to see if they will do as he says. Hebrews 11:17–19 takes Abraham's testing as an illustration of how God relates to us. He checks whether we, too, will operate on the basis of trust in him. Given that God can look into our hearts, it may seem odd that he tests our hearts (1 Thess 2:4). Perhaps it is a sign that he relates to us in the real world, not a virtual or theoretical world. The ancient Jewish commentary Genesis Rabbah comments on this story that testing is a kind of compliment.[12] It is the faithful people that God tests in this way, not the faithless (Ps 11:5). For many people, the greatest tests come not through something God commissions but through something that just happens. Before my girlfriend, Ann, became my fiancée and my wife, we found she had multiple sclerosis, and we lived with that reality for more than forty years. It tested my faithfulness, and I sometimes failed the test.

For God, then, the question that the chapter answers is whether Abraham really lives in awe of him. For Genesis, the chapter is also one of a series of stories that answer the question of how God went about fulfilling his promise to Abraham. God uses the word traditionally translated "fear," which can mean "be afraid," but which often denotes a submission that acquiesces to whatever God expects of us (e.g., Exod 1:17, 21; Luke 1:50). This fear or awe is not very different from love, which also expresses itself in doing what God says.

We don't know how Abraham knew that it was really God telling him to offer up Isaac, but somehow he did. God's words to him underline the enormity of his bidding. But Abraham already knows that God

---

Song of Songs for Everyone (Louisville: Westminster John Knox, 2014); and Goldingay, *Message of Isaiah 40–55*.

12. H. Freedman and M. Simon, eds., *Midrash Rabbah* (London: Soncino, 1939), 1:482–83.

is trustworthy, if also mysterious in some of the things he asks. God has made promises to him and Sarah. And God has squared a circle before. It is within this framework that Abraham hears God speak. You could never do what Abraham does unless you knew you had reason to trust God. That trust enables him to follow God's bidding without hesitation and to know that offering Isaac will not be the end of the story. But neither Abraham nor Isaac knows where the journey will lead; both operate on the basis of trust and obedience.

God only needs Abraham to lift the cleaver over Isaac to establish that he would go the whole way in obedience. God can then stop him, and Abraham finds a ram and offers it instead. He comments that God is shown to be Yahweh Yir'eh (KJV, Jehovah-jireh): "God sees to things."

The story leads into God repeating his promise about a multitude of offspring. Indeed, he turns the promise into an oath that he swears "by myself," on the basis of who I am. If he fails to keep this oath, he will have betrayed himself. He adds that as a result of Abraham's obedience, all the nations will bless themselves by his offspring—that is, they will pray to be blessed in the way Abraham was blessed. The fact that we are thinking about this story is evidence that God kept his promise.

For Israelites, the story may have signified that God doesn't ask them to offer a child as a sacrifice, as he could, and as other peoples of their time thought, and as Israelites sometimes did. Subsequently, as Israel's story continued into the story of the exodus, the people's arrival and flourishing in Canaan, the building of the temple, the restoration of the people, the rebuilding of the temple after the exile, and the deliverance from Antiochus, this story became one that the Israelites would listen to in the context of a relationship with the God whom they could trust. The trustworthiness of this God was newly embodied when God gave up his own Son for his people and for the world, doing what he did not ultimately require of Abraham (Mark 1:11; Rom 8:31–32).

If we ask how God was speaking to the ancestors in Genesis 22, then the kind of interpretation I have suggested is the one that emerges from the chapter. There is nothing to put the ancestors on the track of the idea that the passage may be messianic. Christ is not in Genesis 22, nor does Genesis 22 point to Christ. But Genesis 22 helped Mark and Paul understand Christ.

Proverbs 8:22-31

I was once the principal of a UK seminary, a position that is a cross between being a president and a provost. It meant I had to seek to ensure that the seminary encouraged the development of students as people of God and as potential pastors, teachers, and missionaries, that the seminary was well-known and attracted students, that the budget worked even if there was a financial crisis, that we made good appointments to the faculty, that the faculty received the right support and oversight, and that we developed good programs. It was a demanding job. Leadership places demands on a person. Proverbs 8 is concerned for leaders of various kinds (vv. 15–16), though it is also concerned for ordinary people, and it wants to urge them to listen as smartness (*hokmah*) summons them (v. 1).[13] Translations traditionally have the word "wisdom," but that word is a little high-flown. Proverbs is talking about something down-to-earth.

To commend smartness, Proverbs 8:22–31 draws attention to the fact that God could not have created the world without being smart. Ms. Smartness declares, "God had me from the beginning of his creative work. . . . I was there by his side" (vv. 22, 30). She then describes herself by a word that doesn't occur anywhere else. Some translations have a rendering such as "master of crafts" (CEB). Others have something like a foster child, "one brought up with him" (KJV), which fits with her picture of delighting alongside God as he does his work. Wisdom sounds like something serious, but it then turns out to be something playful. You could infer that creation was itself an outworking of joy. Ms. Smartness was excited about the creation that God was bringing into being, and with humanity itself. Genesis 1 describes creation as good, but it is more solemn about it. Ms. Smartness claps her hands and dances.

God couldn't have created the world unless he had been smart; so people in general and leaders in particular need to cultivate smartness if they are to succeed in their lives and work. The alternative, the context indicates, is to cultivate stupidity. Smartness does mean truthfulness and faithfulness, turning your back on wrongdoing and living in awe of God (vv. 8, 13, 20). Proverbs confronts the temptation of leaders to

---

13. Cf. Michael V. Fox, *Proverbs 1–9*, AB 18A (New York: Doubleday, 2000), 293.

think that it's smart to sidestep truthfulness and faithfulness. Christian leaders remain vulnerable to this teaching in Proverbs, though they may not see themselves that way. As evidence, it seems that every week another Christian leader gets fired for yielding to unfaithfulness rather than evidencing smartness.

Again, Christ is not in Proverbs 8:22–31. But the passage helped shape an understanding of Christ. Its personification of Ms. Smartness pictures her being present at creation as a person distinguishable from God, even while being an aspect of God. So when John needed to speak about Jesus as existing before becoming a human being and as divine yet distinguishable from the Father, he picked up the idea of God's smartness from this passage. The description of Jesus as God's word in John 1 takes up terms that describe Ms. Smartness in Proverbs 8.

There is an amusing footnote to this development. Proverbs speaks as if God "had" Ms. Smartness at creation, and it uses the verb *qanah*, which Eve used when she "had" Cain (it's the verb that lies behind Cain's own name). The Hebrew verb is less common than the English word "had," but it also has a range of meanings. The Old Greek translation of Proverbs uses the word "created" (as the NRSV does); this is a bit misleading in Proverbs, though harmless. But it caused trouble two or three centuries after Jesus, when Christians came to assume that Christ was in Proverbs 8. European theologians read the First Testament in its Greek translation, which made it look as if God had created Smartness, which suggested that he had created Christ. The implication was then that Christ isn't God in the full sense or in the same sense as the Father is God. Finding Christ in the First Testament led to heresy![14] It needn't have that effect, though it serves as a warning as we interpret the Scriptures.

Isaiah 42:1-4

Yet the greater danger of looking for Christ in the Old Testament is that we miss the riches of what God was saying to our ancestors through the prophets. "You as Israel are my servant, as Jacob you're the one I chose, as the offspring of Abraham you're my friend. . . . Don't be afraid, because

---

14. See, for example, Athanasius, *First Discourse against the Arians* 1.5, in *The Orations of St Athanasius against the Arians*, ed. W. Bright, repr. ed. (Cambridge: Cambridge University Press, 2014), 5.

I'm with you" (Isa 41:8–10). God speaks these words to people who have been under the domination of a superpower for half a century.[15] They are understandably depressed, and they think God has abandoned them. They are not exactly wrong. In 587 BC God finally had it with their inclination to ignore everything he said, and he walked out on them. But like a mother who walks out on her children, he couldn't maintain his abandonment, and he decided it had gone on long enough.

God had not previously described Israel as his servant, but he had used that description of people such as Moses and David and (ironically) of Nebuchadnezzar, the head of the world superpower. Being the servant of an important master is a position of privilege and security. Masters are bound to be committed to their servants and to protect them. So this was an accolade and a reassurance.

Of course, servants are also bound to be committed to their masters, to do the work they commission. So God now went on to describe what he planned for his servant to do. His servant is one on whom he puts his spirit (42:1), which again calls to mind David as his servant (1 Sam 16:13). It implies being equipped for the work God wants done. His servant is one who will make God's government go out to the nations. The word for government (*mishpat*) is tricky to translate. The KJV has "judgment" here, which has the advantage of being concrete but sounds negative. The NIV has "justice," which has the advantage of being positive but sounds abstract. *The Message* has "He'll set everything right among the nations," which is a good paraphrase.

Whichever way one translates it, we will wonder, *How would Israel fulfill that commission?* Isaiah 42 is taking up Isaiah 2:2–4, another promise that envisages God "governing" among the nations. Many translations again have "judge" there, and that English verb may be less negative and less misleading than the noun "judgment." Isaiah 2 promises that God will decide things between the nations and thus bring peace there because they won't need to fight; it will happen because God's "teaching" goes out from Jerusalem. Now God notes that foreign shores are waiting for this teaching (42:4), though they may not realize it. Jerusalem as the mountain where God lives and Israel as his servant are the means whereby God's teaching is to issue forth, to sort out the

---

15. On this background, see Goldingay, *Message of Isaiah 40–55.*

world. What that would look like, neither Isaiah 2 nor Isaiah 42 makes clear. Both versions of the promise appear in contexts that indicate how the idea stands in conflict with what Jerusalem and Israel are at the moment. God has his work cut out if he is to achieve his aim. But he is pledged to it. He has made a commitment to Israel as the servant he will use, and he can't get out of that commitment. The following chapters reaffirm that Israel is his servant who is destined to serve him as his witnesses (43:8–12; 44:1–8).

Once again, if we ask how God was speaking to the ancestors in Isaiah 42, then the kind of interpretation I have suggested is the one that emerges from the passage. There is nothing to give the ancestors the idea that the passage is messianic. Christ is not in Isaiah 42, nor does Isaiah 42 point to Christ. But Isaiah 42 contributes to an understanding of Christ, as Matthew 12:17–21 affirms. God's Spirit would rest on Jesus as God's servant and his chosen one, and he would be gentle with people. His healing activity would "fulfill" or "fill up" or "fill out" what God had said. Jesus doesn't reach out to the nations in keeping with Isaiah 42, though this points to a link Matthew doesn't make. Luke hints at it when he describes Jesus as coming to bring about the restoration of Israel (Luke 1:54–55, 69–79). By bringing that restoration, Jesus would prepare the way for Israel to function as God's servant. When people decline to recognize Jesus, it threatens to derail God's plan again, but Paul sees a mysterious divine purpose in this refusal (see Rom 11:1–32). The refusal doesn't mean God has turned his back on Israel, and it was Jews like Paul who took God's teaching out among the nations. As a result, the church comes to share in the servant vocation, so that Isaiah 42 is significant for gentiles who believe in Jesus, as a revelation of God's vision for us.

Conclusion

The First Testament is rich in its portrait of God in his grace and faithfulness and in its account of how he was at work in the world and in Israel. God indeed spoke to our ancestors through the prophets, on the way to embodying that same speaking in Jesus (Heb 1:1–2). But a focus on reading Jesus back into the First Testament means we don't get to hear what it has to say. We learn what we knew already (because we knew it from the New Testament), and we miss the First Testament's own insight. We narrow down the Scriptures to our own narrow interests. We will be wiser to seek to put ourselves into the position of those ancestors and read them afresh.

The British organization the Scripture Union has as one of its main aims to encourage Bible reading. I once heard a preacher comment that if its badge were ever redesigned, it should become a pair of raised eyebrows. The First Testament especially has a vast capacity to raise our eyebrows. Reading Christ into it short-circuits that effect. Reading it for what God was saying to the ancestors can mean we see more clearly how the God-breathed Scriptures speak to us.

RESPONSE TO JOHN GOLDINGAY
(THE CHRISTOTELIC APPROACH)

TREMPER LONGMAN III

Let me start with a confession. I have known and deeply respected John Goldingay, read carefully and even edited a project or two of his, endorsed his books, and had many wonderful conversations with him since 1985, when I met him on my first sabbatical at Tyndale House in Cambridge when he was principal at the Anglican training school in Nottingham. When I saw he was one of the contributors to this volume, I thought he would be the one with whom I disagreed more than anyone. We have many, many topics on which we see eye to eye, but on Christ in the Old Testament we have had our disagreements. However, I could not have been more wrong. If anything, we may disagree on emphasis and on semantics (which may lead him to be critical of my essay), but in my opinion we agree on the main points.

Perhaps my assessment is influenced by the concerns I express about the other three essays. As valuable and insightful as they are in their own way, they do not give enough attention to the Old Testament text in its original setting. They either pass it by and go right to a christological/Christotelic interpretation or impose what can only be an interpretation that can be discerned in the light of the New Testament. Goldingay, on the other hand, lovingly and insightfully dwells on the rich theological message of the Old Testament before thinking about a connection with Christ.

Goldingay indicates his appreciation for the Old Testament's discrete message by calling it the First Testament, rather than the Old Testament, to signal that, though this group of writings is older than the ones in the New Testament, they are no less relevant after the appearance of the New Testament. I believe he is correct to say that "Christ is everywhere in the First Testament story . . . but he is not 'in the First Testament' as someone whom the text mentions" (22).[1]

I appreciate and agree with Goldingay's comments about 2 Timothy 3:15–16 and Hebrews 1:1–2 and how they throw light on "reading the First Testament in light of Jesus" (22). I would have also liked to hear him speak about Luke 24:25–27, 44–49, and John 5:36–40 in terms of the scope of Jesus's illumination of the First Testament. Is it possible, for instance, after doing a first reading of each of the 150 psalms to go on and offer a Christotelic reading,[2] or does reading in the light of Jesus only illumine select psalms?

I also appreciate his emphasis that "while the spiritual meaning of the prophets' messages was the Holy Spirit's message to their own people, everything the First Testament says is also instructive beyond its original context" (23). I also affirm his view that the First Testament's human authors were not aware of how their writings "would benefit people who would eventually believe in Jesus" (23).

While I start talking about *sensus plenior* and the divine author's intended meaning at this point, Goldingay appeals to a distinction between meaning and significance. Meaning would be connected with the author's intended message, while significance refers to "the illumination the message might bring to someone else, which may have little to do with that original act of communication" (24).

I struggle a little with this distinction for a couple of reasons, though it may be my problem, not Goldingay's. This distinction is most familiar to me from the writings of Walter Kaiser,[3] based on the literary theorist E. D. Hirsch.[4] Kaiser and Hirsch have a very rigid understanding of literary meaning determined by the conscious intention of the human author; at least in Kaiser's case, his approach to author-centered

---

1. This quote specifically addresses "the events" of the First Testament. I don't think he intends to rule out other nonhistorical sections of the OT, since his examples from Proverbs and Isaiah also show that he sees a Christotelic significance there (see p. 85 for my definition of *Christotelic*).

2. As I attempt to do in Tremper Longman III, *Psalms: An Introduction and Commentary*, TOTC 15–16 (Downers Grove, IL: InterVarsity Press, 2014).

3. Walter C. Kaiser Jr., *Toward an Exegetical Theology: Biblical Exegesis for Preaching and Teaching* (Grand Rapids: Baker, 1981), 31–34.

4. E. D. Hirsch, *Validity in Interpretation* (New Haven, CT: Yale University Press, 1967).

interpretation in my opinion violates the legitimate concern expressed by the intentional fallacy.[5] I also think that it is difficult to make a clear distinction between meaning and significance.

However, that said, when Goldingay treats actual texts with his meaning/significance distinction, I find myself resonating with his analysis. I wonder, though, whether we might still be able to talk about how the divine meaning may emerge from the type of reasoning he suggests comes about by later authors reflecting on the meaning of First Testament texts. Bottom line, Goldingay's discussion here has given me something to think about further, which enriches my understanding to think about Jesus's relationship to the First Testament.

I do question Goldingay's perspective that "the New Testament tells us nothing new about God's character, nor does it suggest that there was anything about God that the Torah, the Prophets, and the Writings lacked" (26–27). I suppose in one sense that is true, but on the other hand there is more of a "progress in revelation" than he seems to admit. But then again, I think he would agree that while God is the Trinity in the First Testament, we really don't get much of a glimpse of his Trinitarian nature, nor of the afterlife, nor of the devil. He knows that but still does not like the progress metaphor, though I will admit along with him that such progress is more like the tree growing out of the acorn, a filling out of the detail.

Nevertheless, particularly in this day and age I want to absolutely affirm Goldingay's point that "the First Testament God is a God of wrath and the New Testament God a God of love doesn't survive a reading of either Testament" (27). It has become something of a cottage industry these days to argue that God is not violent in his judgments, or to put it another way, that the God depicted in the Old Testament is not the actual God as displayed in Christ on the cross.

We can see the importance that Goldingay puts on the discrete message of the First Testament in most of his interpretive steps, which tease out that message (steps 1–4, 6–7). I also appreciate his awareness that our social situatedness creates lenses through which we read the text.

---

5. Though in my chapter I depend on the work of Kevin Vanhoozer to produce a more nuanced understanding of authorial meaning.

Dr. Dharamraj did as well, but I join Goldingay in encouraging what I call reading in a community, a diverse one at that.

When we look at the New Testament's use of the Old Testament, I think Goldingay is right to conclude that "sometimes the New Testament uses a First Testament text in a way that ignores its inherent meaning" (37). At least I believe that is the case in terms of the human author's conscious human intention, even in the human author's "conscious peripheral vision."[6] On the other hand, I do think there is a continuity between the New Testament use and its Old Testament meaning. I imagine an Old Testament prophet like Isaiah at first being shocked at how Matthew uses his statement about a child being born to a "young woman" (Isa 7:14), but then, perhaps through the process described by Goldingay and reading through the prism of the Greek translation of his words, feeling comfortable with it. Again, at this point I think it useful to talk about *sensus plenior* and divine intention.

In terms of Goldingay's case studies, not surprisingly he brings out the riches of these First Testament texts beautifully, and I have only the occasional question concerning what I would call his first reading of the text. In terms of Genesis 22, I agree with him that the text is not messianic in the sense that Christ is in Genesis 22. However, I do think that this text points to Christ (to me these are two different things) and that is why, as he says, "Genesis 22 helped Mark and Paul understand Christ" (41). I would have loved to see Goldingay unpack in more detail how it so helped them.

I also agree with Goldingay when he says, "Christ is not in Proverbs 8:22–31" (42). And I like the way he describes how Proverbs 8 "helped shape an understanding of Christ" (42). That is what I was getting at in my chapter when I said that the New Testament authors did not identify Christ as Woman Wisdom, but rather associated him with her. I guess I would like to push back on Goldingay's understanding of *hokmah* as "smart" with the result that he speaks of Ms. Smartness. In my opinion, smart moves the concept too much in the direction of IQ, whereas on a practical level wisdom is more like emotional intelligence. Perhaps he

---

6. This phrase comes from G. K. Beale, "The Cognitive Peripheral Vision of Biblical Authors," *WTJ* 76 (2014): 263–93. See my chapter for a critical discussion of this category.

means something like "street smarts," but then that is too restrictive to the practical dimension of wisdom and does not account for its ethical and theological dimensions.[7] So I have a respectful disagreement with Goldingay here because I think that indeed *hokmah* is a rich and complex concept, so well captured by a "high-flown" word like wisdom.

When it comes to Isaiah 42, I think that Goldingay and I are on the same wavelength (and I readily concede that he knows a lot more about Isaiah than I do!). And once again I agree with him when he says that "there is nothing to give the ancestors the idea that the passage is messianic," which helps explain why the Gospels give us the impression that no one seemed to get the "suffering servant" part of the messiah at the time Jesus lived. Again, I agree that "Christ is not in Isaiah 42" (44), but in my opinion that does not mean it does not "point to Christ." It apparently took the resurrection for those who followed Jesus to see this deeper meaning.

Again, I want to thank Goldingay for helping all of us remember that the First/Old Testament contributes on its own terms (its discrete message) to our understanding of God, ourselves, and our world. Overall, I agree with the way he then describes the New Testament's Christotelic appropriation of the First Testament, though I wish he had developed that even further.

---

7. For these three dimensions of wisdom, see my *The Fear of the Lord Is Wisdom: A Theological Introduction to Wisdom in Israel* (Grand Rapids: Baker Academic, 2017), 6–25.

HAVILAH DHARAMRAJ

I heard this story about a person whom the Old Testament introduced to Jesus. A young Hindu man starting university reached his campus accommodation. Entering his room, he found a Bible on his bed. It had been placed there by the UESI (the Union of Evangelical Students in India). He recognized it to be the "Christian book," and never having read it before, he randomly opened it and read the story of Naboth (1 Kgs 21). Soon he found he was reading about himself in the story. He belonged to the category at the bottom of the caste system, the Dalits, a group oppressed across the centuries by the so-called upper castes. "That was my story," he later said about Naboth. "We also suffered false accusations, theft of land, and murder of family members." He went on to read and was taken by surprise that the god here sent his prophet Elijah to confront the government on behalf of the hapless Naboth. "I never knew such a god existed," he exclaimed—a god who took the side of the socially powerless. "I wanted to know more about this god of justice," he said. And that, I think, illustrates what Dr. Goldingay says, "In reading the First Testament, we are wise to look at what it tells us about God and to allow it to draw us into a fuller relationship with the God to whom Jesus wants to introduce people (John 14:6)" (22). As it happened, the young man eventually came to faith in Jesus and now enjoys the God of the Old Testament even more in the light of all that Jesus reveals about him.

The First Testament approach emphasizes that "a focus on reading Jesus back into the First Testament means we don't get to hear what it has to say" (45). The aforementioned young man had the opportunity to hear what the Old Testament had to say. Its message to its ancient audience turned out to be exactly what he, in the twenty-first century, needed to hear. In South Asia we read the Bible in a cultural environment that often easily bridges into that of the Old Testament, whether it be the dynamics of kinship relationships or the vulnerable situation of widows or slavery-like bonded labor. What is more, the literary genres of the Old Testament are the ones we have traditionally used for passing teaching down from generation to generation: poems, songs, proverbs, and most of all, stories. We "get" narrative theology much more readily than the logic of Paul's rhetoric. So I am very content to endorse the value of the First Testament approach.

Further, whether culturally close or distanced, not paying attention to what the Old Testament has to say might drop us into the danger of overlooking a whole swath of very important matters that God wants us to understand and appreciate. I cite here Christopher Wright, a good friend and mentor, from his provocatively titled chapter "Don't Just Give Me Jesus" in his book *How to Preach and Teach the Old Testament for All Its Worth*. God goes to great lengths to reveal in the Old Testament what it means to be human; the fact and deeply damaging consequences of sin; God's intolerance of injustice and oppression; and God's sovereign rule over all the kingdoms of the earth and over all the ages of history. Wright discerningly points out,

> Of course, we can show how all these great themes eventually lead us to Christ. . . . But if . . . all the time we're thinking, "This must be all about Jesus," we will miss all the richness and depth of what God is *actually* saying to us. . . . And that is not only sad—it is tragic. For it leaves people not understanding and applying so much of what there is in the Bible. Indeed, it distracts them away from listening to what God wants to say to them in those texts—and that is a seriously bad thing to do.[1]

As Goldingay says, citing 2 Timothy 3:16, Old Testament texts are "useful for teaching, testing, correcting, and training in right living.

---

1. Christopher J. H. Wright, *How to Preach and Teach the Old Testament for All Its Worth* (Grand Rapids: Zondervan Academic, 2016), 57.

They have this capacity whether or not the authors were aware of saying things that would benefit people who would eventually believe in Jesus" (23). Indeed, we sabotage this capacity of the Old Testament to steer us—followers of Christ—into right living when we straightaway redirect three-fourths of the Bible toward Jesus.

A second observation I would like to make is Goldingay's emphatic position on the priority of the Old Testament, which he highlights through a refrain: "Christ is not in . . ." the texts studied in the chapter. He clarifies: Christ is not *in* the Old Testament "as someone whom the text mentions," "in the way Josiah is in 1 Kings 13 or the way Antiochus is in Daniel 11" (38), that is, as a historical figure. However, "Christ is everywhere in the First Testament story." With that presupposition, he provides steps for reading the Scripture, finishing with the question: "What light does [the text] throw on Jesus?" (36).

I take the liberty of summarizing what I understand to be Goldingay's position with a pair of prepositions, informed by Wright's choice of title for his book: *Knowing Jesus through the Old Testament*:[2] Christ is not *in* the Old Testament, per se, but can be understood *through* the Old Testament. Similarly, with my method, which pairs an Old Testament text with a christological New Testament text, I show how Jesus can be better understood through the study of Isaac, the figure of Wisdom, and the Servant. Goldingay could include into his assertion that even though Christ is not, historically speaking, in the pages of the Old Testament, he can be appreciated through them.

A third and last observation concerns Goldingay's other refrain: the Old Testament "does not point" to Christ. This way of putting it can lead to serious, even if unintended, misconceptions, especially in a multireligious environment as exists in many parts of the majority world, where Christianity lives side by side with Hinduism or Islam or Buddhism, or with all three, as in South Asia.

Let me elaborate my concern starting with how Goldingay explains Jesus's claim that he fulfills the Isaiah text he has just cited (Luke 4:16–21): "The traditional translation 'fulfilled' makes this comment sound as if the testimony was a prediction, but *plēroō* is a more

2. Christopher J. H. Wright, *Knowing Jesus through the Old Testament* (Downers Grove, IL: InterVarsity Press, 1992).

ordinary (yet interesting) word than that" since "Jesus . . . comments that this Scripture has been 'filled' or 'filled out' or 'filled up' in his hearers' ears" (34). Here I am reminded of the British missionary John Nichol Farquhar's writings. Inaugurating a whole new groundbreaking approach to missions that continues to have traction, he cited Matthew 5:17 in an article (1910), a text parallel to the one Goldingay employs (Luke 4:16–21): "Christ's own declaration, 'I came not to destroy but to fulfil,' has cleared up for us completely all our difficulties with regard to the Old Testament . . . which finds its perfect consummation in the life, death, resurrection and teaching of Jesus Christ."[3]

Farquhar appears to understand the verb "to fulfil" in much the same way—in the sense of filling out into a "perfect consummation" rather than as predictive. However, while Goldingay applies the text in "connection with the Torah and the Prophets" (34), Farquhar moves beyond the Judeo-Christian canon to ask, "Can it be that Christ Himself was thinking of pagan faiths as well as Judaism when He said, 'I came not to destroy, but to fulfil'"? Farquhar goes on to explain how "Christianity is the fulfilment and crown of each" of the Indian sub-continent's many religions.[4] Whether this is so or not, the point here is that if—as Goldingay rightly affirms—"Christ is everywhere in the First Testament story," this is certainly not the case in the scriptures of other faiths; and if the latter are understood as pointing to Christ and being deployed accordingly in missions, then the potential of the Old Testament to lead up to Jesus needs to be not just acknowledged but celebrated in language that leaves no room for misconception! To emphasize that the Old Testament "does not point to Christ" without adding an explanatory qualifier could be problematic. At the very least, we could affirm that the Old Testament has the *potential* to point to Christ.

Here, what might help is *not* to separate out the meaning of an Old Testament text from its significance or application. I agree that

---

3. Cited in Geoman K. George, "Early 20th Century British Missionaries and Fulfilment Theology: Comparison of the Approaches of William Temple Gairdner to Islam in Egypt, and John Nichol Farquhar to Hinduism in India," in *Christian Witness between Continuity and New Beginnings: Modern Historical Missions in the Middle East*, ed. Martin Tamcke and Michael Martens, Studien zur Orientalischen Kirchengeschichte 39 (Berlin: LIT, 2006), 17.

4. Cited in George, "Early 20th Century British Missionaries and Fulfilment Theology," 17.

"the difference between meaning and significance is worth preserving, because letting Genesis or Isaiah and Galatians or Matthew have their separate meanings gives us two texts to learn from. If we assimilate Genesis and Isaiah to Galatians and Matthew, we have only one meaning" (33). However, this separation of meaning and significance reminds me of how, over the last century and a half, Indian Christian theologians have separated ancient Sanskrit texts and philosophical concepts from their original meaning within Hinduism and baptized them with a whole new significance in the light of the cross. Indigenous hymns have borrowed phrases from the praise of other deities, phrases that originally had nothing to do with Jesus. Whether that is helpful to do is a matter for a different discussion. The point here is that, unlike texts and concepts adapted from other faiths where separation of meaning and significance becomes imperative, the texts and concepts of the Old Testament are in unity and in agreement with the New Testament that such clinically precise separation may not be necessary or helpful. Goldingay's remark on the continuity of the two parts of the Christian canon is germane here: "the New Testament tells us nothing new about God's character, nor does it suggest that there was anything about God that the Torah, the Prophets, and the Writings lacked" (27). This being the case, it might be more exact to speak of *layers* of meaning, as we do with an artfully composed piece of prose or poetry. All the layers may not be in the mind of the narrator or composer. Certainly, there were no christological layers in the mind of the Old Testament writers. Those belong to the reader—whether that is the New Testament writer reading the Old Testament to help him understand the person and work of Jesus, or all those who, down the ages of the history of the church, have read the Old Testament and understood Jesus better through its pages.

Goldingay's emphasis on the priority of the First Testament is well made, especially considering the growing illiteracy of the global church with the first thirty-nine books of the Christian canon. However, as the West becomes increasingly plural in culture and religion, and with the center of gravity of the emerging church shifting to the global South, there is the need to describe the Old Testament's relationship to Jesus in language that incontestably and unambiguously privileges the Old Testament over the sacred texts of other faiths.

JASON S. DEROUCHIE

I will address two main parts of Dr. Goldingay's methodology: (1) How Jesus relates to the First Testament's[1] meaning and significance and (2) typology's nature and role.

Jesus and the First Testament's Meaning and Significance

Goldingay helpfully states that "a message's meaning is what the giver of the message was seeking to communicate to the recipient" (24). Problematically, however, he further asserts that "Christ . . . is not 'in the First Testament' as someone whom the text mentions. Its message to God's people does not invite them to think in terms of him" (22). Moreover, "To read Jesus back" into the First Testament Scriptures results in our missing "what they have to say" (21). In contrast, Goldingay's case studies disclose that he often fails to read carefully even the close context, which helps identify that the First Testament authors themselves were indeed hoping in the promised Messiah. Furthermore, his approach runs counter to the claims of the New Testament itself.

---

1. Jesus would agree with Goldingay that the Hebrew Scriptures are not "old, antiquated, and out-of-date" (21). Yet a number of redemptive-historical factors lead me to think the title "Old Testament" is better than "First Testament." In this essay, I will refer to the Old Testament as the First Testament, but the reader should keep in mind that Moses anticipated the old covenant's end and the need for the new (e.g., Deut 4:25–31; 30:1–14), and his teaching guided the later prophets' hopes (e.g., Isa 54:1–55:5; Jer 31:31–34).

Jesus in Genesis 22:1-19

In his discussion of Genesis 22:1–19, Goldingay maintains that "there is nothing to put the ancestors on the track of the idea that the passage is messianic" (41). But what of the fact that the book's *toledot* structure ("these are the generations of . . .") and the promise of "offspring" throughout the Abrahamic narrative directly tie the story back to the "offspring" promise in Genesis 3:15, upon which the entire world's hope rests? The offspring promise is the means by which God will overcome the problem of sin and its consequences, as curse once again gives rise to divine blessing. By missing the close context, Goldingay fails to note that God promised Abraham not only that he would become a nation (Gen 12:2; cf. 35:11) but also that from this nation would rise a royal *person* who would overcome enemy hostility (49:8–10), bring God's blessing to the nations (22:18), expand God's kingdom (22:17; 24:60; 26:3–4), and make Abraham "the father of a multitude of nations" (17:4; cf. 35:11). The only descendant of Abraham who realizes such hopes is Jesus Christ (Luke 1:68–75; Gal 3:16, 29).

Jesus in Proverbs 8:22-31

Goldingay maintains that "Christ is not in Proverbs 8:22–31" and that "it caused trouble . . . when Christians came to assume that Christ was in Proverbs 8" (42). Yet Goldingay's exegesis of the text never accounts for how the book's opening in 1:1 invites us to read the whole in the light of the historical and prophetic context of the Davidic covenant. Furthermore, he never addresses how the book's early calls to the royal "son" to pursue wisdom (e.g., 1:8, 10; 2:1) anticipate the character of the messianic king or how the allusion back to 8:22–31 in 30:3–4 calls us to consider who the unnamed "son" is who stands as one of the "Holy Ones" who deserves to be known and feared (9:10; 30:3). While Goldingay recognizes some allusion to the wisdom tradition in John 1:1, he fails to note that Jesus himself seems to allude to Proverbs 30:4 in John 3:13, thus identifying himself with the wisdom of Proverbs 8:22–31 and the "son" of 30:4.[2]

---

2. Many commentators on John 3:13 direct readers to Proverbs 30:4a. See, for example, J. H. Bernard, *A Critical and Exegetical Commentary on the Gospel according to St. John*, ed. A. H. McNeile, 2 vols., ICC (Edinburgh: T&T Clark, 1929), 1:111; Raymond E. Brown, *The*

Again, Goldingay's exegesis fails to account for the close and continuing contexts, which causes him to miss the First Testament's meaning.

Jesus in Isaiah 42:1–4

Goldingay says, "Christ is not in Isaiah 42, nor does Isaiah 42 point to Christ" (44). Instead, the "servant" of this text is the people, and the New Testament shows in texts like Matthew 12:17–21 that Jesus's coming prepares "the way for Israel to function as God's servant" (44). But this approach fails, for the nation of Israel as a whole does not stand as a covenant for themselves (Isa 42:6) or operate as a light for the nations to deliver prisoners (42:6–7). Rather, this is the role of the servant-person (cf. 49:3, 6–9). Intriguingly, in an earlier publication, Goldingay sees further significance in the servant's anonymity in 42:1–4 by noting that "Jacob-Israel cannot fulfil this role" but needs "someone to fulfil it."[3] Thus, Jesus himself asserts that Isaiah's claim that the servant "was numbered with the transgressors" (Isa 53:12) was "written about me" and "is reaching its fulfillment" (Luke 22:37). Jesus is addressing the meaning of the words themselves and not just their significance.

Does the First Testament Prophesy about Christ?

Goldingay appears to commit the word-thing fallacy when he asserts that the First Testament does not prophesy about Christ because it does not announce "Jesus" by name like it did for Josiah (1 Kgs 13:1–2). Similarly, the messianic hope of Micah 5:2 (5:1 MT) is only a matter of significance and not meaning since the term *Messiah* does not appear. However, the "shepherd" (5:4 [5:3 MT]) from Bethlehem (5:2 [5:1 MT]) is an eschatological David, who like the original David, would certainly be an "anointed one" or "messiah" (cf. 1 Sam 16:13; 2 Sam 5:3).

Gospel according to John (I–XII): Introduction, Translation, and Notes, AB (New Haven, CT: Yale University Press, 1966), 145; D. A. Carson, *The Gospel according to John*, PNTC (Grand Rapids: Eerdmans, 1991), 201; Leon Morris, *The Gospel according to John*, 2nd ed., NICNT (Grand Rapids: Eerdmans, 1995), 197; Colin G. Kruse, *John: An Introduction and Commentary*, 2nd ed., TNTC 4 (Downers Grove, IL: InterVarsity Press, 2017), 112. Furthermore, Köstenberger notes that John 3:13 "may allude to Prov. 30:4a." Andreas J. Köstenberger, "John," in *Commentary on the New Testament Use of the Old Testament*, ed. G. K. Beale and D. A. Carson (Grand Rapids: Baker Academic, 2007), 435. I thank my doctoral fellow Brian Verrett for reminding me of Jesus's allusion in John 3:13.

3. John Goldingay, *The Message of Isaiah 40–55: A Literary-Theological Commentary* (New York: T&T Clark, 2005), 153–54.

Furthermore, the one Isaiah tags "Immanuel" (Isa 7:14) and a child-king (9:6) could still refer to Jesus of Nazareth, even though the prophet never applies the name Jesus or the title "Messiah" to him. Goldingay himself finds "Antiochus . . . in Daniel 11" (38)—a text that never names him, and this fact identifies the fallacious nature of his earlier comments.

Given Goldingay's position regarding the First Testament containing no references to the Messiah, he asserts, "It's hardly surprising that John the Baptizer wonders if Jesus is really the one who was to come (Luke 7:18–19)" (33). Against Goldingay, however, John's claim assumes that the First Testament actually anticipated someone to save (cf. Luke 2:25, 38), and Jesus's response identifies himself as the servant-person for whom Isaiah was looking. Any offense to the imprisoned John would arise only if he failed to hope in the completed work that Christ was inaugurating.

Goldingay denies that Jesus's response to John in Luke 7:22–23 bears any link with Isaiah's words. But Goldingay ignores the close context, missing that the prophet associates the very epoch that Isaiah 35:5–6 describes with the promised king, servant, and anointed conqueror![4] Goldingay further fails to see Isaiah 61:1–2's messianism since he limits First Testament "prophecy" to a particular genre, standing against the New Testament authors who view "prophecy" and "fulfillment" (i.e., *plēroō*, "to fulfill") in much broader terms (Matt 11:13; cf. Luke 16:16). Jesus prophetically fulfills not only explicit promises but also recorded events like the exodus (Matt 2:15; cf. Hos 11:1), legal material from Moses (Matt 5:17–18), and depictions like the servant's role in bringing healing (Matt 8:17; cf. Isa 53:4).

The New Testament's Claims Regarding the First Testament's Meaning

For Goldingay, when the New Testament links Christ to First Testament promises, we learn about how the "later writer" received or applied the First Testament text (i.e., reception history) rather than "the meaning of the original text" (25). But this understanding fails to explain the New Testament data. Luke tells us that Jesus "interpreted" the First Testament, causing others to "understand the Scriptures" (Luke 24:27,

---

4. Cf. Isaiah 35:2 with 40:5; 35:4 with 63:1–6; 35:6–7 with 32:2 and 49:10; 35:8 with 19:23 and 62:10–12.

45). The verbs speak not of *applying* but of *interpreting* and *understanding* what "is written" in the text. More appears operative here than merely addressing the First Testament's lasting significance (cf. 1 Cor 2:13; 2 Pet 1:20–21).

Goldingay asserts, "One cannot prove from the First Testament that Jesus is the Messiah" (35). But is this not exactly what Paul did when "reasoning and persuading them about the kingdom of God" (Acts 19:8 ESV; cf. 28:23)? And why did Luke commend the Bereans (Acts 17:11)? Furthermore, often the New Testament argument's logic hinges on Jesus residing in the First Testament's meaning (e.g., John 5:45–47; Acts 2:22–36; 13:32–37). Far from Goldingay's claim that the First Testament's "message to God's people does not invite them to think in terms of [Jesus]" (22), Peter said that "God . . . foretold . . . that his Messiah would suffer" through "*all* the prophets" (Acts 3:18, emphasis added; cf. 2:30–31; 3:24). Jesus himself asserted that the account about the servant in Isaiah 53:12 was "written about me" (Luke 22:37). To claim that the New Testament authors only applied Isaiah to Jesus but did not view him as part of the original meaning is to say more than the texts allow.

Typology

Goldingay's understanding of typology resembles mine, except that he does not treat typology as prophetic in nature. Therefore, for Goldingay, types are only literary features of significance, not meaning, and they are known only in retrospect (*a posteriori*). In contrast, I suggest that typology is related to meaning inherent in the original and not just the significance drawn from it. A case in point is that we learn that Miriam was a "prophetess" when she first sang the Song of the Sea (Exod 15:19–21). This song portrays the first exodus (15:4–10) as a foreshadow that ensures coming future victories (15:13–18). Because Moses viewed the original exodus typologically (i.e., as indirect prophecy), he later associated a second exodus with a messianic royal figure (Num 24:7–9). And on this basis, Isaiah linked a second exodus with a coming Spirit-empowered king (Isa 11:1–12:6) by recalling the words of Exodus 15:2 (Isa 12:2).

Goldingay claims, "In the First Testament, the priests, the sacrifices, and the sanctuary are not shadows of something else" (31). But Paul asserted that features of the old covenant associated with "food . . . drink . . . a festival . . . a new moon or a Sabbath" are all "a shadow" whose "substance belongs to Christ" (Col 2:16–17 ESV). Moreover, Hebrews' author argued that everything associated with the old covenant tabernacle was "a copy and shadow of what is in heaven" and that God "warned" Moses of this very fact, saying, "See to it that you make everything according to the pattern shown you on the mountain" (Heb 8:5; cf. Exod 25:40). God's speech to Moses in Exodus 25:40 identifies that the prophet himself recognized the typological nature of the earthly tabernacle, and Scripture suggests that he saw the potential for advancement from type to the antitype. In Leviticus 26:11–12 Yahweh promised that he would dwell and walk among the people in a special way (beyond the tabernacle experience) *if* they perfectly obeyed. Jesus, representing Israel the people, perfectly obeyed and thus secured such realities for everyone in him (2 Cor 6:16; cf. Ezek 37:27). *Moses*, thus, knew that the tabernacle bore a built-in obsolescence, such that when the pattern became sight, there would no longer be a need for the earthly replica.

An added feature of typology that highlights its prospective nature is the presence of identifiable patterns within the biblical story. Authors by design draw attention to repeated events, character experiences, or scenarios and do so to identify a predictive cycle, guided by God, that will climax in future fulfillment. Examples include the motifs of "parting waters" leading to "new creation" (Gen 1–2; Exod 14–15; Josh 3–4; Isa 11–12) and of "the sin of the two sons" (Gen 34; Lev 10; 1 Sam 2; 8:1–3; 2 Sam 13–18). Authors generate links between texts that are neither random nor accidental but are instead purposeful and that drive ahead to literary resolution.

Conclusion

Goldingay claims that the First Testament's inherent meaning never related to Christ Jesus and that typology is only a literary device telling us how later authors found significance concerning Christ in the First Testament. But such perspectives run counter to the New Testament's own claims regarding both the First Testament texts and the New Testament authors' approach. The First Testament prophets foresaw and hoped in Jesus's day (Matt 13:17; John 8:56). By the Spirit's help, they interpreted their Scriptures (2 Pet 1:20–21), searching them and praying to learn more about Jesus's person and time (1 Pet 1:10–11). New Testament figures like Jesus (Luke 24:27) and Paul (1 Cor 2:13) interpreted what the Spirit revealed to be the meaning of the prophetic writings themselves and of Jesus's teaching (Rom 16:25–26). Interpreting the First Testament texts within their close, continuing, and canonical contexts enables one to recognize that Christ is central to the First Testament's meaning and hope.

RESPONSE TO JOHN GOLDINGAY
(THE PREMODERN APPROACH)

CRAIG A. CARTER

If Dr. Goldingay is right, then most of the Christian church has been reading the Bible wrongly most of the time for most of church history. If he is right, it is a good thing the German higher critics of the nineteenth century came along to inform us that the non-messianic rabbinic Jews had been reading the Hebrew Bible correctly all along. Most premodern biblical commentary on the Old Testament is embarrassingly deficient. The central dogmas of Trinity and incarnation rest on the New Testament alone. From Marcion to the German Christians of the 1930s, heretics have declared the Old Testament to be a Jewish, and therefore not a Christian, book. Goldingay would not agree with them, but it seems to me that he has hollowed out the Christian argument as to why they are wrong to a dangerous degree.

Goldingay asserts several times that the Bible is a metanarrative that comes to a climax in Jesus Christ. But what does he mean by this statement? He seems to be saying that we can have a Christian interpretation of the Old Testament (which he calls the First Testament). But the way we obtain this Christian reading of the Hebrew Scriptures is by reading into them our Christian preunderstanding. Goldingay thinks we have no choice but to do so.

For Goldingay, we become Christians by reading the New Testament, and then we claim that the Hebrew Bible can be read as the precursor to the New Testament. This appears to leave the interpretation of the Hebrew Scriptures open in such a way that two opposing interpretations could both be right. The rabbinic Jewish reading that supposes that Jesus was not the Messiah and the messianic Jewish reading that sees

Jesus as the Messiah could both be right. But only the first would be the *inherent meaning* of the Hebrew Scriptures themselves. This is a huge theological problem for Christian faith insofar as the claim of the church has always been that our Trinitarian and christological dogma, which is foundational to saving faith, is the true meaning of the Bible, not just our opinion of its significance.

Goldingay makes three key moves in this chapter that need to be examined. First, he uses a hard and fast distinction between meaning and significance. Second, he claims that Christ is not in the Old Testament, going so far as to say that "one cannot prove from the First Testament that Jesus is the Messiah" (35). Third, he claims that the New Testament writers use Old Testament texts in a way that "looks unrelated to their inherent meaning" (32). Taken together, these three moves render the apostolic interpretation of the Hebrew Scriptures untenable and undermine the unity of the Bible as a two Testament witness to Jesus Christ. This is not Goldingay's intention, to be sure, but it is the unintended consequence of his rejection of the premodern church's approach to understanding Christ in the Hebrew Scriptures.

Meaning and Significance

The first move involves a hard distinction between the meaning of the text and its "significance or application." I find the concept of "application" to be very problematic as it is used, for example, in inductive Bible study. The three steps of inductive Bible study are often set forth as observation, interpretation, and application. This is a widely used approach in evangelical churches. When I teach laypeople this method of Bible study, I am sure to define application as something the Holy Spirit does rather than as something we do. We observe the text carefully, and then we attempt to place it in its immediate literary context, its context in the book of the Bible, and its canonical context. Placing the text in its proper context is the essence of "interpretation." Then I say that when one spends time reading and rereading the text carefully, praying over it, observing every detail you can, and setting it in its proper context, one usually finds that in this process the Spirit opens your eyes to see ways in which the text applies to your life. It is not something you gin up artificially or choose arbitrarily; it arises organically out of the text as the Spirit who inspired the text illumines your understanding of what God is saying to you through it. The result can be encouragement, comfort, conviction of sin, insight into the nature of God, or a new desire to worship or obey. The point is that if God's word is to be a means by which Christ is Lord of our lives, we cannot be in charge of deciding how it is applied to us.

This concern for ensuring that the Bible is the vehicle by which God speaks authoritatively into our situation through his word has been key to the Christian understanding of Scripture from the days of the church fathers on. Reading Scripture is a means of sanctification through the Spirit; it is a spiritual discipline. The effect of hiving off "significance" or "application" from meaning is to bring the word of God under human control and domesticate it. When we read either Testament, we should come face-to-face with our Creator and Redeemer, and we should believe what we learn and obey the commands we find. Bible reading is discipleship, and it should move us to obedience and worship.

For God to be Lord of our lives, God must determine the significance of the text, and the way theology has traditionally understood that to happen is through divine authorial intent as the determining factor in what the text means. Its inherent meaning is what God says through the text. This is something we discover, not something we decide. As I show in my book *Interpreting Scripture with the Great Tradition*,[1] the church historically has seen levels of meaning in the text, although the terminology used to describe this phenomenon has varied considerably. One way of doing so, going back to John Cassian, and becoming prominent in the medieval period, is to speak of the fourfold sense of Scripture consisting of the literal sense plus a threefold spiritual sense. The tradition represented by Thomas Aquinas and Nicholas of Lyra has spoken of the extended or expanded literal sense. Augustine spoke of the christological sense. All levels of meaning beyond the human authorial intent are seen as part of divine authorial intent.

Divine authorial intent is present because of the inspiration of Scripture. First Peter 1:10–12 is the *locus classicus* for the distinction between human and authorial intent. The prophets are pictured as seeking to grasp what person or time the Spirit of Christ in them

---

1. Craig A. Carter, *Interpreting Scripture with the Great Tradition: Recovering the Genius of Premodern Exegesis* (Grand Rapids: Baker Academic, 2018), chaps. 5–7.

was indicating through their inspired utterances. The human author understood much of what the text says, but not all. As Paul indicated in 1 Corinthians 10:11, although the Old Testament texts obviously were written for their own time, they can be said to have been written down for our instruction as well. The spiritual or extended literal or christological sense is the divine authorial intent that is found in the text in addition to the human authorial intent. This feature of the Old Testament is what makes it relevant to all generations of readers throughout history. And since the aspect of the text that is "for us" is part of the meaning, it is objective and binding, not subjective and under our control as readers.

The meaning versus significance distinction reduces the meaning of the text to human authorial intent only. It can lead to two equally unhelpful outcomes: either seeing the Old Testament text as irrelevant or making it relevant by reading our ideas into it. Both moves render its authority moot. It is messier and more complex to see a spiritual sense in addition to the literal or an extended literal christological sense, but it has the merit of allowing us as readers to submit to the word of God as found in the text of the whole Bible.

Is Christ in the Old Testament?

Goldingay repeatedly makes statements to the effect that Christ is not in the Old Testament. Christ is not in Genesis 22, he claims. Christ is not in Proverbs 8 either. There is nothing messianic in Isaiah 42. He says categorically, "Thus, one cannot prove from the First Testament that Jesus is the Messiah" (35).

The degree to which this upends two thousand years of Christian theology cannot be minimized. This position implies that Paul's opponents in those synagogue debates during his missionary journeys were right. We are told that when Paul and Silas came to Thessalonica, Paul sought to convince the Jews there that Jesus is the Messiah (Acts 17:2–4). Paul's message was that Jesus is the Christ of the Hebrew Scriptures. The objection that the Messiah would never have ended up on a Roman cross was an obvious one, and Paul met it head-on. In doing so, he was merely following the example of Jesus.

After his resurrection, Jesus rebuked the disciples on the Emmaus road for being "foolish" and "slow of heart to believe all that the prophets have spoken" (Luke 24:25 ESV). He asked, "Was it not necessary that the Christ should suffer these things and then enter into his glory?" (v. 26 ESV). Then we are told that "beginning with Moses and all the Prophets, he interpreted to them in all the Scriptures the things concerning himself" (v. 27 ESV). Jesus and Paul taught that the Old Testament testified to Christ. The early church fathers took their cue from them in seeing Christ as the content of the Old Testament and its central theme. They would not have conceded that they were reading Christ into the Old Testament, which brings us to the third move Goldingay makes that is concerning.

Reading Christ into the Old Testament

Goldingay says this about Paul's use of allegory in Galatians 4: "His interpretation of the story uses the words of Genesis to throw light on salvation in Christ in a way that looks unrelated to their inherent meaning" (32). Goldingay's position is that it was all right for Paul to use the Scriptures in this way, but it would be wrong for us to do so. But this makes Paul and the other New Testament apostles bad examples for interpreters. As Andrew Louth pointedly asks, "How can one accept their results if one does not accept their methods?"[2] As Louth and many others point out, the church fathers followed the apostles in their methods of interpretation, and we see the fruits of their exegesis in the ecumenical creeds.

The Definition of Chalcedon of 451, having stated the doctrine of the two natures of Christ and the hypostatic union, adds, "just as the prophets taught from the beginning about him, and as the Lord Jesus Christ himself instructed us, and as the creed of the fathers handed it down to us."[3] The "creed of the fathers" is the Niceno-Constantinopolitan Creed of 381, which is an expansion of the Creed of Nicaea of 325. The fathers who defined the dogmas of Trinity and incarnation believed that the dogmas contained in the creeds constitute the true teaching of the

---

2. Andrew Louth, *Discerning the Mystery: An Essay on the Nature of Theology* (Oxford: Clarendon, 1983), 100.

3. Jaroslav Pelikan and Valerie Hotchkiss, eds., *Creeds and Confessions of Faith in the Christian Tradition: Volume I: Early, Eastern and Medieval* (New Haven, CT: Yale University Press, 2003), 181.

whole Bible. This is the essence of the ecumenical Christian faith and has been since its beginning.

Conclusion

Jesus Christ is the theme of the whole Bible. From Genesis 1 to the end of Revelation, he is the sun around which all else revolves. The meaning of the Old Testament is Christ, and he is found there as the literal sense defined by divine authorial intent. We do not read him into the Scriptures; we meet him there.

REJOINDER

JOHN GOLDINGAY

I'm grateful to my co-contributors for their comments, which make me clarify or qualify some points.

The First Testament indeed refers to the Messiah, in the sense that it declares God's intention to fulfill his promises about a coming Davidic ruler. But it doesn't call him the Messiah; nor do its promises about this ruler amount to a portrait that corresponds with who Jesus is. This fits with several facets of the New Testament's accounts of Jesus, to which I refer in my chapter. John the Baptizer can't see that Jesus behaves messianically, and Jesus responds to him not by quoting messianic texts but by drawing attention to things he has actually been doing, none of which corresponds to a text that refers to the Messiah (Matt 11:2–6). And when Peter recognizes him as the Messiah, Jesus both congratulates him and bids him not to tell anyone, then goes on to try to get the disciples to understand that he has to be killed and be raised from death, which they did not expect of the Messiah—which all links with the fact that his own preferred title is "Son of Man" (Matt 16:13–21). So Jesus is the Messiah, but that is not the only important thing about him. This also fits the opening verses in Hebrews (Heb 1:1–2) about God having spoken in various ways by the prophets (one of them being their promises of a coming Davidic ruler) but having now spoken by a Son (who in himself is the Messiah, and also the exalted Son of Man, and the Lord, and the persecuted prophet who makes his suffering an offering to God to compensate for his people's wrongdoing).

In this connection, I overstated the point about it being impossible to prove from the First Testament that Jesus is the Messiah. Acts does record that Paul did so. It would be better to say that the main way Paul and other New Testament writers relate the First Testament to Jesus is in using it to help believers understand the Jesus in whom they believe. And my guess is that Paul's argument in Acts involved more than an appeal to messianic texts in the narrow sense—in effect, he would be arguing that Jesus is the embodiment of that wider range of First Testament texts.

First Testament realities such as the sacrifices did turn out to foreshadow Jesus, but for the people to whom God gave the rules about such matters, they were not shadows but realities, and we have so much to learn from them when we consider what God meant them to signify for his relationship with Israel and their relationship with him. They were realities, though they also turned out to be things that were in some ways overshadowed by what came about in Jesus. I write just after All Saints Day, and when I was a pastor in California, on this day each year I would reflect that the joy of worshiping in our multiethnic congregation was a foreshadowing of the worship described in Revelation 7. It was both a present reality and a foreshadowing. I expect there are other present realities that I will recognize to have been foreshadowings when I get to the new Jerusalem, but I don't realize now that they are shadows. They are simply realities. Temple, priesthood, and sacrifices were the second kind of foreshadowings. For Israel, they were simply realities of God's relationship with them. The writer of Hebrews, looking back, could see them as foreshadowings.

I appreciated Dr. Carter's description of the way he encourages his congregation to engage in the study of the Scriptures and his description of the organic way in which the Holy Spirit brings out the significance of a text for us. I agree with him that the application of the Scriptures to us is the Holy Spirit's business, but I wouldn't make the rather sharp distinction he makes between interpretation as our business and application as the Holy Spirit's business. In practice there is more interweaving between these two stages, and the Holy Spirit is involved in both. Sometimes an insight about the significance or application of a text makes it possible to see more clearly the inherent meaning of the text. A classic example is Paul's wrestling with the enigma of his people's refusal to recognize Jesus (cf. Rom 9–11), during which wrestling he receives a revelation from God about the interpretation of the First Testament story as a whole.

In connection with Paul's use of the First Testament, Dr. Carter goes on to comment that "Goldingay's position is that it was all right for Paul to use the Scriptures in this way, but it would be wrong for us to do so. But this makes Paul and the other New Testament apostles bad examples for interpreters" (67). I don't say that, and I don't think it. I note in my chapter that God has sometimes spoken to me through words of Scripture in a way that did not correspond to the text's inherent meaning. This is a reality about how the Holy Spirit sometimes works. The New Testament's own use of the Scriptures in a way that does not correspond with their inherent meaning is an outworking of their being *theopneustos*, God-breathed (2 Tim 3:16). A number of Dr. Carter's other comments attribute to me views that I do not hold or express, such as that "most premodern biblical commentary on the Old Testament is embarrassingly deficient" (63). I might add, as I suspect he would, that most modern biblical commentary is embarrassingly deficient.

I note with enthusiasm Dr. Dharamraj's description of people coming to know Jesus *through* the First Testament, her comment that in some contexts one needs to privilege the First Testament, and her observation that when setting the First Testament alongside other people's sacred texts one needs to affirm the special relationship between the First Testament and Jesus. These features of her chapter cohere with my convictions (which I think Dr. Longman also shares) that God spoke to his people in the First Testament in ways that they could understand even though they did not know about Jesus, and that we have much to gain by reading it with them as God's message to us, without reading Jesus into it.

CHRISTOTELIC APPROACH

TREMPER LONGMAN III

Introduction to the Approach

Through their numerous citations and allusions to the Old Testament, the New Testament authors make it abundantly clear that the former anticipates the Messiah who is Jesus. As we will explain in more detail below, Jesus himself told his disciples that the Scriptures, meaning what we call the Old Testament, looked forward to his coming (Luke 24:25–27, 44–49). For these reasons alone, it appears incontestable that a Christian reading of the Old Testament recognize that Jesus is indeed in the Old Testament.

Even so, questions remain. For instance, if the Old Testament anticipates the coming of the Messiah, why did so few—indeed, from the gospel accounts, nobody—quite get it? Why, after the crucifixion, are the Messiah's followers confused and dismayed (Luke 24:17) rather than excited and expectant? And why does it appear that it all begins to make sense to them in the light of the resurrection in a way that it hadn't before?

In this chapter, I argue that while perhaps they should have known better (otherwise how should we understand Jesus's charge that the two disciples on the road to Emmaus were "foolish" [Luke 24:25]), the deeper meaning of the Old Testament becomes much clearer in the light of the resurrection. Indeed, I believe the textual evidence indicates that the Old Testament writers themselves would often have been surprised at how their writings anticipated Jesus, the suffering and victorious Messiah.

Thus, this chapter presents what has been called a Christotelic approach to the question of Christ in the Old Testament. Christ is the goal (the *telos*) of the Old Testament, so that, as Augustine famously said, "The New is hidden in the Old and the Old is revealed in the New."[1]

I also will suggest that a proper understanding of Christ in the Old Testament requires that the Christian interpreter read an Old Testament text twice. The first reading brackets the fuller knowledge acquired in the further revelation of the New Testament. In other words, we read the Old Testament in its original context as addressed to its contemporary audience in order to hear the "discrete voice" of the Old Testament. The second reading then seeks to understand the passage in the light of the coming of Christ.

Nature of Scripture

Scripture is God's word to his human creatures. While God discloses himself in many different ways (through image bearers, nature, our conscience, and more), nowhere does he reveal himself more clearly than in the words of the Bible. That is why the church recognizes the Bible as its canon, the standard of its faith and practice.

That the Bible is the word of God raises questions about the relationship between divine and human authorship, which we will explore in the next section. Here I simply affirm that since God is its ultimate author, then it is true that Scripture is true in everything that it teaches, which is the best understanding of the doctrine of inerrancy against some who believe that inerrancy entails certain interpretive conclusions.

But we always must remember that while Scripture is without error in all that it affirms, our interpretations are not inerrant. That is why we have differences about the intended meaning of biblical texts, including how Christ relates to the Old Testament. Still, the Bible is clear in what matters. In this we affirm the Westminster Confession of Faith:

---

1. Augustine, *Questions on the Heptateuch* 2.73, in *Writings on the Old Testament*, The Works of Saint Augustine: A Translation for the 21st Century, trans. Joseph T. Lienhard and Sean Doyle (New York: New City Press, 2016), 125 (Exodus, 73).

> All things in Scripture are not alike plain in themselves, nor alike clear unto all: yet those things which are necessary to be known, believed, and observed for salvation, are so clearly propounded, and opened in some place of Scripture or other, that not only the learned, but the unlearned, in a due use of the ordinary means, may attain unto a sufficient understanding of them.

That the Bible is God's word also implies an organic unity or coherence to the books of the Bible. The Bible is composed of a wide variety of different types of books (historical, poetic, prophetic, epistolary, apocalyptic) written over a period of centuries by authors and editors, some of whom we know by name but many whom we do not, who lived in significantly different historical contexts and addressed a wide variety of contemporary issues. Yet the Bible, while being written for us, was not written to us.[2] Issues of genre as well as literary and historical setting are important as we consider how the New Testament relates to the Old Testament.

One important consideration is that we should not prematurely and superficially impose a New Testament perspective on an Old Testament text. Old Testament authors wrote their books to be understood by and to address the concerns of their contemporaries. So while we can get a fuller understanding of Old Testament texts in the light of the New Testament, believing that the original readers or the author would have been aware of that fuller meaning is an error.

Let's consider two examples. Genesis 3 opens, "Now the serpent was more crafty than any of the wild animals the Lord God had made" (v. 1). This walking[3] serpent clearly speaks and acts at cross-purposes with God, successfully luring Adam and Eve into violating God's command not to eat from the tree of the knowledge of good and evil. What would the original audience have thought of the serpent? Many Christian readers would say that the serpent is the devil, also known as Satan, and might point to a passage like Revelation 12:9 to make their point: "The great dragon was hurled down—that ancient serpent called the devil,

---

2. The turn of phrase here is John H. Walton's (personal communication).
3. Implied because the serpent's later punishment included being reduced to slithering on the ground (Gen. 3:14).

or Satan, who leads the whole world astray." They would be correct to make the connection back to Genesis 3:1 but wrong to think that the ancient author and audience would have made that connection. There is nothing in the Old Testament that gives indication that the character of Satan was so clearly understood during that time period.[4]

What would they have thought then? Reading Genesis 3 in the light of its contemporary setting (or more generally in the context of the Old Testament) suggests that they would have understood the serpent as a symbol of personified evil. Walking serpents were representative of evil forces in the ancient Near East.[5]

An organic, coherent relationship exists between the Old and New Testaments, but they are not identical or related in a static way. We find both continuity and discontinuity as we move from the Old Testament to the New Testament, which are based at least in part on what theologians have called the progression of revelation. That is, God over time reveals more and more about himself to his people. For example, we learn more about the Trinity, the afterlife, and many other teachings and concepts as we read the New Testament. That there is both continuity and discontinuity between the Testaments is expressed in Jesus's well-known statement at the beginning of the Sermon on the Mount:

> Do not think that I have come to abolish the Law or the Prophets; I have not come to abolish them but to fulfill them. For truly I tell you, until heaven and earth disappear, not the smallest letter, not the least stroke of a pen, will by any means disappear from the Law until everything is accomplished. (Matt 5:17–18)

---

4. Ryan E. Stokes, *The Satan: How God's Executioner Became the Enemy* (Grand Rapids: Eerdmans, 2019).

5. John H. Walton points out that in the Adapa text one of the divine doorkeepers to heaven is Ningishzida who is depicted as a serpent and is the "guardian of demons who lives in the underworld." John H. Walton, "Genesis," in *Genesis, Exodus, Leviticus, Numbers, Deuteronomy*, ZIBBCOT 1 (Grand Rapids: Zondervan, 2007), 33. He also talks about how in Egypt serpents were associated with magical, dark wisdom and with the figure of Apophis, a chaos monster. Indeed, Tiamat, the goddess of chaos who resists the forces of creation in the Enuma Elish is thought to be serpentine in appearance. She certainly gives birth to serpentine demonic figures. In what may be pictorial representations of Tiamat, she is depicted as a walking serpent.

Jesus places a heavy emphasis on continuity, but he also asserts discontinuity. When the purpose of an Old Testament passage is "accomplished," it has been fulfilled and is no longer relevant or observed in the same way as during the Old Testament period. The New Testament provides the pattern for us as we see what continues and what does not. Obvious examples of the latter include sacrifices, circumcision, food laws, and holy war.

The covenants provide further guidance on the question of continuity and discontinuity. A biblical theology of covenant in the Bible is full of nuance and generates disagreements on many questions. Was there a covenant of Adam? What is the precise relationship between the various covenants? My point here is simply that the relationship between the historical covenants is neither pure continuity nor pure discontinuity, and this is certainly true of the covenants of the Old Testament and the new covenant of the New Testament.[6]

We can see this in a classic passage that announces the future new covenant in relationship to the old, particularly in terms of the Mosaic covenant. The discontinuity is clear in Jeremiah 31:31–32:

> "The days are coming," declares the Lord,
>   "when I will make a new covenant
> with the people of Israel
>   and with the people of Judah.
> It will not be like the covenant
>   I made with their ancestors
> when I took them by the hand
>   to lead them out of Egypt,
> because they broke my covenant,
>   though I was a husband to them,"
> declares the Lord.

This passage goes on, however, to describe the new covenant in a way that signals there will be continuity:

---

6. For a helpful survey of the main schools on this issue, see Benjamin L. Merkle, *Discontinuity to Continuity: A Survey of Dispensational and Covenantal Theologies* (Bellingham, WA: Lexham, 2020). I find myself somewhere between what he calls progressive covenantalism and covenant theology.

"This is the covenant I will make with the people of Israel
 after that time," declares the Lord.
"I will put my law in their minds
 and write it on their hearts.
I will be their God,
 and they will be my people.
No longer will they teach their neighbor,
 or say to one another, 'Know the Lord,'
because they will all know me,
 from the least to the greatest,"
  declares the Lord.
"For I will forgive their wickedness
 and will remember their sins no more." (Jer 31:33–34)

The new covenant does not abolish the law but puts it on the hearts and minds of the people. God will continue to be their God, and they will be his people. The promise that God will forgive the people's wickedness should not be taken to imply that the Israelites never had their sin forgiven. The new covenant does not abolish the relationship between God and his people depicted by the old covenants. The new makes it more intense, intimate, internal, and immediate.

The New Testament confirms this understanding in its depiction of the new covenant established by Jesus (Luke 22:20; 1 Cor 11:25; Heb 8:7–13) as a fulfillment of the old covenants. Jesus, as the Messiah, fulfills the Davidic covenant (2 Sam 7). According to Paul, he is the promised seed of Abraham (Gal 3:15–29). Jesus is the fulfillment of the Mosaic covenant as the divine Lawgiver (Matt 5–7), law keeper, and the one who suffers the penalty of the law on our behalf. How he fulfills the Noahic covenant is more complicated, but related is the idea of a covenant of Adam that is a covenant of creation, leading us to understand the Noahic covenant as a covenant of re-creation. We should see the fulfillment of the creation and re-creation covenants in the language of Jesus as the Second Adam (Rom 5:12–21; 1 Cor 15:21–22, 45–49).

I do not have space for a full presentation of a biblical theology of covenant, but I hope I have provided enough to demonstrate the continuity and discontinuity between the Old and New Testaments. One practical implication of the continuity and discontinuity we find in the relationship between the Testaments is *the necessity of attending to the message of the Old Testament before considering the passage from a New Testament perspective.*

In other words, we must begin by listening to what Brevard S. Childs, an interpreter who practices what others call christological/telic interpretation, calls the "discrete voice" or "discrete witness" of the Old Testament.[7] Walter Brueggemann concurs, calling for a reading of the Old Testament apart from the New Testament that preserves the "wild and untamed" theological witness of the Old Testament.[8] We must first read a passage of the Old Testament from the vantage point of its original authors as they address the first intended audience, also called the "implied readers." Here we consider the benefits of a historical-grammatical or historical-critical approach. Only after we interpret the text from the perspective of the original author and first readers should we proceed with a second reading from the perspective provided by the New Testament.

Reading the Old Testament as a Christian is analogous to watching a movie or reading a book or piece of literature a second time. One's first interpretation of a passage must be based on how the text would have been understood by its original audience. This honors the fact that the books of the Old Testament were not written to us but to an ancient audience and preserves the "discrete voice" of the Old Testament witness to God. However, a Christian cannot stop at that point but must read the text a second time, utilizing the full perspective of the New Testament as well. While some believe that such a reading entails a problematic Christian appropriation of Jewish literature, I agree with the Jewish scholar Jon Levenson of Harvard University, who recognizes that "Christian exegesis requires that the Hebrew Bible be read ultimately in a literary context that includes the New Testament. To read the Hebrew Bible on its own would be like reading the first three acts of *Hamlet* as if the last two had never been written."[9]

---

7. Brevard S. Childs, *Biblical Theology of the Old and New Testaments: Theological Reflections on the Christian Bible* (Minneapolis: Fortress, 1993), 76.

8. Walter Brueggemann, *Theology of the Old Testament: Testimony, Dispute, Advocacy* (Minneapolis: Fortress, 1997).

9. Jon D. Levenson, *The Hebrew Bible, the Old Testament, and Historical Criticism: Jews and Christians in Biblical Studies* (Louisville: Westminster John Knox, 1993), 9.

Authorial Intent

Any textual communication involves an *author* producing a *text* directed to an *audience*. The various biblical books are texts composed by authors directed to an audience, yet there are many nuances and complications with each of the three elements of this transaction. For example, considerable evidence shows that most biblical books were not written by a single author but by multiple authors over time, most of whom we cannot name. However, our interest is in the canonical final form of the text, and so we think of the author as the final author/redactor who brought the text into its final form, the one we read in our Bible today. When we speak of the reader, we remind ourselves that the audience of biblical books was the contemporary audience receiving the final form of the book—not those of us reading the book today. Sometimes we can specify the date of the final form of a book (e.g., Samuel–Kings during the exile; Nahum before the fall of Assyria in 612 BC), but often we cannot pinpoint an exact date or there is debate over when a biblical book came into its final form.[10] Nonetheless, we can say that all books of the Old Testament reached their final form well before the coming of Christ, thus justifying the insistence that we read Old Testament texts in their discrete setting in the Old Testament time period *before* reading them from a New Testament perspective.

Despite these nuances, we should insist on an author-centered understanding of meaning. An author writes a text to communicate a message to readers, and readers examine the text to hear the voice of the author. However, since the mid-twentieth-century work of the New Critics, many argue that this view commits the intentional fallacy.[11] How, we might ask, can anyone get into the mind of the author, especially one separated from us by time and culture? I agree that attempts to get into the mind of the author are wrong-minded and problematic. After all, what access do we have to biblical authors except through the text they

---

10. Or for that matter, the various earlier redactional stages of a book. For instance, I would understand Proverbs to have an origin at the time of Solomon, but Proverbs 25:1 makes it very clear that it had not reached its final form (no matter what Solomon's relationship to that material "compiled" by the men of Hezekiah). Jeremiah 36 shows that there was an edition of that book produced around 605 BC, but we don't know how many later editions existed before the book came to its final form, but almost certainly after the lifetime of Jeremiah.

11. W. K. Wimsatt and M. Beardsley, "The Intentional Fallacy," reprinted in *The Verbal Icon: Studies in the Meaning of Poetry* (Lexington: University Press of Kentucky, 1954), 3–18.

have written? We can't interview them or ask questions, and even if we could (speaking as an author myself), they might not remember or even fully know what meanings they have put into play through unconscious intertextual references.[12]

Our only access to an author's intended message is through a careful study of their literary production. As Kevin Vanhoozer has forcefully argued,[13] when we interpret a text, we are making claims—not about what was in the author's mind—but about the meaning produced in the text itself. As Geoffrey Strickland has said, when we interpret a text, we are making hypotheses about the author's meaning, and our hypothesis is as strong as the justification we can give it from the text itself.[14]

Thus, the goal of interpretation is to read the text to discover the author's meaning. Such study involves a close reading of the text, paying attention to historical context and literary context, particularly genre, style, and structure. The discovery of meaning comes about through the work of historical-grammatical exegesis.

That said, another dimension of authorial meaning emerges when we attend to the Bible's claim that it is the word of God. The text may have been written by Moses, David, Solomon, Jeremiah, or some unnamed human author, but the Bible claims (and I accept the claim) that God is the ultimate author of Scripture.

This claim raises the question of the relationship between the human authors of Scripture and the ultimate divine author. One of the difficulties of answering this question is that we can't get into the mind of the human authors to understand what they had in mind, which raises questions about how one can speak of the cognitive peripheral vision (using G. K. Beale's term[15]) of the Old Testament authors except by making a case from the text itself that the meaning assigned to their texts in the New Testament was plausibly in their minds. For me, in a number of instances I do not believe such a case can be made. Therefore, I think it is correct to speak of a deeper meaning of a text (*sensus plenior*),

12. This statement is true especially for literary texts like those we find in the Bible.
13. Kevin J. Vanhoozer, *Is There a Meaning in This Text? The Bible, the Reader, and the Morality of Literary Knowledge* (Grand Rapids: Zondervan, 1998).
14. Geoffrey Strickland, *Structuralism or Criticism? Thoughts on How We Read* (Cambridge: Cambridge University Press, 1981).
15. See G. K. Beale, "The Cognitive Peripheral Vision of Biblical Authors," *WTJ* 76 (2014): 263–93.

one of which the human author would *not* have been consciously aware. The human author of such texts would have been surprised to see them used in the way they were. Yet this conclusion does not mean the human author would have concluded that such use was inappropriate, particularly in light of the resurrection.

Luke 24

Luke 24 reveals Jesus's own perspective on how he relates to what we call the Old Testament. His words clearly impact our own approach to the question at hand. Luke 24 relates Jesus's words and actions in the brief period between the resurrection and the ascension, and he devotes all his teaching during this time to the question of Old Testament hermeneutics. This significance is underlined by the fact that the gospel writer includes two encounters with disciples in which Jesus repeats essentially the same lesson.

The first occasion is the famous walk with two followers on the road to Emmaus. Jesus, whose identity was kept from them at first (Luke 24:16), joins them and asks about the subject of their conversation. They are amazed that he seems ignorant of the big news about Jesus, whose death has stunned them. Further, they have heard reports from some women disciples who found his tomb empty.

Jesus's response to them is instructive:

> "How foolish you are, and how slow to believe all that the prophets have spoken! Did not the Messiah have to suffer these things and then enter his glory?" And beginning with Moses and all the Prophets, he explained to them what was said in all the Scriptures concerning himself. (Luke 24:25–27)

Later in the same chapter, Jesus is speaking to a broader group of disciples:

> He said to them, "This is what I told you while I was still with you: Everything must be fulfilled that is written about me in the Law of Moses, the Prophets and the Psalms." Then he opened their minds so they could understand the Scriptures. (Luke 24:44–45)

What is undeniable is Jesus's contention that the Scriptures the people of God possessed at the time *in some sense* anticipated his coming and work. He refers to what Christians call the Old Testament, using nomenclature that was current among the Jewish people in the first century AD, the expression "Moses and all the Prophets," and in the second instance the tripartite terms, "the Law of Moses, the Prophets and the Psalms."[16] These are variants referring to the same collection of books. The Law (*Torah*) of Moses is the first five books of the Old Testament. The Prophets (*Nevi'im*) refer to the books of Joshua, Judges, Samuel, and Kings (the Former Prophets), as well as Isaiah, Jeremiah, Ezekiel, and the Twelve Minor Prophets (the Latter Prophets). Psalms is one way to refer to the third part of the Hebrew canon, which is more widely known as the Writings (*Ketuvim*) and refers to a miscellaneous group of books too numerous to list here.[17]

Jesus's two statements to his disciples suggest that the entire Hebrew Bible anticipated his coming and work—not just some isolated prophecies. Jesus does not say precisely how the Old Testament looks forward to his coming, and this is a question we will take up shortly. His words also raise an interesting question in the light of the initial response to his crucifixion and resurrection.

To put it bluntly, from what we read in the gospel accounts, no one seemed to "get it" before the resurrection. We do not hear of people anticipating the crucifixion—far from it. And after Jesus's death, when his followers visit the tomb, they are shocked to find it empty. From what we can tell about messianic expectation in the first century AD and in the centuries before, no one was expecting a fully divine, fully human messiah who would end up on a cross to die for people's sins. If anything, most people expected a very human messiah who would reestablish David's kingly line and cast off Israel's oppressors. There were variations to this, like the view that there would be two messiahs, one

---

16. See Roger T. Beckwith, *The Old Testament Canon of the New Testament Church* (London: SPCK, 1985), 105–9.

17. But containing all the books found in the Protestant canon of the Old Testament that are not found in the first two sections. As we can see, the order of the books in the Hebrew Bible (known as the Tanak [an acronym based on the first letters of its three sections]) in our English translations is based on the Septuagint.

kingly and one priestly. But nothing leads us to think that anyone had the slightest idea that the work of Jesus would take the course it did.[18]

This situation leads to the present debate as to whether Christ's presence in the Old Testament was something that could be discerned ahead of time or whether Christ's death and resurrection were a prerequisite to seeing Christ in the Old Testament.

Expected or Surprising?

Jesus tells his disciples that the whole Scripture (Hebrew Bible) anticipated his coming, but from what we read in the New Testament, no one seemed to have understood that it was looking forward to a messiah who would die and be raised. Was Jesus's coming something that *should* have been expected? Or was it a surprise that could only be understood after the fact?

This question has led to a sometimes-bitter debate among Christian scholars who believe the Old Testament anticipates Christ. On the one hand, some scholars insist that the message concerning the Messiah fulfilled in Christ *must* have been understood by the author and the original readers and others in advance of his life and work. This issue is connected to the question of how the New Testament cites texts from the Old Testament. Those who believe that the Christ-significance of the Old Testament should have been clear to the disciples at the time of Christ also tend to believe that the Old Testament authors themselves were aware of the messianic sense of their words. G. K. Beale, for instance, argues that the meaning ascribed to an Old Testament passage by the New Testament must have been at least in the "cognitive peripheral vision" of the Old Testament author.[19] On the other hand, other scholars, such as Peter Enns and Richard Hays, point to the lack of awareness at the time of Jesus's death and resurrection as well as the oft-surprising uses of Old Testament passages in the New Testament.[20]

---

18. See Stanley E. Porter, ed., *The Messiah in the Old and New Testaments* (Grand Rapids: Eerdmans, 2007), for an excellent survey of what we know about messianic expectation at the time. In particular, see the chapter by Loren T. Stuckenbruck, "Messianic Ideas in Apocalyptic and Related Literature of Early Judaism" (pp. 90–116).

19. Beale, "Cognitive Peripheral Vision."

20. Peter Enns, *Inspiration and Incarnation: Evangelicals and the Problem of the Old Testament*, 2nd ed. (Grand Rapids: Baker Academic, 2015); Richard B. Hays, *Reading*

The debate has generated its own terminology. The first school of thought labels their approach "christological interpretation," while at least some advocates of the second approach prefer the term *Christotelic*. Christological, combining Christ with *logos* (in the sense of "essence"), highlights the belief that Christ is an essential part of the Old Testament method. Christotelic, combining Christ with *telos* ("goal"), suggests that rather than Christ being an essential part of the Old Testament message, he is the goal of the Old Testament and is not able to be seen until the goal is fulfilled.

Perhaps, rather than seeing these as two opposing viewpoints, we can consider both as providing legitimate perspectives on the relationship between the Old and New Testaments. To say that Christ can *only* be seen in the Old Testament after the fact cannot adequately explain Jesus's statement to the two disciples on the road to Emmaus: "How foolish you are, and how slow to believe all that the prophets have spoken!" (Luke 24:25). In other words, they should have known. The Law and the Prophets spoke about his coming and the nature of his work.

On the other hand, when we look at the way the New Testament appropriates the Old Testament in reference to Christ and the fact that no one understood it, we can say that Christ's presence in the Old Testament becomes clearer in the light of his death and resurrection. Moreover, the New Testament uses the Old Testament in many ways that almost certainly were not in the mind of the original human author (see above on the divine author). Beale's appeal to the cognitive peripheral vision of the Old Testament author is as desperate as it sounds. Explanations often given for how the Old Testament author could have understood the New Testament use are strained to the extreme.

In my opinion, both a Christotelic and a christological approach to the Old Testament seem warranted for a Christian understanding of the Old Testament. I tend to use these terms interchangeably when I talk about the *Christocentric* nature of the Old Testament.

Backwards: Figural Christology and the Fourfold Gospel Witness (Waco, TX: Baylor University Press, 2016).

Interpretive Steps for Readers
Criteria for Identification

Criteria are standards or principles by which to judge or evaluate a matter. In christological interpretation of an Old Testament passage, the criteria are important to prevent arbitrary connections from being drawn. In some areas, criteria are straightforward and can be listed as a series of bullet points. During the initial phase of the COVID-19 vaccine distribution, for example, there was a very straightforward list of criteria for who was allowed to receive the vaccine:

- Seniors over sixty-five years of age
- Essential frontline workers
- People ages sixteen to sixty-four with underlying medical conditions

Of course, the last two of these criteria have further criteria to define who is considered an essential frontline worker and what is considered an underlying medical condition.

Reading literature is not the same as deciding who gets a vaccine. Some interpreters want to turn literary studies into a science, arguing that a certain number of lexical or conceptual links between biblical texts establish a connection with Christ. Or they require that the New Testament utilize an Old Testament text in a christological direction before a connection can be made. These are not insignificant matters, but they are not essential or determinative for interpretation. They are significant because they encourage and support the suggestion of a christological connection. In other words, one might sense a connection and propose it to oneself or to a broader audience, but in order to persuade others, you will need a persuasive argument. The eminent literary scholar Benjamin Harshav makes this point when he says of literary interpretation in general, "We must distinguish between the cognitive act of actual understanding or experiencing literature, which may be largely intuitive, and the reasoned account for and justification of specific structures and meanings understood and realized in a text."[21]

---

21. Benjamin Harshav, *Explorations in Poetics* (Stanford, CA: Stanford University Press, 2007), 175.

The same is true of the later church's christological understanding of Old Testament texts. If these interpreters saw a christological connection, we ought to pay attention and give the matter our thoughtful consideration. However, while that may sometimes help to confirm a connection in our minds (see comments on Gen 22 below), at other times there are reasons to depart from earlier Christian interpretation. The latter is my conclusion, for example, about allegorical interpretations of the Song of Songs, which not only interpret the man to represent Christ and the woman the church, but also press details of the text in an arbitrary manner (e.g., Hippolytus's understanding of the sachet of myrrh lodged between the woman's breasts in 1:13 as Jesus Christ who spans the Old and New Testaments).[22]

Jewish reception of the Old Testament, by definition, does not lead in a christological direction. But it seems to me that the New Testament authors read the Old Testament with Jewish eyes and thus, under divine inspiration, were influenced in their reading of the Old Testament by Jewish interpretation. A good example of this is when Paul speaks of the rock in the wilderness as Christ who traveled in the wilderness with the Israelites (1 Cor 10:4). Jewish interpretation does not identify the Messiah with the wilderness rock, but it does understand the rock to travel through the wilderness. Paul did not originate that understanding; nor did he derive it from the Old Testament.[23]

Biblical interpretation is an art, not a science. The text itself provides limits on our interpretation; we as readers cannot arbitrarily impose meaning on the text (like saying Jesus is a sachet of myrrh in Song of Songs 1:13). We must be convinced ourselves and be able to convince others of a connection *by an appeal to the biblical text.* As I have read Scripture christologically through the years, I have found there are many different ways to see Christ in the Old Testament. What is important is to always read the Old Testament text first—without appeal to Christ—to listen to its discrete voice. Afterward we step back and read that same text a second time from the full vantage point of the gospel, in the light of the resurrection. I will now illustrate this practice through three passages: Genesis 22, Isaiah 42, and Proverbs 8.

22. Tremper Longman III, *Song of Songs*, NICOT (Grand Rapids: Eerdmans, 2001), 35–38.

23. Enns, *Inspiration and Incarnation*, 139–41.

Specific Steps for Readers

As illustrated in the three examples, the most important principle for reading the Old Testament is to read the text two times. In the first reading, the twenty-first-century Christian reader must imagine themselves among the original audience intended by the human author of the text. This reading must account for the passage's genre and historical context. In the second reading, Christians read the text in the light of the further revelation of the New Testament. Here, as Peter Enns well puts it, Christians should be guided by "an intuitive, Spirit-led engagement of Scripture, with the anchor being not what the Old Testament author intended but how Christ gives the Old Testament its final coherence." He rightly encourages readers to ask themselves, "What difference does the death and resurrection of Christ make for how I understand this part of the Old Testament?"[24]

This intuitive, Spirit-led reading does not reduce itself to some kind of formulaic methodology, but it calls on the reader to justify the connections they draw from the Bible itself in order to persuade others that the connections they draw are not simply arbitrary. These might include key words, common themes, or similar patterns of plot (the stuff of typology). We look to see how the New Testament authors appropriated the Old Testament—not just in terms of specific quotations (which are often shaped by first-century Jewish interpretive practices rather than historical-grammatical considerations) but in other ways as well (for instance the well-known presentation of Jesus's life and ministry in relationship with the exodus story).

Apply the Approach: Three Case Studies
Interpreting Genesis 22:1-19
First Reading

One of the most consequential moments in Genesis is God's call to Abraham to go to "the land I will show you" (Gen 12:1). Encouraged by the promise of blessing and that God will make him into a great nation (vv. 1–3), Abraham thus departs for what turns out to be the land of

---

24. Enns, *Inspiration and Incarnation*, 148–49.

Canaan with the hope that he will eventually receive the land and have numerous descendants—the prerequisite to becoming "a great nation."

Soon Abraham grows exceedingly frustrated that he and Sarah have no children, even into their old age. One of the major themes of the Abraham narrative is his journey of faith in the face of what appears to be God's failure to deliver on his promise. Many of the episodes of the story of Abraham have to do with how he responds to the threats and obstacles to the fulfillment of the divine promises. Does he respond with faith or with fear? In spite of the New Testament's use of Abraham as a paragon of faith (Heb 11:8–12), the stories we read mostly illustrate his fear that he cannot depend on God. He tries to manufacture an heir in his own power. In Genesis 15:2, for instance, the reference to Eliezer of Damascus reveals that he believes he won't have children and thinks his household servant will become his heir, according to the custom of the day. God renews his covenant in response and reassures Abraham that he will indeed fulfill his promises through another ancient Near Eastern custom, the passing through of the pieces (15:12–21).

Though "Abram believed the Lord, and he credited it to him as righteousness" (15:6), Abraham soon doubts again and tries to manipulate the fulfillment of the promise by taking on a concubine, Hagar, and having a son, Ishmael, with her. God again must come and reassure Abraham of his intention to fulfill his promise.

The promised moment finally comes when Abraham is a hundred years old. Sarah gives birth to Isaac (21:1–7), God fulfills his promise, and Abraham's journey of faith comes to a successful conclusion. Or so we think until Genesis 22:1: "Some time later God tested Abraham." While the reader knows that what follows is a test, Abraham does not know this when he hears the command, "Take your son, your only son, whom you love—Isaac—and go to the region of Moriah. Sacrifice him there as a burnt offering on a mountain I will show you" (22:2).

What does Abraham think about this? Is he horrified? Afraid? Incredulous? The narrator intentionally does not tell us, simply reporting that "early the next morning Abraham got up and loaded his donkey" (22:3). He then undertakes the journey with Isaac and two servants to Mount Moriah.

The omniscient narrator could have let us know what Abraham thought and felt but does not. The effect for readers is an emphasis on Abraham's obedience. Toward the end of his life, a life of mostly faltering faith in God, Abraham's actions communicate complete trust. Does he hope God will stay his hand from the act? There are hints in the story that he does. As he and Isaac start up the mountain, he tells the servants, "Stay here with the donkey while I and the boy go over there. We will worship and then we will come back to you" (22:5). And in response to Isaac's question about a lamb for the offering, Abraham responds, "God himself will provide the lamb for the burnt offering, my son" (22:8).

While these are just hints, it is also clear that if God had not told Abraham to stop, he would have gone through with the deed: "Then he reached out his hand and took the knife to slay his son" (22:10). But God, as the reader already knows he will, intervenes: "Do not lay a hand on the boy" (22:12). God provides a substitute ram.

The story makes it clear to the reader that Abraham would have followed through with the sacrifice of his beloved son. He had confidence in the God who had given him and Sarah this son at an advanced age, and he trusted God completely. Because of Abraham's actions here ("because you have done this and have not withheld your son, your only son," 22:16), God would bless him and make his descendants numerous. He would give his descendants land and bless all the nations of the world through his offspring. Why? "Because you have obeyed me" (22:18). As James would later point out, faith without works is dead (Jas 2:14–26).

Second Reading

Before moving on to our New Testament second reading, we should take note of an important later Old Testament reference to the place of this momentous event. Mount Moriah is mentioned one other place in Scripture, 2 Chronicles 3:1: "Then Solomon began to build the temple of the Lord in Jerusalem on Mount Moriah." Of course, the mountain on which Solomon built the temple is better known as Mount Zion, but there are various ways to think of the relationship between Zion and Moriah. For example, it could be the same name for different mountains, or perhaps Moriah is a range and Zion a peak. What is important is that this reference makes a connection between the place where Abraham took Isaac and the place of the later temple.

God had provided a substitute sacrifice for Isaac, and the temple was the place where later Israelites would offer atonement sacrifices for their sins, animals that were accepted as their own substitutes. When we turn to the New Testament, Jesus fulfills both the symbolic function of the temple ("the Word became flesh and made his dwelling among us," John 1:14), the place where God made his presence known, as well as offering himself on the cross "for [the people's] sins once for all" (Heb 7:27).[25] When Abraham went to Moriah, God provided a ram as a substitute. In Romans 8:31–32, Paul said that it was the Father's will that Jesus go to the cross: "He . . . did not spare his own Son, but gave him up for us all."

Genesis 22 is never directly cited in the New Testament, but Christian readers will immediately hear echoes of God's call to Abraham to sacrifice "your son, your only son, whom you love" (Gen 22:2) in God's announcement to Jesus at his baptism: "You are my Son, whom I love; with you I am well pleased" (Mark 1:11; see also Matt 3:17; Luke 3:22; and 2 Pet 1:17; these passages also reflect Isa 42:1 in their background).

This Christotelic reading has an ancient background, and the early church fathers also noted the connection. As one example, consider the poem of Melito in the second century:

> As a ram he was bound,
> he says concerning our Lord Jesus Christ,
> and as a lamb he was shorn,
> and as a lamb he was crucified,
> and he bore the wood on his shoulders,
> Going up to slaughter like Isaac at the hand of his father,
> but Christ suffered.
> Isaac did not suffer,
> For he is a type of the passion of Christ which was
> to come.[26]

---

25. For how Jesus fulfills the symbolic purpose of the tabernacle/temple, see Tremper Longman III, *Immanuel in Our Place: Seeing Christ in Israel's Worship* (Phillipsburg, NJ: P&R, 2001), 3–74.

26. Melito of Sardis, *On Pascha: With the Fragments of Melito and Other Material Related to Quartodecimans*, trans. Alistair Stewart-Sykes (Crestwood, NY: Saint Vladimir's Seminary, 2001), 76.

Interpreting Proverbs 8:22-31
First Reading

Proverbs 8:22–31 has generated great interest throughout the history of interpretation, partly because of its critical role in the book of Proverbs and partly because of the theological damage that has been caused through misunderstanding its meaning in the Old Testament as well as its connection to Christ. Though our treatment here is brief, we must treat this passage with care.

The book of Proverbs has two main sections following a preamble (1:1–7) that introduces the book and its main purpose to make its readers wise. The remainder of Proverbs 1–9 contains a collection of discourses either from a father to his son or from Woman Wisdom to all the men she addresses. The second part contains proverbs per se, namely, short observations, admonitions, or prohibitions. These proverbs seem random in organization, in spite of valiant efforts to discover a deep structure, as well as practical rather than theological in content. Proverbs 10:4 is illustrative of the practical nature of many of the proverbs: "Lazy hands make for poverty, but diligent hands bring wealth."

When some Proverbs scholars argue that proverbs are just good practical advice, they ignore the broader context. Proverbs 1–9 provides a hermeneutical lens through which to read the second part of the book and imparts theological significance to the concept and practices of wisdom. One way the book communicates wisdom's theological foundation is through the figure of Woman Wisdom.

Proverbs introduces Woman Wisdom as early as the first chapter, but our focus is on her description in Proverbs 8. First, we need to first consider her role in Proverbs 9. Proverbs 9 is a turning point in the book, the last chapter of the first part. Proverbs 9 requires the reader to make a choice: will I dine with Woman Wisdom (9:1–6) or with Woman Folly (9:13–18)? To dine with someone is to enter into a more intimate relationship with them. But who do these women represent?

Our focus is on Woman Wisdom, and Proverbs 8 intentionally introduces her to us before we make the decision whether to accept her invitation. Woman Wisdom represents all the virtues of wisdom (e.g., she is trustworthy, honest, just, prudent, etc.), and she eschews all the vices of folly (e.g., wickedness, perversity). In Proverbs 8:22–31, Woman Wisdom tells us of her connection to God's work of creation.

Much interpretive angst has been experienced over these verses (as can be seen in the footnotes to most English Bible translations). Without getting into too much detail here,[27] there is an unnecessary tendency on the part of some translators to distance Woman Wisdom from a connection with what we might call the "firstborn of creation." We will return to this issue in our second reading of the passage. For now, what we know is that Woman Wisdom is described as present during the creation process. She observed how God put the cosmos together from the very start. Her claim may well go even further if the one-time occurring Hebrew word 'amon (translated in the NIV as "constantly") should be rendered "artisan." This would suggest that Woman Wisdom not only observed God's creation of the cosmos but participated in it.

God created everything by his wisdom, so the implicit message here is that if one wants to navigate this world successfully, they should accept Woman Wisdom's invitation to enter into a relationship with her. She observed and participated in the process of putting it all together.

In its Old Testament setting, the symbolic significance of Woman Wisdom is found in the fact that her house is on the highest point of the city (Prov 9:3). Minimally, she represents God's wisdom, or to put it another way, she is a personification of God's wisdom. But the location of her home at the highest point of the city suggests we should read further meaning into this. The only house that would have been built on that location is a temple, implying that Woman Wisdom stands for Yahweh himself.

Thus, wisdom starts with a relationship with Yahweh,[28] meaning that the very concept of wisdom and the attitudes and behaviors associated with wisdom are deeply theological. Going back to Proverbs 10:4, if someone is a hard worker, they are acting like someone who has a relationship with Woman Wisdom, but if they are lazy, then they betray the behavior of someone who has dined with Woman Folly. And since her house is also at the highest point of the city (Prov 9:14), Woman

---

27. Those interested in my understanding of these issues may consult Tremper Longman III, *Proverbs*, BCOTWP (Grand Rapids: Baker Academic, 2006), 203–13.

28. Of course, this truth is also taught in Proverbs 1:7: "The fear of the Lord is the beginning of knowledge." One can't even get started in wisdom without having the proper relationship with God. See Tremper Longman III, *The Fear of the Lord is the Beginning of Wisdom: An Introduction to Wisdom in Israel* (Grand Rapids: Baker Academic, 2017).

Folly represents all the false deities that seek to seduce God's people to worship them.

Second Reading

In its Old Testament context, Proverbs 8 presents Woman Wisdom as a personification of God's wisdom, representing God himself in contrast to the false gods represented by Woman Folly. The New Testament makes it clear that Jesus is the epitome of the sage, the godly wisdom teacher.

One of the rare things we learn about Jesus's youth is that he was "filled with" and grew in wisdom (Luke 2:40, 52), as illustrated by his interaction with the teachers in the temple courts (2:41–50). When Jesus began to teach, the people were overwhelmed by his wisdom (Mark 1:27–28). His preferred teaching vehicle was the parable, the pedagogical tool of the sage and the later equivalent to the "proverb." Paul tells the Colossians that Jesus is the one "in whom are hidden all the treasures of wisdom and knowledge" (Col 2:3; see also 1 Cor 1–2). Proverbs 8:21–32 more specifically describes Woman Wisdom's connection to creation. She both observed and participated in the creation of the cosmos.

With this background in mind, and in addition to the New Testament's description of Jesus as the epitome of wisdom, we should take special note of those passages that associate him with Woman Wisdom. First, in response to a dispute with Jewish leaders, Jesus caps off his argument by saying, "But wisdom is proved right by her deeds" (Matt 11:19). It is subtle but clear that Jesus is referring to Woman Wisdom. In Colossians Paul describes Jesus as the Son who "is the image of the firstborn over all creation," reminiscent of the description of Woman Wisdom as the firstborn of creation. Like Woman Wisdom, Jesus, too, was involved in creation: "In him all things were created: things in heaven and on earth, visible and invisible, whether thrones or powers or rulers or authorities; all things have been created through him and for him" (Col 1:15–16). The reference to power, rulers, and authorities reminds one of Woman Wisdom's claim that "by me kings reign and rulers issue decrees that are just; by me princes govern, and nobles—all who rule on earth" (Prov 8:15–16). In addition, while certainly echoing Genesis 1, one can also hear Proverbs 8 in the Gospel of John's magisterial opening: "In the beginning was the Word, and the Word was with God and the Word was God. He was with God in the beginning. Through him all things were made; without him nothing was made that has been made" (John 1:1–3). Finally, and perhaps more speculatively, in the opening to the letter to the church at Laodicea, Jesus is described as the "beginning" or "ruler of God's creation" (Rev 3:14),[29] which may also be a conceptual reference to Woman Wisdom in Proverbs 8.

These passages lead us to conclude that various New Testament writers associated Jesus with Woman Wisdom. When Christians read Proverbs, they might think of the choice presented in Proverbs 9 as a choice between dining (entering into an intimate relationship) with Jesus or dining with Woman Folly who represents a false god, making any thing or person other than the triune God the most important thing in one's life.

There is also the danger of misunderstanding here. I have been careful to use the verb *associate* rather than *identify* because the New Testament does not claim that Woman Wisdom is Jesus as if Proverbs 8 is a prophecy of Jesus. Woman Wisdom represents God's wisdom. The New Testament authors recognize that Jesus is the perfect expression of God's wisdom (Col 2:3), thus the association. Proverbs 8 is a poem using imagery and should not be pressed in a literalistic manner, particularly as applied to Jesus. Jesus is not the firstborn of creation (a created being), and treating Proverbs 8 as a literalistic description of Jesus—rather than a poem exploring God's wisdom associated with Jesus—leads to the Arian heresy.[30]

Interpreting Isaiah 42:1-4
First Reading

Of our three test cases, Isaiah 42:1–9 is the most difficult.[31] The difficulty is not its appropriation in the New Testament, as the New Testament authors clearly saw Jesus as the suffering servant described here and in later songs that describe him (49:1–6; 52:13–53:12[32]).

---

29. The ESV, NLT, and NRSV translate "the beginning of God's creation," showing an even closer connection with Proverbs 8:30 than the NIV.

30. Longman, *Proverbs*, 212–13.

31. While the assignment is to look at Isaiah 42:1–4, the unit actually continues until verse 9.

32. Some would add Isaiah 50:4–6, but the speaker there is not identified as the servant and, in my opinion, is the prophet himself.

The question is what the original audience would have heard and even what the prophet might have known.[33] And this will raise the related question: on what basis did the New Testament authors think the suffering servant passages of Isaiah applied to Jesus?

First, some comments on Isaiah 42:1–9 that set the passage in context. God, the speaker, draws attention to his servant whom he upholds. He is God's chosen one and the object of his delight. God promises to put his Spirit on him so that he will bring justice to the nations. This servant will bring justice but will do so with compassion, and his justice will spread to the furthest parts of the earth ("the islands," v. 4). God, the Creator, addresses the servant, telling the servant that he will support him and make him a covenant for the people and a light for the gentiles. He will give sight to the blind and free the prisoners. God concludes by asserting sole claim to glory and right to praise over against the idols. What he has announced here is something that will take place in the future ("before they spring into being I announce them to you," 42:9).

Who, then, is this servant? What role does the servant play? To answer this question, we now appeal to the broader context. When we read the broader context, only one answer is given, and it is given time and time again. The servant is Israel. No one else is ever identified as the servant in Isaiah's so-called Servant Songs or its immediate context.[34]

> But you, Israel, my servant,
>> Jacob, whom I have chosen. (Isa 41:8)

> But now listen, Jacob, my servant,
>> Israel, whom I have chosen. (Isa 44:1)

> Remember these things, Jacob,
>> for you, Israel, are my servant.
> I have made you, you are my servant;
>> Israel, I will not forget you. (Isa 44:21)

---

33. Though, again, we can only analyze his writing since we can't get into his mind.

34. Earlier in the book Eliakim (Isa 22:20) and David (37:35) are called God's servant, and starting in Isaiah 54:17 there is a shift from singular "servant" to plural "servants."

> For the sake of Jacob my servant,
> > of Israel my chosen. (Isa 45:4)

The context is clear that the servant in our passage is none other than Israel itself.[35] No other person or group is so identified. So why is this identification so controversial?

Some believe the New Testament appropriation of this passage (Matt 12:15–22, citing Isa 42:1–4) can be justified only if it is a prophecy of the Messiah himself. We will address this concern in our second reading. Others, often arguing in support of the idea that this passage speaks of Jesus and not Israel, point out that in the broader context Israel is far from living up to the role of the servant. In Isaiah 41:10–16, for instance, Israel as God's servant is fearful and discouraged. In 42:18–22, far from healing the blind, servant Israel is itself blind and deaf.

How can fearful, sinful Israel be the servant who will bring justice to the world and light to the gentiles? For some this problem is only intensified when we read 42:1–9 in the context of the later Servant Songs, particularly when the servant is described more like an individual rather than a group, one whose suffering is on behalf of others (53:4). Is this not grounds for us to say that we ought to think Isaiah had in mind a future individual in Isaiah 42, perhaps identified with the expected messiah described earlier in the book (9:1–7; 11), rather than Israel?

This perspective is tempting when viewed on this side of the resurrection, but that is the point of our first reading: we want to describe the discrete message of the Old Testament. And in support of the position that an individual was not in the conscious purview of the prophet nor his audience is the fact that from what we know about messianic expectation in Second Temple Jewish literature as well as the Gospels themselves, no one was thinking in those terms. No one was expecting a suffering messiah, or if they were, they are not mentioned in the Gospels. Indeed, when Jesus talked about his suffering and death, the disciples were incredulous (e.g., Mark 8:31–33).

---

35. The Septuagint makes this identification explicit when it renders 42:1, "Iakob is my servant; I will lay hold of him; Israel is my chosen; my soul has accepted him" (NETS).

And when we think about it more carefully, the supposed tension between the servant and Israel, particularly if we think in terms of the faithful remnant, is not an obstacle. The servant passages are looking to the future, not the present. In the present, Israel is sinful, particularly in the matter of idolatry that is the object of prophetic derision in this part of Isaiah. But according to our passage, God in the future will put his Spirit on him and he will bring justice to the nations (42:1). In support of the position that the servant is the faithful remnant and not Israel as a whole, we can even imagine that in the future the faithful servant will play the role of bringing Israel back to God (49:5–6). The reason some may think the servant is an individual figure (and in a more intense way in 52:13–53:12) is because the servant is a personification of the faithful remnant of Israel, similar to the "man of affliction" personified in Lamentations 3.

Second Reading

A contextual reading best understands the Servant Songs, including our passage, to refer to the faithful remnant of Israel. But does that exhaust the full divinely intended meaning of these passages? The New Testament authors certainly did not think so.

Reading the Servant Songs in the light of the resurrection, the New Testament authors knew that Jesus was the full realization of the servant. He was the Israel of one; in the words of Geoffrey Grogan, they knew that "Jesus was the perfect expression of what God intended Israel to be,"[36] or more specifically as Raymond Dillard put it, the "remnant of one, the embodiment of faithful Israel, the truly righteous and suffering servant."[37]

Thus, Jesus is God's servant in whom he delights and on whom he put his Spirit (Isa 42:1; cf. Mark 1:11; Matt 3:17; Luke 3:22; 1 Pet 1:17; with Gen 22:2 also in the background). Jesus is the humble bringer of justice on earth (Isa 42:3). He comes to make all things right. He is the one who is the covenant for his people as the one who establishes the new covenant that fulfills the Old Testament covenants, and he is

---

36. Geoffrey W. Grogan, "Isaiah," in *Proverbs–Isaiah*, EBC, rev. ed. (Grand Rapids: Zondervan, 2008), 457.
37. In Tremper Longman III and Raymond B. Dillard, *Introduction to the Old Testament*, 2nd ed. (Grand Rapids: Zondervan, 2006), 315.

the light for the gentiles (Isa 42:6; cf. 49:6; Luke 2:32; Acts 26:23). He brings sight to the blind, and he releases the prisoners (Isa 42:7; Matt 11:5; Luke 4:18). The realization that Jesus fulfills the expectation of this first Servant Song led Matthew to cite the entirety of Isaiah 42:1–4 and apply it to Christ (Matt 12:18–20).

In the light of the resurrection, the New Testament authors recognized Jesus as the ideal Israel and thus saw the connection with the Servant Songs of Isaiah. I should point out that the Servant Songs are not the only New Testament passages where a New Testament connection rested on the realization that Jesus is the Israel of one. When Jesus experienced the devil's three temptations in the wilderness (Matt 4:1–11), he was resisting temptations to which Israel succumbed, three times citing the book of Deuteronomy—Moses's final sermon to the Israelites before they entered the promised land in which he warns them not to sin as their forebears did in the wilderness. Jesus is the obedient Son of God in contrast to and in fulfillment of the expectations of Israel. Paul makes the argument that Jesus is the fulfillment of Israel, the seed of Abraham, in that the promise made to Abraham ultimately was fulfilled in "one person, who is Christ" (Gal 3:16 NRSV).

Did Isaiah have in mind the Messiah when he wrote the Servant Songs? Would Abraham, or the author of Genesis, have thought that a single individual would be the fulfillment of the promise of the seed? While we cannot get into their minds, the idea that they did stretches credulity. However, if Isaiah or the author of Genesis had lived after the resurrection themselves, I believe they would have agreed that it was right to speak of Jesus as the realization of their expectations.

Significance of Approach

We worship the triune God, and we understand that Jesus is our mediator and the one who died for our sins and was raised in power. Accordingly, most Christians are drawn to the New Testament and many struggle with how to read the Old Testament. To believe Jesus's own testimony that "all the Scriptures" anticipated his coming (Luke 24:27) reminds us that the Old Testament remains vitally relevant to our faith and practice.

In my opinion, this understanding of the relationship between Christ and the Old Testament should inform how pastors and teachers present the Old Testament. Christian preaching and teaching should engage in both readings of the text. While not neglecting the message communicated to the original audience in its full theocentric power, the preacher and teacher should also be sensitive to the Christotelic significance of the passage when read in the light of the whole canon.

RESPONSE TO TREMPER LONGMAN III
(THE FIRST TESTAMENT APPROACH)

JOHN GOLDINGAY

Dr. Longman writes, "The human author of such texts would have been surprised to see them used in the way they were. Yet this conclusion does not mean the human author would have concluded that such use was inappropriate, particularly in light of the resurrection" (82). I like that way of putting it! How can we think further about the implications?

The New Hidden in the Old, the Old in the New?

I don't think, as Dr. Longman believes, that the Scriptures indicate that "the New is hidden in the Old and the Old is revealed in the New," Augustine's observation on Exodus 20:19–20 (74). The people ask Moses, rather than God, to speak to them. Moses responds that they needn't be (negatively) fearful, because God just wants them to fear him (in the positive sense). Augustine said that fear pertains more to the Old Testament and love to the New, then added the comment about the Old and the New. But the contrast doesn't work. People in the First Testament weren't usually fearful of God, and people in the New Testament are expected to live in the fear of God (e.g., Heb 10:26–31; 1 Pet 2:17).

Augustine's comment gained a life of its own, however, as a way of thinking about Christ and the First Testament. Does the Trinity hide in Genesis 1; then does Jesus's victory over Satan hide in Genesis 3:15, does the nature of Jesus's atonement hide in Leviticus, and does Jesus's suffering hide in Psalm 22 and in Isaiah 53—with the result that their reference is then clear in the New Testament? While the Creator was the God who is Trinity, that fact is not hiding in the text in Genesis 1.

101

While Satan was active in Eden, that fact is not in Genesis 3, nor is Jesus's victory over Satan hiding there; the text describes an ongoing conflict, not a final victory. Leviticus indicates how God provided for Israel to find cleansing, and Hebrews uses Leviticus to help it understand Jesus, but Jesus's atonement is not hiding in Leviticus. Psalm 22 provides persecuted people with a way of praying, and the Gospels cite this psalm to make sense of Jesus's suffering, but Jesus's suffering is not hiding in the psalm. Isaiah 53 has a vision of someone who is persecuted turning his persecution into an offering, and the New Testament again finds this passage helps provide an understanding of Jesus's suffering, but Jesus's suffering is not hiding there.

The nearest thing to an example of the New Testament saying that something is hiding in the First Testament is Paul discovering from there the dynamics of God's concern to reveal himself to the nations through his own people's resistance (Rom 9–11). This example tests and proves the rule that things are clear in the First Testament itself, because Paul sees himself as drawing out the First Testament's own clear implications in light of what has now happened in Jesus's death, his people's declining to believe in him, and God's commissioning the task of telling the nations about him.

"It appears incontestable that a Christian reading of the Old Testament recognize that Jesus is indeed in the Old Testament" (73). I guess I do contest it, but at least I can claim that the New Testament is not Christian either, since it says that Moses and David are in the First Testament, but not that Jesus is!

God the Ultimate Author of the Scriptures?

Is God the ultimate author of Scripture? In the way the Scriptures themselves speak, God is the immediate author of the Ten Commandments, but otherwise, he is more a speaker than an author. Luke thinks he himself is the author of his Gospel, the Psalms look as if they are authored by human beings, Paul claims to be the author of his letters; none suggest that in any sense God is the author. Nor do the Scriptures speak of God as the author behind the authors.

Second Timothy 3:15–16 does say that the First Testament Scriptures are both sacred and God-breathed (I assume the same applies to the New Testament, though it cannot say so because it was still being written). Human beings wrote them and other human beings recognized that they were true and important, and that's how they became the Scriptures. Luke (for instance) wasn't sacred when it was written, but it became sacred. The New Testament does imply that the First Testament Scriptures have God's authority, which fits with the image of them being sacred.

Intriguingly, the statement that the written Scriptures are God-breathed does fit with the fact that God is more a speaker than a writer. It's a paradoxical statement, and a kind of metonymy or catachresis or transferred epithet, because speech is what one breathes out; one does not breathe out writings. Had Paul said that the Scriptures were God-authored, it would have been less puzzling, but that isn't what he said. I think we can see the significance of saying that they were God-breathed by considering other references to the Spirit's involvement in the origin of the Scriptures (e.g., Mark 12:36; Acts 28:25). The New Testament writers knew that the Scriptures often had a capacity to speak beyond their original context, and they take this capacity to reflect an involvement of the Holy Spirit with the Scriptures in general, not just with prophecy. The Scriptures have the extraordinary extra significance that attaches to prophecy. Prophecy itself is thus a term or concept that got extended to apply to the Scriptures as a whole (cf. Heb 1:1). Prophecy's distinctive feature is that it involves speaking out words that God originally generates. God is indeed their ultimate author, and he is their direct author in a way that doesn't apply to narratives, psalms, or proverbs. Would it still be better to say that God is the ultimate speaker of the Scriptures? The New Testament has a couple of intriguing references to God speaking the Scriptures now (Heb 3:7; 10:15). Perhaps they *become* God-breathed, maybe in some new way?

So the Holy Spirit being the Scriptures' ultimate speaker could imply, for instance, that in Genesis 1 he knew that Father, Son, and Holy Spirit could have said, "Let us make. . . ." Such meanings could be within what might be called the Holy Spirit's "peripheral vision," though not the human author's. Is it in this connection that one can think of the Scriptures having a "fuller sense"? Though I would prefer to think in terms of a fuller significance. It would fit with the New Testament's usage, where it talks about Jesus "filling" scriptural texts. Translations have him "fulfilling" them, but the word (*plēroō*) is the ordinary word meaning "fill." It suggests filling up the texts or filling them out.

Incidentally, the New Testament commonly speaks in terms of plural "Scriptures," while singular "Scripture" generally indicates reference to a particular passage. Does Dr. Longman think there are any exceptions? It is even clearer that the Scriptures never refer to the Scriptures as "the word of God." The expression "the word of God" either refers to the gospel message or to a particular message.

First and Second Readings?

I like the image of a first and second reading, which enables us to distinguish and affirm the authorial meaning of the text and its possible broader implications. But the New Testament passages that refer back to First Testament passages don't suggest that the two readings are sequential, certainly not in that order. Matthew did not undertake a reading of Isaiah 42, then ask how it might apply in ways that go beyond what the prophet meant in the context, and thus generate a second reading (which is indeed what I would do). He starts from his knowledge of Jesus and goes back to Isaiah. The second reading comes first. Perhaps one should rather say that the two readings interweave. Thus Acts 28:23–28 reports how Paul found that many Jews in Rome would not accept his message about God's reign. This recurrent experience makes him go back to the Scriptures to find insight into this puzzling phenomenon, and he finds it in Isaiah 6. He thus also comes to have more of an understanding of Isaiah 6 by going back to it. But the New Testament writers don't imply that the Scriptures have a deeper meaning, which they themselves are in a position to reveal. The historical meaning of, say, Genesis 22 or Proverbs 8 or Isaiah 42 is utterly profound. It could not be made deeper.

Dr. Longman notes that Jesus calls some of his disciples foolish for not getting the significance of the Prophets (Luke 24:25). "Perhaps they should have known better," he comments (73). I wonder at what point and how they should have known better? If they heard Genesis 22, Proverbs 8, or Isaiah 42 read in synagogue before they met Jesus, it's not obvious that they should have realized that these passages were about the Messiah. The point at which they could know better was when they could look back from cross and resurrection. That was the aha moment, the moment when a second reading became possible.

Progressive Revelation?

Is there really "progression of revelation" within the Scriptures, as Dr. Longman argues? There are important things in the New Testament that aren't in the First Testament, but the image of progressive revelation is more misleading than illuminating. To start with, the key truths about God and humanity were clear from the beginning.

Dr. Longman gives two examples of things that might be understood in terms of progress, the Trinity and the afterlife. But surely these do not illustrate how "God over time reveals more and more about himself" (76). They illustrate how God does something new and it has a spinoff in new insights. It became possible to see that God is Father, Son, and Holy Spirit because Jesus came as an embodiment of God and the Spirit of Jesus continues to be a powerful presence since Jesus has gone to be with his Father. To describe God revealing more and more about himself surely does not clarify the dynamic of the way it happens.

The same and something extra applies regarding afterlife. There's nothing new about the idea of afterlife. Paul did not come to believe in an afterlife because of believing in Jesus; as a Pharisee he would have believed in it already. The Pharisees' basis for believing in an afterlife would have been the faithfulness of God or the kind of argument Jesus uses in Mark 12:18–27 in arguing with the Sadducees, who disagreed with the Pharisees over the question. What is then new for Paul is the same consideration as applies to the Trinity: not that there will be an afterlife but that Jesus's death and resurrection provide a new basis for believing in our resurrection.

Dr. Longman continues, "The New Testament provides the pattern for us as we see what continues and what does not. Obvious examples of the latter include sacrifices, circumcision, food laws, and holy war" (77). But some converse considerations apply. Sacrifices needn't stop with Jesus's coming (Acts 21:26). Circumcision came in with the Abrahamic promise and it needn't stop with Jesus's coming (Acts 16:3). Food laws came in with the exodus and needn't stop with Jesus's coming (Rom 14–15). Rather differently, if there ever was such a thing as holy war, Israel gave it up at least six centuries before Jesus (one might see 2 Kgs 23:29–30 as an example). The first three practices must no longer be requirements attached to membership of the covenant people, but that again shows that their status relates not to progress in revelation but to a new stage in what God is doing with his people. Yes, for the most part these practices are "no longer relevant or observed in the same way" (77), but they are still theologically and behaviorally relevant.

This fact links with another consideration that makes the language of progressive revelation misleading. It gives people a reason to ignore parts of the First Testament that they can view as out-of-date. Neither of us wants people to do that!

HAVILAH DHARAMRAJ

I much appreciate in Dr. Longman's chapter the layered reading of the Old Testament text. The first reading pays attention to the historical matrix in which the text is embedded. In the case of Genesis 22, the first reading concludes with this as the point of the narrative: Because Abraham displayed a God-trusting obedience, God "would give his descendants land and bless all the nations of the world through his offspring" (90). In the case of the Wisdom poem, the question of how its first audience might have understood the protagonist leads to this answer: "She represents God's wisdom, or to put it another way, she is a personification of God's wisdom. But the location of her home at the highest point of the city suggests . . . that Woman Wisdom stands for Yahweh himself" (93). In the case of the Servant Song, Longman asks who the text might be speaking of as the servant, and his answer is consonant with the historical situations of exile and restoration: the faithful remnant within Israel is personified as the servant.

I would take each of Longman's first readings further toward an application to Christian living. Thus, with Genesis 22, I might point out that Abraham is an exemplar of the old hymn that exhorts us to "trust and obey." When the story is taught in Sunday school, that is the usual takeaway of Genesis 22. The Sunday school teacher may finish off with a reference to Jesus as the perfect example of God-trusting obedience, but that comes after Abraham has been (re)commended as worthy of emulation. Isn't this the way the writer of Hebrews constructs his appeal? After setting up his Hall of Fame of faith heroes, he concludes, "Therefore, since we are surrounded by such a great cloud of witnesses, let us throw off everything that hinders and the sin that so easily entangles. And let us run with perseverance the race marked out for us" (Heb 12:1). And then, like our hypothetical Sunday school teacher, the exhortation segues into a Christ-based appeal: "fixing our eyes on Jesus, the pioneer and perfecter of faith" (12:2). Though hermeneutical approaches such as the Christocentric method may not favor it, there is value in the Old Testament for both edification and caution. After all, "all Scripture . . . is useful for teaching, rebuking, correcting and training in righteousness" (2 Tim 3:16), and it is the early church's Scripture, the Old Testament, that Paul is referring to. In this story, Abraham works wonderfully well as an exemplar.

In the second case study, Longman nicely ties the text into its literary matrix of Proverbs 1–9 and shows us how it contributes to the big question that the argumentation of eight chapters is leading up to: "Will I dine with Woman Wisdom (9:1–6) or with Woman Folly (9:13–18)?" (93). I recall as a child laboriously translating the Latin legend painted over the stage of a friend's school assembly hall: *Reverentia Jehovae est Caput Sapientiae.* Working with the English cognates, I figured it was "the fear of the Lord is the beginning of wisdom," a text familiar from sermons I had heard and Bible verses I had memorized. There was no doubt at all in my mind that the aphorism was meant for Christian children to internalize. There was no conflict about the divine name being not Jesus but Jehovah. That is how the Common Reader reads the Wisdom books. God speaks to the twenty-first century Christian through these Before-the-Common-Era texts of practical and philosophical wisdom, just as he did to its ancient audience. Perhaps as they read Proverbs 1–9 the Common Reader might think of the wise and foolish builders of Jesus's parable (Matt 7:24–27). But there is no sense of inadequacy arising from having read just Proverbs 9 for one's morning devotions; no compulsion to link Wisdom with Jesus to "complete" one's reading. Proverbs 9 would still throw out its implicit but hard-hitting question and would still compel the reader to choose wisely in the decisions they make that day, decisions that honor their commitment to Christ.

In the last case study, the first reading identified Isaiah's servant as faithful Israel, personified. In this case, the necessity to hold on to the first reading is even stronger. Longman rightly emphasizes the contrast between sinful Israel and faithful Israel. "How can fearful, sinful Israel be the servant who will bring justice to the world and light to the gentiles?" (97). Of course, it cannot be. It is the Israel persistently loyal to YHWH that can be the servant described in the song. Lingering on this first reading, the Common Reader may well apply to themselves the expectations God has for his people: to be agents of justice. And we know that Christians urgently need to stand up against injustice in any part of the world today. Moving too quickly to a second reading would interfere with the Isaiah text speaking to us. Once we've associated the servant with Jesus, the message of the text gets redirected away from us and toward a future in which God will set right all wrongs.

To summarize: the first reading is well able to teach, rebuke, correct, and train the twenty-first-century Christian (2 Tim 3:16). Viewing it as inferior to the second reading—which Longman does not do—is deeply disrespectful to about 77 percent of the word of God, the Old Testament. Having said that, I rejoice in the second reading: Jesus as the sacrifice that Isaac could never be; the association between Woman Wisdom and Jesus; and Jesus as the perfect servant who brings justice to the world. To me, the first readings more often lead to confession and repentance; the second readings mostly lead to adoration and worship. Longman does well in giving us two readings, and even better by keeping the two readings discrete.

My second observation concerns Longman's *deployment of the Christocentric reading of the Old Testament*. Here he first sets out the two camps: "Christological, combining Christ with *logos* (in the sense of 'essence'), highlights the belief that Christ is an essential part of the Old Testament method. Christotelic, combining Christ with *telos* ('goal'), suggests that rather than Christ being an essential part of the Old Testament message, he is the goal of the Old Testament and is not able to be seen until the goal is fulfilled" (85). He then persuasively argues why neither camp need be wrong: in the Emmaus road conversation, Jesus affirms that there is enough in the Hebrew Bible for the disciples to have understood his person and work; conversely, from the way New Testament writers carefully interpret the Hebrew Bible to show Jesus as the Messiah, we may gather that this exercise is more productive after the facts of Jesus's death and resurrection.

Holding both positions as valid enriches the reading of the text.

As Longman's case studies show, the retrospective view is easily illustrated. For example, Longman lists an array of Gospel and Pauline texts that make the association between Jesus and Woman Wisdom. Similarly, he shows us how the New Testament writers identified in Jesus the ideal Israel of the Servant Songs.

An example of the prospective view is perhaps found in the case of Genesis 22. Longman presents the ram substituting for Isaac on Moriah, and the substitutionary sin offerings later made in that same location, as pointers that the Emmaus disciples could have extrapolated to make sense of the crucifixion of Jesus. This—taken together with all those other forward-looking texts in the Psalms, the Law, and the Prophets—should perhaps have helped them "get" what had just happened to their rabbi.

Here I would add another factor: the theological developments of the Second Temple period (I acknowledge that this is better known to the Common Academic than the Common Reader). While substitutionary animal deaths were the norm in Israel's cultus, the only exception was the substitutionary human death presented in one of Isaiah's Servant Songs: the servant "poured out his life unto death. . . . He bore the sin of many, and made intercession for the transgressors" (Isa 53:12; cf. vv. 4–11). This exception, this idea that a human could substitute for other humans, gets picked up again. Under the Seleucid persecution of the second century BC, the death of the martyrs is interpreted similarly in literature both before and after the death of Jesus. Second Maccabees (between 150 and 120 BC) presents a family of mother and seven sons being put through ghastly torture to coerce them to renounce their faith. The last and youngest brother to die makes this speech: "I, like my brothers, give up body and life for the laws of our ancestors, appealing to God to show mercy soon to our nation . . . and through me and my brothers to bring to an end the wrath of the Almighty that has justly fallen on our whole nation" (2 Macc 7:37–38 NRSV). The understanding here is that the blood of the faithful absorbs the wrath that the faithless have invited upon themselves. In another instance, these deaths prepare the way for military victory of the resistance movement led by Judas Maccabeus. As he musters his forces and strategizes against the enemy, the population entreats God. "They implored the Lord to . . . hearken to the blood that cried out to him, to remember also the lawless slaughter of the innocent babies." God heeded this cry to consider their blood as atoning for the sin of the people. "As soon as Makkabaios got his army organized, he became insuperable . . . for the wrath of the Lord had turned to mercy" (2 Macc 8:2–5 NETS; see also 4 Macc 6:28–29; 17:22).

It is true that the Judaism of the Second Temple period is far from monochromatic. And it is true that death is not part of the expected messiah's profile. However, developing understandings of Old Testament concepts—such as vicarious human death and postmortem vindication through resurrection—were the ethos in which Jesus "began to teach [his disciples] that the Son of Man must suffer many things . . . and that he must be killed and after three days rise again" (Mark 8:31). If this is so, the disciples had sufficient opportunity to understand the work of Jesus, even on this side of his death and resurrection.

My final observation is this: Longman is right that *biblical interpretation is an art, not a science.* It "does not reduce itself to some kind of formulaic methodology, but it calls on the reader to justify the connections they draw from the Bible itself in order to persuade others that the connections they draw are not simply arbitrary" (88). Even though the New Testament heavily references the Old Testament, there is still plenty of Old Testament that is not cited or alluded to or echoed in the New. Longman recommends that "key words, common themes, or similar patterns of plot" are some things to look for. Here I would add that usually themes and patterns are safer to work with. *The Jesus Storybook Bible* is a wonderful example.[1] From "The Girl No One Wanted" (Leah) to "The Forgiving Prince" (Joseph) to "Daniel and the Scary Sleepover," its selection of Old Testament texts is discerning and delivers persuasively the promise of the book's subtitle: *Every Story Whispers His Name.* With themes and patterns—whispers—the Common Reader can more readily "justify the connections" and learn the art of understanding Jesus through the Old Testament.

---

1. Sally Lloyd-Jones, *The Jesus Storybook Bible* (Grand Rapids: Zondervan, 2007).

JASON S. DEROUCHIE

Longman rightly affirms Scripture's "organic unity" (75). He also rightly upholds "that a Christian reading of the Old Testament [must] recognize that Jesus is indeed in the Old Testament" and that "the entire Hebrew Bible" "*in some sense* anticipated his coming and work" (83).

Nevertheless, Longman's exegesis in his case studies provides no evidence that Jesus is part of the Old Testament itself. Indeed, he consistently identifies Christ as standing outside the Old Testament and only as the "goal" (*telos*) to which it points. Thus, the "deeper" or "fuller meaning" regarding Christ was (1) usually unknown to the original human Old Testament authors, (2) apparent only after Jesus's resurrection (*sensus plenior*), and (3) something that would have "surprised" the Old Testament authors, although they would approve of it "in the light of the resurrection" (73–74).

Evaluating Longman's Interpretive Steps

Longman instructs Christians to read the Old Testament twice—first to grasp the Old Testament "in its original context as addressed to its contemporary audience," and second "to understand the passage in the light of the coming of Christ" (74). The necessity of this double reading arises since the Old Testament's intended audience is those who received "the final form of the book—not those . . . reading the book today" (80). As such, on the first reading of the Old Testament text, in order "to listen to its discrete voice," we make no "appeal to Christ"; only on the second reading do we interpret "from the full vantage point of the gospel, in the light of the resurrection" (88).

This proposal wrongly assumes that God ever intended those who know the final chapter to read Scripture's earlier parts as if they are ignorant of the end. The New Testament's authors give no evidence that they interpreted their Scriptures as if Christ had not come. Instead, after meeting Jesus, Paul sought to convince his hearers "about Jesus both from the Law of Moses and from the Prophets" (Acts 28:23 ESV; cf. 19:8; Rom 16:25–26). The apostle's encounter with Jesus reshaped all his biblical interpretation, not just his second step. The apostle never "brackets the fuller knowledge acquired in the further revelation of the New Testament" (74). Longman's own *Hamlet* illustration strongly supports this conclusion. He rightly notes that we would only bracket off acts 1–3 from acts 4–5 if Shakespeare never intended them to be part of the same story; but they are part of the same story, so we must read them together. So, too, with Scripture! God *always* intended that the Christian Bible include both Old and New Testaments, so at no stage of interpretation should we attempt to treat either Testament apart from the other. Longman maintains both that the Bible is "an organic unity" and that we should temporarily "bracket" off the New Testament from the Old Testament. These two approaches are inherently contradictory. I contend that as Christians who have by nature already encountered Jesus, our *first* reading of the Old Testament must account for the end of the story in order to read the whole rightly from the beginning.

Furthermore, the Old Testament authors regularly identify that they wrote to and for *future* generations associated with the new covenant more so than their contemporaries. For example, though Moses's audience remained largely spiritually disabled (Deut 29:4 [29:3 MT]), his words would matter for the transformed, heart-circumcised saints participating in the age of restoration (30:6–8; Rom 2:29). Most of Isaiah's contemporaries were unable to receive his word (Isa 6:9–10; 29:9–12; 30:9), but God called him to write his scroll for a future people who would hear and see (29:18–19; 30:8; Matt 11:5, 15).[1] Again, the Lord charged Jeremiah to "write in a book all the words that I have spoken to you" *because* "days are coming" when God would return his people from exile and one of their own would rule over them in the "latter days"

---

1. The same blindness remained through the Old Testament era and into the New Testament (e.g., Jer 5:21; Ezek 3:7; Matt 13:14–15; Rom 11:8). But Jesus came to give sight to the blind and understanding to the foolish.

of healing and spiritual understanding, days associated with the new covenant (Jer 30:2–3, 17, 21, 24 ESV; cf. 31:31, 33; Zech 2:9, 11; 6:15). The Old Testament even claims that only the "wise" would understand certain things from the prophets at "the time of the end" (Dan 12:9–10; cf. John 13:7). Peter noted that God "revealed to [the OT prophets] that they were not serving themselves but you" (1 Pet 1:11–12). To "read the Old Testament texts in their discrete setting in the Old Testament time period" *requires* that we equally recognize that we as new covenant believers are regularly the implied readers.

Next, Longman's exegesis appears to bracket off reading a passage even in light of its close literary context, let alone its broader Old Testament context. He stresses that the first reading "must account for the passage's genre and historical context" (88), and this is about as far as he goes in his case studies. Yet faithful interpretation requires more. I attempt to show in my own essay that careful wrestling with the close literary context of each book actually pushes one to read each passage within its broader continuing and complete context and clarifies that each case study passage is indeed about Messiah Jesus.

Longman also wrongly pits the Spirit's work against himself. Citing Peter Enns, Longman claims that the Spirit leads our second reading "with the anchor being not what the Old Testament author intended but how Christ gives the Old Testament its final coherence" (88).[2] Yet the apostle Peter identifies that God's Spirit carried the Old Testament prophets along and predicted Christ's tribulation and triumph through them as they searched and interpreted earlier Scriptures (1 Pet 1:10–11; 2 Pet 1:21). Rather than leading us away from his original intent, our Spirit-led engagement with the Old Testament text leads us to embrace what the Old Testament prophets wrote about—Jesus's suffering and resurrection.

Finally, Longman fails to sufficiently account for the New Testament's clear testimony regarding how much the Old Testament prophets knew about Jesus and his coming. Jesus declared, "Your father Abraham rejoiced that he would see my day. He saw it and was glad" (John 8:56 ESV). The patriarch delighted in the Messiah and his coming era from

---

2. Longman here cites Peter Enns, *Inspiration and Incarnation: Evangelicals and the Problem of the Old Testament*, 2nd ed. (Grand Rapids: Baker Academic, 2015), 148–49.

a distance. Thus, we read, "Many prophets and righteous people longed to see what you see but did not see it, and to hear what you hear but did not hear it" (Matt 13:17; cf. Luke 10:24). And again, "Isaiah . . . saw Jesus' glory and spoke about him" (John 12:41). These Old Testament saints "all died in faith, not having received the things promised, but having seen them and greeted them from afar" (Heb 11:13 ESV). Their faith was future-oriented, related to the coming kingdom and the perfecting work of Christ found in the new covenant (11:40; 12:2; cf. 10:14; 12:23–24).

Evaluating Longman's Case Studies

Longman's hermeneutical missteps become very apparent in his case studies. Far from identifying the "discrete voice" of Genesis 22:1–19, Longman's first reading fails to place the story within the close context of Genesis as a whole. He never reflects on how God's promise of offspring to Abraham relates to the offspring promise in Genesis 3:15; nor does he identify that Isaac is *not* the offspring but the one through whom God will name him (21:12). Longman speaks of "the promise," which appears identified with Yahweh's declaration that the patriarch would "receive the land and have numerous descendants—the prerequisite to becoming 'a great nation'" (89). But he fails to note how the book's hope is not only in a *people* but in a *person* who overcomes the curse and God's enemies and brings divine blessing to all the earth's nations (e.g., 3:15; 22:17–18; 24:60; 49:10).

In case study two, Longman helpfully notes that Woman Wisdom "is a personification of God's wisdom" (93). However, he fails to assess Proverbs 8:22–31 in light of its close context. He neither interprets Wisdom's call within the historical and prophetic setting of the Davidic covenant (1:1) nor recognizes Wisdom as God's "son" (30:3–4), which in context bears allusions to earlier messianic prophecies (30:1 with Num 24:3, 15; 2 Sam 23:1) and which Proverbs depicts with royal overtones. This failure causes him to believe that Woman Wisdom is not "Jesus as if Proverbs 8 is a prophecy" about him (95). Additionally, Longman claims that "Jesus is not the firstborn of creation," for he is not a created being (95). However, this is Paul's exact language (Col 1:15), and Longman's view wrongly assumes that "firstborn of creation" refers to a created being and that Proverbs 8:22 teaches that Wisdom is created.

In case study three, Longman avers that the New Testament authors "applied" Isaiah's suffering servant passages to Jesus and believed they "describe him," although they originally referred "to the faithful remnant of Israel" (98). Yet the only one Isaiah has identified thus far as being endowed with God's Spirit (42:1) and as bringing justice to the nations (42:1, 4) is the anticipated king (11:2, 5), whose very names are closely tied to God himself (9:6–7; cf. 7:14). Indeed, how apart from Jesus Christ's preceding work does the faithful remnant "bring justice to the nations," operate as "a covenant for the people and a light for the gentiles," "open eyes that are blind," and "free captives from prison" (42:1, 6–7; cf. 49:8–9)? Is the remnant truly "righteous," having "done no violence" (53:9, 11; cf. 50:5, 8–9)? Did the remnant ever die a substitutionary death, rise to life, "justify many," and "bear their iniquities" (53:5, 11)? Longman never answers these questions.

Furthermore, Longman fails to assess the close context to recognize that Isaiah identifies the remnant *not* as the (singular) servant but as the servant's "offspring" (Isa 45:25; 53:10; 54:3; 59:21; 65:23; 66:22)—the "many" (52:14–15; 53:11–12) multiethnic (plural) "servants" (54:17; 56:6, 8; 65:13–15; 66:14) whom the servant-person justifies (45:25; 53:11). He also misses how Isaiah links the suffering servant and anointed conqueror with the royal figure from earlier in the book (e.g., 9:7 with 42:1, 4; 9:7 with 55:3; 11:2 with 42:1 and 61:1; 11:5 and 32:1 with 59:17; 11:8 with 53:2). We do not need to jump to the New Testament to see "Jesus as the ideal Israel"; Isaiah himself already made this identification (49:3, 6; cf. 45:25).

Finally, Longman moves beyond the "discrete voice" of the Old Testament itself and says that Isaiah could not have had in view an individual because "what we know about messianic expectation in Second Temple Jewish literature as well as the Gospels themselves" shows us that "no one was thinking in those terms" (98). Thus, Longman illegitimately limits prophetic ability and intention based on communal perception. Moreover, prior to Jesus's resurrection, David along with "all the prophets" and Simeon foretold with Jesus that he would die and rise (Mark 8:31; Luke 2:34–35; Acts 2:30–31; 3:18). Yes, Israel's majority was blind and deaf (Mark 4:11–12; Rom 11:7–8), but the remnant could see, for through Christ "the veil is taken away" (2 Cor 3:16).

Conclusion

Longman claims the idea that Abraham, Moses, Solomon, or Isaiah would have hoped in an individual messiah "stretches credulity" (99), suggesting that my approach naively believes that the Old Testament prophets could not have spoken about the Christ in detail. I disagree based on my exegetical arguments from the close, continuing, and complete contexts. I appreciate that Longman recognizes the need to interpret the Old Testament "in the light of the whole canon" (100). Nevertheless, his two-readings approach supplies an interpretive strategy that has no precedent in Scripture. To act as though Christ has not come at any stage in our biblical interpretation is to restore a "veil" over our hearts (2 Cor 3:14–16) and to act as a "natural" rather than "spiritual" person who cannot accept the things of God (1 Cor 2:13–14). Lastly, Longman's exegesis in his first readings fails to account for the numerous clues in the close contexts of all his case studies that signal that the human author was anticipating an individual messiah.

RESPONSE TO TREMPER LONGMAN III
(THE PREMODERN APPROACH)

CRAIG A. CARTER

I agree with many of the points made by Dr. Longman in this chapter. However, this approach suffers from certain internal tensions that characterize all attempts to use modern hermeneutical principles to arrive at traditional, orthodox conclusions. There are hints throughout the chapter that Longman is uneasy with some of the premodern interpretations of Old Testament texts, but he is clear that he wants to preserve the basic teaching that Jesus fulfills the Old Testament prophecies and is Israel's Messiah. Yet, in his approach, he seems to accept the modern reduction of the meaning of the biblical text to what the original author meant to convey to the original audience in the original situation. This definition of the meaning of the text means that whatever is not consciously known and asserted by the human author at the time of writing cannot be said to be the meaning of the text itself, in which case it is difficult to see how Longman's christological interpretation can be evaluated as anything other than reading Christ into the Old Testament text. Holding together modern methodology and premodern conclusions is not easy, so I will explore some of the tensions in my response.

Nothing that follows is meant to impugn Longman's motives in wanting to uphold an orthodox Christology; the question is whether this approach of a first reading using the historical-critical method followed by a second reading that considers the history of Christian interpretation is adequate for maintaining orthodoxy in the long run. One reason for doubt is that this approach would not have been sufficient to establish Christian interpretations of the Old Testament in the first place. When Paul was arguing in the synagogues that Jesus of Nazareth is the one foretold in the Old Testament, he did not have two thousand years of Christian interpretation upon which to draw. He would have had the facts of Christ's birth, life, death, resurrection, and ascension, but the proper interpretation of the meaning of these events was itself the focus of the disagreement. His opponents would not have denied the existence of the historical Jesus; they would have disagreed with what they considered to be Paul's overblown interpretation of the significance of the man from Nazareth. Even if he was an amazing teacher and performed miracles, they still found it impossible to believe that the messiah would have ended up on a Roman cross. As for the resurrection, the problem was not that they ruled out the possibility of a miracle; it was, rather, the unlikelihood that the messiah would allow himself to die as a common criminal in the first place.

It comes down to whether the Isaianic suffering servant figure should be identified with the Danielic Son of Man and the Davidic king as the messiah who comes twice, once to die for the sins of the world and the second time in the clouds of glory to rule and reign. Is that how the Hebrew Scriptures should be interpreted as a whole? Jesus apparently thought so. Is it likely that Israel's messiah would have been rejected by the leaders of the nation? Again, Jesus believed it had been predicted by Isaiah (Matt 13:13–15). He knew God's prophets, from Abel to Zechariah, had been rejected (Luke 11:51). If the apostles had not been convinced that the Hebrew Scriptures describe exactly the kind of messiah that Jesus was—a suffering, rejected messiah—they would not have had the confidence to proclaim him as the fulfillment of Scripture.

According to apostolic testimony, this confidence originated with Jesus himself and was taught to the apostles by the risen Lord himself, as Luke 24 indicates. Many individual aspects of Jesus's reading of Scripture had Second Temple precedents, but no one put it all together the way he did until after his resurrection from the dead and his teaching ministry prior to the ascension. The Holy Spirit continued to teach the apostles after the ascension as they obeyed the Great Commission. None of this means that the New Testament interpretation of the Old is reading new meaning into it that it did not have before. The problem of the lack of understanding of the meaning of the Old Testament prior to the resurrection was a flaw in the readers, not a lack of meaning in the text, which is why Jesus rebukes the disciples on the Emmaus road as "foolish" and "slow of heart to believe all that the prophets have spoken!" (Luke 24:25 ESV).

Human Authorial Intent versus the Plain Sense of the Text

First, let us examine the tension between human authorial intent and what we can call the "plain sense" of the text. The term *plain sense* has been taken to mean different things in the history of interpretation, but for our purposes here let us use it to refer to what the text itself says, as opposed to all that might or might not have been in the mind of the original human author or how the first readers might have understood it.

Many modern interpreters claim that we need to limit the text's meaning to the human author's intent to anchor meaning in something objective and stable so that we don't get wild, arbitrary, subjective readings that are all over the place. After two centuries of higher criticism, how is that going? A quick survey of higher critical commentaries on Isaiah, for example, shows that hardly any two commentators agree on much of anything in terms of date, authorship, interpolations, theological meaning, and so on. The focus on human authorial intent makes for very subjective interpretation.

We do not know what was in the mind of Isaiah or David or Moses. We should note that the Christian tradition has never claimed that whatever it was that they were thinking was inspired. Paul spoke of Scripture as breathed out by God (2 Tim 3:16), and when Peter spoke of prophetic speech, he said that "men spoke from God as they were carried along by the Holy Spirit" (2 Pet 1:21 ESV). The church always speaks of the inspiration of prophecy itself or of the text of Scripture, but not of authors. Besides, if something an author thought but did not write down was inspired, we would have no way of knowing it.

Human authorial intent may sound objective and scientifically discoverable, but it is not easy to determine. The speculative reconstructions of biblical criticism—the priestly writer, the Johannine community—are often at odds with each other and usually impossible to prove. In many cases, we do not even know the identity of the original author or the final redactor. Nor is it clear whether the final editor felt at liberty to make alterations and expansions. The answer probably varies from case to case. What if a later reactor's intention contradicts the original author's intention?

One of the worst features of the modern reduction of what used to be called "the literal sense" to conscious human authorial intent is the introduction into Scripture of contradictions. It seems that the dozens of authors did not all intend the same things. So, if the meaning of the text is only what they intended, it is not surprising that interpreters see the texts as saying incompatible things. The only way some texts can be harmonized is by seeing in them more than just conscious, human authorial intent. We must see divine authorial intent in them, and when we do the contradictions fade because there is only one God and only one divine intent that is witnessed to in various ways in various texts.

Distinguishing Divine versus Human Authorial Intent

This brings us to the second tension: the tension between divine and human authorial intent. In the New Testament we read,

> Concerning this salvation, the prophets who prophesied about the grace that was to be yours searched and inquired carefully, inquiring what person or time the Spirit of Christ in them was indicating when he predicted the sufferings of Christ and the subsequent glories. It was revealed to them that they were serving not themselves but you, in the things that have now been announced to you through those who preached the good news to you by the Holy Spirit sent from heaven, things into which angels long to look. (1 Pet 1:10–12 ESV)

Here Peter explains that the prophets who wrote the Scriptures did not fully understand their own inspired utterance in detail.

What we see in Peter's description of prophetic writings is an important distinction between human authorial intent (what the prophets wrote) and divine authorial intent (what the Spirit of Christ was "indicating"). The Old Testament text contained more meaning than the human author could grasp because the divine author intended that meaning. Because the text is "God-breathed," divine authorial intent can be said to be in the text even though it exceeds the conscious understanding of the original human author and the first hearers/readers.

What we need is a more expansive sense of divine authorial intent, one that goes beyond (without contradicting) the original human author's conscious intent. This sort of divine authorial intent is supernatural. No atheist allows for divine speaking or intending. But if biblical interpretation is, as I hold, a matter of "faith seeking understanding," then searching for the expanded literal (christological) sense is a natural move. This is how we can speak of the meaning always being there in the text all along even though very few saw it until after the resurrection of Christ.

The Historical Sense versus the Literal Sense

A third tension is seen in the fact that the literal sense can be defined as the original human author's conscious intent or as the divine author's intent. But what if it is both? The former excludes the latter, but the latter includes the former. Divine authorial intent is not *less* than the human authorial intent, but it can be *more*. Often they are basically identical. But at times, especially in Old Testament texts with a christological reference, the expanded or extended literal sense can be much larger than the human authorial intent. An expanded literal sense must be based on and not a contradiction of the human author's intended meaning, which prevents arbitrary interpretation. Divine inspiration preserves the human author from error even when inspiring the human author to write something that has more meaning than even that author can grasp at the time.

It is crucial not to detach the christological sense from the literal sense. Modern hermeneutics does so by reducing the historical meaning to the naturalistic meaning, that is, by excluding the category of the supernatural from the description of the meaning of the text. There is an implicit denial of the presence of the supernatural activity of God in history in the naturalistic definition of history. So, from a Christian metaphysical perspective, there is no conflict between a literal sense that is both christological and fully historical at once. Christian metaphysical assumptions are required for sound hermeneutics because the meaning of the text cannot be understood properly if divine authorial intent is either denied or bracketed, and only Christian metaphysical assumptions enable us to hold the divine and human authorial intent together.

Conclusion

In this chapter, Longman is trying to affirm the modern, historical-critical method without letting it rule out a Christian reading of the

Old Testament. He hopes that by strategically retreating from some Christian interpretations (such as the christological interpretation of the Song of Songs) he can maintain a plausible Christian interpretation as a kind of add-on reading to the primary, historical reading. The problem comes when there is a conflict between the historical-critical and christological readings. In that case, his approach has insufficient resources for affirming a Christian reading as *superior* to the modern one. Therefore, it is probable that this approach will create a false sense of peace between two opposing approaches to interpretation and, in the long run, result in a long, slow secularization of our reading of the Old Testament.

REJOINDER

I have to confess to being a bit mystified by Dr. Carter's critique of my chapter. I don't see myself in his description of me. I don't accept, as he thinks I do, "the modern reduction of the meaning of the biblical text to what the original author meant to convey to the original audience in the original situation" (118), nor do I believe that "whatever is not consciously known and asserted by the human author at the time of writing cannot be said to be the meaning of the text itself" (118). I very clearly state that I am not a historical critic, as he calls me. I never claimed that we could "know what was in the mind of Isaiah or David or Moses" (120) but rather call for an evaluation of the author's writerly performance *a la* Kevin Vanhoozer, and thus I avoid the so-called intentional fallacy.[1] I do not think, as Dr. Carter seems to think, that the literal sense has to be a choice between the human and divine intention. I have to be open to the possibility that I did not communicate well on these matters, but I suspect that Dr. Carter is working with a stereotype of a historically oriented interpreter. I ask the reader to go back and judge for themselves from my chapter and not from his critique.

In terms of Dr. Goldingay's critique, let me first reiterate that we largely agree on the most important things. I enthusiastically affirm his perception of the importance of understanding the First Testament in its original setting (what I call the "first reading"). I also appreciate, though I describe it differently, his recognition that the "fuller significance"

---

1. Kevin J. Vanhoozer, *Is There a Meaning in This Text? The Bible, the Reader, and the Morality of Literary Knowledge* (Grand Rapids: Zondervan, 1998).

(what I would call the fuller sense of the Old Testament) finds its appropriate referent in Christ. I believe that our differences are the result of his understandable desire to defend the First Testament from too quick a christological appropriation, a desire I share. While he questions my use of Augustine's language of Christ "hiding" in the Old Testament, I still think it is helpful as a metaphor for the idea that although Christ is not explicitly found in the Old Testament, in the light of the New Testament, we can recognize him there.

Goldingay himself says that we learn from the New Testament something that we can't see in the Old Testament (what I mean by progressive revelation), namely, that it was the triune God who created all things, including human beings. So reading Genesis 1 in the light of the New Testament allows us on a second reading to affirm what was "hidden" from the original author and audience. In terms of Jesus in the Old Testament, which I say is incontestable, Goldingay responds, "I guess I do contest it, but at least I can claim that the New Testament is not Christian either, since it says that Moses and David are in the First Testament, but not that Jesus is!" (102). I find this perplexing since Jesus himself said that he is in the First Testament as he "explained to them [the two disciples on the road to Emmaus] what was said in all the Scriptures concerning himself" (Luke 24:27). But again, let me reiterate that I deeply appreciate Dr. Goldingay's defense of a first reading of the Old Testament.

To respond in detail to Dr. DeRouchie's critique of my chapter would take another chapter, though in a sense my response to his "Redemptive-Historical, Christocentric Approach" does a lot of that work. I want to begin by saying that I appreciate that he rightly understands my approach, but with one caveat. I think he misses the point that I do take seriously Jesus's comment that the two disciples were "foolish" and "slow to believe all that the prophets have spoken" (Luke 24:25). While I don't believe that Old Testament saints would have or could have read the Old Testament anything like Dr. DeRouchie does in his case studies, Luke 24:25 suggests that they should have gotten the idea in at least general terms. I can only urge readers to go back and look at texts like Deuteronomy 29:4; 30:6–8; and Isaiah 29:9–12 to see that they do not teach that Old Testament authors were writing with future audiences in mind, as Dr. DeRouchie suggests. His criticisms of my treatments of the case studies are simply repeats of his overclever, overclose readings of the texts, which I question in my response to his original chapter. I think the very idiosyncratic nature of his interpretations are also a reason to question them. If space permitted, I would raise the question whether we should or can interpret the Old Testament exactly like the New Testament authors did. But I will end by lamenting how much is missed in terms of the Old Testament's theological and practical teaching by ignoring the "discrete message" of the Old Testament.

Finally, I think I may wrongly criticize Dr. Dharamraj's chapter for going too quickly to a christological/telic reading and not appreciating what I call the "first reading" of an Old Testament text. Or maybe, in self-defense, she makes it much clearer in her response to my chapter than in her original contribution that she, too, appreciates the importance of the Old Testament's "discrete message" to our understanding of God and our relationship with him. I continue to have trouble understanding the importance of speaking through the voice of the Common Reader, but as I say in my first response to her, I deeply appreciate her sensitive Christian readings of the Old Testament. Her response to my view clarifies that she, too, wants to read the Old Testament on its own terms as well as from a Christian perspective, further deepening my appreciation of her approach to the issue of Christ in the Old Testament.

Thus, I continue to advocate the view that Christian interpreters should start by reading an Old Testament text in its original setting (first reading). Then, after learning from the rich message of the text in its "discrete meaning," Christians should then read the Old Testament in the light of the fuller revelation of the New Testament, fully expecting to see how the passage or book anticipates the coming of Christ.

RECEPTION-CENTERED, INTERTEXTUAL APPROACH

HAVILAH DHARAMRAJ

Introduction to the Reception-Centered, Intertextual Approach

I want to begin by talking about the "Common Reader." This could be you. The Common Reader—as they listen to the Sunday sermon or reflect on the Bible passage that comes up for morning devotion—makes connections. These connections are often made instinctively and might link one text with another text: *Isn't Boaz a bit like Jesus, looking out for the needy? Surely this text in Isaiah fits Christ as the Gospel of John describes him in the opening chapter.* The exercise the Common Reader is performing here is reading an Old Testament text with spectacles, the lenses of which are the person and work of Christ, familiar from the New Testament. This approach to reading Jesus in the Old Testament can be called the Reception-Centered, Intertextual Approach. The Common Reader is the receptor of these texts, and they intuitively set Old and New Testament texts in conversation with each other.

Common Reader is a technical term[1] and is equivalent to what the publishing world might call a "general reader." In simplistic categories, the critic reads to evaluate, the scholar reads for knowledge, and the

---

1. The term belongs in the discipline of comparative literature, in which pairs of texts are not necessarily chosen from within the Christian canon. For an introduction, see Havilah Dharamraj, "The Curious Case of Hagar: Biblical Studies and the Interdisciplinary Approach of Comparative Literature," *Journal of Asian Evangelical Theology* 23.2 (2019): 49–71.

Common Reader reads for pleasure. In my use of the term here, the Common Reader is one who has familiarity with the Bible because they read the Old Testament and seek to correlate it with Jesus. The degree of familiarity will vary from one Common Reader to the next, but the Common Reader's inputs are not confined to the textual. Virginia Woolf's description might work for the Common Reader looking to find Jesus in the Old Testament: "Above all, he is guided by an instinct to create for himself, out of whatever odds and ends he can come by, some kind of whole."[2]

Traditionally, the "intertextual method" of reading texts side by side has been largely *production-centered*, seeking to establish how an older work historically influenced and shaped the writing of a later one, technically called *causality*. The goal is to discover the *purpose* of the intertextual relationship. An example of reading a text intertextually, with *causality* in mind, would be setting the story of the Levite's concubine (Judg 19:22–26) alongside the story of Lot's last night in Sodom (Gen 19:4–8). The events of the two fateful nights are unmistakably in parallel. In Hebrew sixteen words—almost one-fourth of the vocabulary—are identical. Another twenty-four expressions are in close parallel. Even the length of the text is identical, sixty-nine words in each account. The narrator of the Judges story is intentionally evoking the Sodom account. His point couldn't be clearer: the Levite thought he had found a secure halting place among his own countrymen. Yet he had arrived in what was virtually Sodom. It could be argued that the chronologically later text (Judges) is *caused* by the earlier text (Genesis). The *purpose* is to show that Israel at this stage is so Canaanized that it is indistinguishable from Sodom, a byword for wickedness and perversity. *Causality* and *purpose* mark production-centered intertextuality, a largely author-centered, historical endeavor.

What we are considering is different. It is *reception-centered* intertextuality,[3] which intentionally resists speculating about how one text may

---

2. Virginia Woolf, *The Common Reader* (New York: Harcourt, 1953), 2–3.

3. For a helpful tabulation comparing production-centered and reception-centered intertextuality, see Ellen van Wolde, "Texts in Dialogue with Texts: Intertextuality in the Ruth and Tamar Narratives," *BibInt* 5 (1997): 5–7. For a survey of methods in use see B. J. Oropeza, "Intertextuality," in *The Oxford Encyclopedia of Biblical Interpretation*, ed. Steven L. McKenzie (Oxford: Oxford University Press, 2013), 1:453–63. For a comprehensive bibliography of reading on intertextuality, see B. J. Oropeza and Steve Moyise, eds., *Exploring Intertextuality:*

be dependent on another. Instead, the Common Reader pairs one text with another, say, the suffering servant of Isaiah 53 with a crucifixion narrative. The pairing is directed by a dominant theme—technically an *icon*—shared by the texts. When one text (T1) is paired with and engaged with another (T2), the transcript of the conversation between the two becomes a third text (T3). Discovering the *effect* of this intertextual conversation is the purpose of this method. In sum, *iconicity* and *effect* are the unique identifiers of the reception-centered intertextual method, a largely reader-centered, literary investigation.

More recently, this clean line between author- and reader-centered intertextuality, between the historical and the literary, has been smudged. John Barton argues that "the absolute polarization of these two approaches is probably exaggerated."[4] At best, they are "devices for describing different reading emphases, but ultimately, hermeneutics cannot be hermetically sealed off into one approach or the other."[5] The two are both autonomous *and* interdependent.[6] That said, this chapter will adopt a reception-centered reading emphasis.

So how does the Common Reader pair up one text with another? To answer this, it is helpful to consider what is called the *public meaning* of a given piece of literature, another technical concept from the discipline of comparative literature. *Public meaning* is the corpus of meaning(s) of the text generated by a collective or a community. Indeed, as a literary work "moves through time and space it accrues meaning, sheds meaning, provokes meaning."[7] In historiography, this is the *longue durée*—the long stretches of time over which imperceptible changes can happen. With the Bible, the *longue durée* of circulation and transmission of the text (perhaps including orality in some parts of the present-day world)

Diverse Strategies for New Testament Interpretation of Texts (Eugene, OR: Cascade, 2016), xviii–xix.

4. John Barton, "*Déjà Lu*: Intertextuality, Method or Theory?" in *Reading Job Intertextually*, ed. Katharine J. Dell and William L. Kynes, LHBOTS 574 (New York: Bloomsbury, 2013), 7. Barton prefers to use for these two approaches the terms *temporal* and *spatial*.

5. Katharine Dell, "Introduction," in *Reading Job Intertextually*, ed. Katharine J. Dell and William L. Kynes, LHBOTS 574 (New York: Bloomsbury, 2013), xxii.

6. Dell, xxii, following Ferdinand de Saussure, *Course in General Linguistics* (Chicago: Open Court, 1983), 87.

7. Michael Lucey, "A Literary Object's Contextual Life," in *A Companion to Comparative Literature*, ed. Ali Behdad and Dominic Thomas (Chichester: Wiley-Blackwell, 2011), 128.

creates *public meaning*.[8] The Common Reader is familiar with the *public meaning* of these narratives—meaning that is mediated through sermons, liturgy, hymns and contemporary worship songs, the visual arts, the plastic arts, the performing arts, and more. When the Common Reader comes to the biblical text, they bring to their reading "acquisitions that are not simply personal." These are acquisitions "that are related to that person's trajectory through a particular social universe, related to her or his interaction with that universe."[9]

The choosing of intertexts, then, comes from both the Common Reader's intuitive reading and the influence on such reading by the Common Reader's particular social universe. This being the case, one Common Reader will pair up intertexts different from another. This is a measure of subjectivity that any reader-response method such as this presumes. We will return to discuss this further.

Part 1: The Nature of Scripture

Our use of reception-centered intertextuality begins with the presupposition that the sixty-six books of the Protestant canon are in conversation with each other. Take, for example, the book of Ruth. It neatly bridges two great periods of history. Commencing with "the days when the judges ruled," it finishes off with a genealogy that ties it to the books of Samuel.[10] Or think of Deuteronomy and how well it distills the essence of the books of the law before it launches us into the books of history, where the yardstick for the evaluation of its protagonists refers back to Deuteronomy. Michael Fishbane says it with insistence and emphasis: "Intertextuality is the core of the canonical imagination," since "a canon . . . presupposes the possibility of correlations among its parts."[11] What we are postulating is that intertexts abound, both within each Testament and across the Testaments. Our endeavor is to identify them and get them talking to each other.

A second presupposition in this method concerns the reader. When

---

8. Lucey, 121.

9. Lucey, 121.

10. Alternatively, Ruth is located after Proverbs in some Hebrew manuscripts, such that Ruth embodies the woman of worth of Proverbs 31. In another ancient tradition (*Baba Bathra* 14b), Ruth is placed before the Psalms, signaling the Davidic focus of both books.

11. Michael Fishbane, "Types of Biblical Intertextuality," in *Congress Volume: Oslo 1998*, ed. André Lemaire and Magne Sæbø, VTSup 80 (Leiden: Brill, 2000), 39.

the Christian Common Reader comes to the text, they bring to the reading inputs from a variety of locations—socioeconomic, cultural, political, religious, and denominational. This default setting influences the icon the Common Reader picks out in the text. I'll illustrate this by imagining what ospel texts a Common Reader might pair with the plague narrative (Exod 7–12). A lower caste Indian Christian might identify the governing icon of the plague narrative politically, as liberation from oppression, and identify an intertext highlighting Jesus's championing of the marginalized, such as his defense of the woman of disrepute at the house of Simon (Luke 7:36–50). For a Kiwi Christian, coming from a more equitable social location, the icon may be the irresistible power of YHWH and the intertext of choice might be Jesus's calming of a stormy sea (Matt 8:23–27). The religiously plural location of South Asian Christians may prompt them to major on the victory of YHWH in the cosmic battle against the gods of Egypt (Exod 12:12), and the intertext they identify might be Jesus exorcising the unclean spirits from the demoniac (Mark 5:1–13).

The third presupposition of this reader-centered method is that authorial intention is not a driving consideration in the association the Common Reader makes between one text and another. Authorial intent is what governs production-centered intertextuality, and is what concerns inner-biblical exegesis, inner-biblical allusions, and cross-canonical echoes. Certainty that one text has influenced the composition of another is not always easy to nail down. Meanwhile, the openness of reception-centered intertextuality may appear to encourage the Common Reader down the slippery slope of associating a given text with just about any other text. In the three case studies in part 3 of this chapter, I hope to demonstrate that the method has inbuilt hermeneutical checks and balances.

Part 2: Interpretive Steps for Readers

The task of locating Jesus in the Old Testament using reception-centered intertextuality can be systematized into five steps. The method is heuristic—that is, we proceed by trial through the first four steps. In the fifth step, we assess the outcome.

First, the Common Reader comes upon a certain Old Testament text (T1) and finds in it christological resonance. The resonance emerges out of two considerations: the Common Reader's study of the text and the public meaning of the text as they have experienced it. Given this, public meaning is likely to be specific to the Common Reader's social location. The resonance might be detected at the story level (as we shall see in the case of the binding of Isaac) or at the level of parallel ideas (as in the Wisdom poem and the Servant Song).

Second, the Common Reader identifies a dominant theme of the potentially christological Old Testament text—technically, its icon. Perhaps this is one of several icons in the text. As I said, the location of the Common Reader might have a significant influence on icon detection.

Third, the Common Reader looks for a New Testament christological text (T2) that appears to carry the same icon. The choice of T2 depends on two considerations: the Common Reader's degree of familiarity with the Bible and the public meaning of the New Testament text as they have experienced it. Because the icon identified in T1 may vary from one Common Reader to another, the text pairs selected are not likely to be identical.

Fourth, the intertexts (T1 and T2) are put into conversation with each other. Here the Common Reader will need resources for the study of texts that will help with the exposition of the icon and provide sufficient background information, whether ancient West Asian or Greco-Roman. At this stage, the Common Reader will be either affirmed or not on two counts: (1) whether the icon being pursued is a significant one in both the texts; and (2) whether the intertextual conversation (T3) emerging out of the study appears forced or flows naturally. If the intertexts are not in free-flowing dialogue with each other, we will have to abandon the pair and start afresh. If they are in spontaneous conversation, the effect of T3 will be to help the Common Reader see how the pair of intertexts, one in the Old Testament and the other in the New Testament, work together through dialogue to offer a reading of Jesus that honors both the texts and the reception of these texts across the centuries within the communities of faith that have been shaped by them.

Fifth and finally, since the method is heuristic—that is, it proceeds by trial—it must now be evaluated. This is done by assessing T3, the transcript of the intertextual dialogue. T3 should deepen the reading of each text (T1 and T2) toward orthodox Christian faith and practice. An insightful and rich reciprocal reading affirms the identification of the icon in T1 and validates the pairing of T1 with T2. Returning to the introductory paragraph of this chapter, it would be reasonable to say that the method and the steps laid out here simply systematize what many a Common Reader—or Common Preacher!—does anyway, guided by the "readerly" urge to make christological sense of the Old Testament.

Part 3: Applying the Approach: Three Case Studies

The following three case studies will help us understand how reception-centered intertextuality works for the Common Reader who is looking to locate Jesus in the Old Testament.

Case 1: The Ordeal of Isaac: Genesis 22:1-19

Our first case study is a familiar Old Testament text: Genesis 22, the story of the Ordeal of Isaac. In Judaism the narrative is called the *Akedah*, from the verb "to bind," which is what Abraham does with his son before he lays him on the altar (v. 9).

Let us postulate a Christian Common Reader in the Indian city of Mumbai, where Christian communities have lived for centuries alongside Jews and Muslims. This Common Reader starts by noticing the story level parallels between Isaac and Jesus: both carry to an appointed place the wood intended for their death. As for public meaning, the Common Reader has heard Isaac both preached from the pulpit and endorsed in devotional readings as the son who willingly submits himself to the will of his father, Abraham, much like Jesus submitted to his Father. Given this Common Reader's multireligious environment, they have experience of the Akedah in religious public settings outside of the Christian community. In Jewish tradition, Isaac said to Abraham, "Father, I am a young man and am afraid that my body may tremble through fear of the knife and I will grieve thee, whereby the slaughter may be rendered unfit and this will not count as a real sacrifice; therefore bind me very firmly" (Genesis Rabbah 56.8). Similarly, Islamic traditions variously have the son asking to be tied tightly so that he will not squirm; asking that his shirt be pulled back so that it will not become stained with blood; requesting that his father return his shirt to his mother for her comfort.

The icon that emerges from personal reading and from public meaning is this: the willing son. The Common Reader looks for a christological intertext that shares this icon. They could choose a gospel narrative but decide on the poem in Philippians 2:6–11. Again, public meaning helps make this choice. The Christ poem is familiar, being read both at Advent and Lent in the Revised Common Lectionary. Graham Kendrick's "The Servant-King" might remind that Jesus came "not to be served but to serve, and give [his] life that we might live."[12] Having settled on a pair of intertexts, Genesis 22 (T1) is put into conversation with Philippians 2:5–11 (T2). I will show how they speak to each other on at least three significant themes (T3).

First, there is the shifting identity of the protagonist. In the Christ hymn, Jesus is featured rather differently from Paul's usual depiction of him. Elsewhere, Paul speaks of Jesus as commissioned and sent by God, but here the "angle" (as journalists would call it) is on what Jesus himself does (cf. Gal 2:20; Rom 5:18–19).[13] As the poem opens, what Jesus does stands out against what he does not do. He is in the "form of God," which we could simply understand as a "mode of being."[14] He does not grab at the rights and privileges of this form. He does not think of taking advantage of the equality with God that this form confers on him. Rather, this is what he does do: he pours himself out (cf. 2 Cor 8:9) into another form, a form that is so starkly in contrast to that which he enjoyed, that it should drop the Philippian audience's jaw as they allow themselves to be amazed by it. Jesus takes on the form of a slave. He who was *kyrios*, Lord, becomes *doulos*, a slave. In India the Common Reader would have to imagine a wealthy landlord's son choosing to become a bonded laborer in a stone quarry or brick kiln, and that would be but an anemic parallel. In keeping with the worst that a slave might expect in first-century Palestine, Jesus takes his form of being a slave to its vicious end—death. Not just death, the hymn reminds its audience, but "even death on a cross!" (Phil 2:8). By that, Jesus allows upon himself the kind

---

12. Graham Kendrick, "The Servant-King" (Thankyou Music, 1983).

13. Morna D. Hooker, "Philippians," in *New Interpreter's Bible*, vol. 11, ed. Leander E. Keck (Nashville: Abingdon, 2000), 501.

14. Gerald F. Hawthorne, *Philippians*, WBC 43 (Waco, TX: Word, 1983), 83–84. On *morphē*, see Gordon Fee, *Philippians*, IVP New Testament Commentary Series (Downers Grove, IL: InterVarsity Press, 1999), 93–94; Hooker, "Philippians," 504, 507.

of end that might occupy a slave's nightmares—not just a nightmare of life slipping away with each tortured gasp, but stripped of any remaining honor that dignified a slave's wretched existence.

In the Akedah, there are two minor actors who hardly receive any attention. Without any speaking lines, they silently frame the Moriah event (Gen 22:3, 19). Read alongside the Philippians hymn, these two servants become the measure of the shift in Isaac's "mode of being" across the story. In the Hebrew, the same word *na'ar* ("young man") describes both servants (22:3, 5, 19) and Isaac (22:5, 12). Isaac's transformation begins at the foot of the mountain. The servants (*ne'arim*; "young men") wordlessly defer to Abraham's instructions, and Isaac (*na'ar*; "boy") allows the wood for the sacrifice to be laded—not on the servants, as the princeling might expect—but on himself. Though he accepts the servant's role without demur, he still can do what the servants cannot and have not done so far. He addresses the puzzle of the obviously missing piece: the sacrificial lamb. He asks because a son has the freedom to ask his father. But when that father begins to bind him as one would bind a lamb for sacrifice, the son's transformation to servant appears to be complete. As much as the servants wordlessly obey their master's instructions to "stay here with the donkey," Isaac wordlessly becomes the object of his father's actions. That he has spoken boldly earlier throws his later silence into stark relief. This is a period when a chieftain—such as Abraham was—or a king might offer up his firstborn son in exchange for the deity's favor.[15] And in that process, the son, while invested with the "form" of a son, is overwhelmed with yet another form, a form that disallows his right to resist—even to resist death.

A second theme arising from a conversation between the two texts is the voluntary action of the protagonist. When Jesus took on the form of a slave, he did not cease to be in the form of God.[16] Rather, it is in willingly pouring himself into human form that he reveals the selfless sacrifice that only God can make, which sits in contrast to the selfish

---

15. Child sacrifice appears to have been alive in ancient Israel. See Deuteronomy 12:31; 18:10; 2 Kings 16:3; 17:17; 21:6; 2 Kings 23:10; cf. Jeremiah 7:31. Arguably, Judges 11:30–40 is a cautionary tale on such practice. See Baruch Levine, *Leviticus*, JPS Torah Commentary (Philadelphia: Jewish Publication Society, 1989), 258–59 (excursus 7, "The Cult of Molech in Biblical Israel").

16. Hooker, "Philippians," 508.

and grasping instincts of humans. The emphatic position of the pronoun ("himself") and the Greek verb form "strongly suggest that this act was voluntary on the part of the pre-existent Christ."[17] In summary, "Christ's self-giving was accomplished by taking, his self-emptying was achieved by becoming what he was not before, his kenosis ['pouring out'] not by subtracting from but by adding to."[18]

Early Jewish tradition (Genesis Rabbah 56.8) calculates Isaac's age to be thirty-seven at the time his father took him on a journey that ended in him being tied up and hoisted onto an altar. Even if we were to ignore Jewish mathematical exercises on the Akedah, it occurs to us that a young man who could carry a load of wood up a mountain would have the capacity to put up a stout resistance if he had a mind to. As it happens, he did not have a mind to resist. There is no indication in the Old Testament that sacrificial animals were tied before they were slaughtered, but Isaac willingly submits to binding.

That brings us to the third point of contact between the two texts: the exaltation. While in other places, Jesus's exaltation is spoken of as following on the heels of the resurrection (e.g., Rom 8:34; 1 Cor 15:27), here resurrection is elided altogether.[19] The poem hurries on to the antithesis of Christ's self-invoked humiliation—his exaltation. Is Jesus exalted post-resurrection to a position higher than he had? A reasonable argument is: if Christ was already equal to God, then how could he be said to be exalted to anything higher? If he was not already equal to God, how could he truly be said to be in the form of God?[20] It appears then that when the poem speaks of an ascent to the "the highest place" (Phil 2:9), it should be read as expressing "excess" rather than position.[21] Or it could be read that while his post-crucifixion position is not necessarily higher, the exaltation lies in that his position is now declared across the three tiers of the universe—"in heaven and on earth and under the earth"—and is professed by every human knee and tongue (cf. Rom 1:3–4; 10:9; Matt 28:18; Acts 2:36).[22] What is professed is the "name" of

---

17. Hawthorne, *Philippians*, 85.
18. Hawthorne, 86.
19. Hooker, "Philippians," 501–3.
20. Hooker, 507.
21. Fee, *Philippians*, 99.
22. Hooker, "Philippians," 510.

Jesus, that "Jesus Christ is Lord [*kyrios*]" (Phil 2:9–11). This is a stupendous claim the poem makes, because its audience recognizes that *kyrios* is the rendering of the sacred name, YHWH, right through the Greek translation of their Scripture, the Septuagint. Even the Septuagint's verb for YHWH's exaltation "over all the earth" and "far above all gods" is the same as in the Philippians poem (*hyperypsoō*, Ps 96:9 LXX [ET 97:9]).[23] Indeed, it becomes clear to the first-century reader that the fulfillment of YHWH's oath—"By myself I have sworn . . . : Before me every knee will bow; by me every tongue will swear" (Isa 45:23)—is now redirected to Jesus, reassigning to him the high honor of receiving the homage of all peoples.[24]

The Akedah ends not dissimilarly. The divine oath made to Abraham echoes the language of excess: "I swear by myself . . . I will surely bless you and make your descendants as numerous as the stars in the sky and as the sand on the seashore" (Gen 22:16–17). This is because "you have done this and have not withheld your son, your only son" (v. 16). Implicitly nested into this affirmation is Isaac's willing cooperation with Abraham's act. YHWH said of the father, "You have obeyed me" (v. 18).

What, the intertextual method would ask, is the effect obtained by reading these two literary masterpieces side by side? For a story that is often overpowered by Abraham, the father of faith, the Christ hymn throws Isaac into relief. Because of the hymn, we better appreciate the princeling self-transformed into a servant. The Akedah plumbs the depths of the anguish of an obedient son whose "father turns his face away."[25] Indeed, in the artistic depictions of the ordeal of Isaac over the centuries, Abraham's face is turned away from Isaac, looking heavenward, and in one of Rembrandt's two paintings of this scene (1636), Abraham's hand covers Isaac's face. Isaac's willingness to be bound collides head-on with the human instinct to live. We try—and fail—to imagine that the horror of a violent death can be overwhelmed by the desire to submit to the will of a human father.

From reading the Christ hymn through the Akedah, we understand the

---

23. Hawthorne, *Philippians*, 91.
24. Fee, *Philippians*, 100.
25. Stuart Townend, "How Deep the Father's Love for Us" (Thankyou Music, 1995).

Son of God and his act better because of the son of this patriarch of Israel. From this story, we are able to move to the story of Jesus and understand better that despite the dark night of Gethsemane, it was true that "to obey, as a slave must obey, was his delight."[26] While the hymn follows a trajectory across the borders and orders of the three-storied universe, cosmic in its reach, showcasing the extreme degree of divine condescension, the lesser story of Isaac, playing out in a small family of three, long ago but not so far away, makes the inconceivable somewhat conceivable.

Stepping back to evaluate the validity of the pairing of texts, I submit that I have studied T1 and T2, respecting the rules that govern what is called "close reading." The effect of the intertextual conversation (T3) is consistent with, and edifying to, orthodox faith and practice. It exhorts us to be Christ-minded (Phil 2:5); it moves us to a deep appreciation of the work of Christ.

Case 2: Wisdom's Priority in Creation: Proverbs 8:22-31

Our second case study for discovering Jesus in the Old Testament is Proverbs 8:22–31, the self-attestation of the ancient origins of Lady Wisdom.

Let us assume a Common Reader for whom the public meaning of this text is in a context with a significant presence of Jehovah's Witnesses. Perhaps there is a Kingdom Hall down the road from where this Common Reader lives (as in my case, in India) or they received an unsolicited visit from a pair of Jehovah's Witnesses (also as in my case, when I resided in the UK). Their theologically problematic distinctive is a denial of the deity of Christ. Wisdom's claim that "the Lord [YHWH] created me as the beginning of his ways, for the sake of his works" (Prov 8:22 NETS) is superimposed on Christ, "the firstborn" of God "over all creation" (Col 1:15). The inference is that Christ is not coeternal with God the Father but is simply his creation, and thus less than God. Right at the start, then, the Common Reader has a ready-to-use pair of intertexts. The icon common to the Wisdom poem (T1) and the Christ hymn (T2) is the relationship between God and the one celebrated in the text.

At least three concepts in the Wisdom poem resonate with the Colossians hymn. The first is the preexistence of the one celebrated in the text.

---

26. Hawthorne, *Philippians*, 95.

The Hebrew text of the opening line of the Wisdom poem is fraught with difficulties. "The Lord brought me forth [*qnh*] as the first of his works," Wisdom declares (Prov 8:22). Some English versions render *qnh* in its regular sense of "acquire" (CSB), and by derivation, "possess" (KJV, ESV). A second semantic cluster is "create" (LXX, CEB, NASB, NET, NRSV), "make" (HCSB, MSG), and "form" (NLT). A third rendering, "to give birth to," is an extension of "create." This is the sense in which the NIV speaks of YHWH bringing forth Wisdom, stopping short of using the birthing metaphor, which runs through (perhaps) the rest of the poem. "I was formed [*skk*] long ages ago," says Wisdom (Prov 8:23), using a word that biblical poetry uses to describe the human fetus coming together: "For you created my inmost being; you knit me together [*skk*] in my mother's womb" (Ps 139:13; cf. Job 10:11).[27] What is more, Wisdom twice applies a feminine metaphor to the process of her creation: "I was given birth [*hyl*]" (Prov 8:24–25). The English hardly does justice to the verb *hyl*, which means "to writhe." Here it would audaciously apply to YHWH, writhing in the pangs of labor, to give birth to Wisdom. Lastly, the poem ends with Wisdom describing herself as '*amon* at YHWH's side (v. 30). One alternative rendering of '*amon* is "nursling" or "child." If birthing is the motif that describes the origin of Wisdom, then Bruce Waltke is right: "Wisdom has an organic connection with God's very nature and being, unlike the rest of creation that came into existence outside of him and independent of his being."[28] Waltke would also be right, then, that Wisdom is preexistent but not coeternal with God.[29] When was she born? She was the "first of his works, before his deeds of old," born "long ages ago, at the very beginning, when the world came to be" (Prov 8:22–23). The antiquity of Wisdom stretches back to a remote point when time had yet to start ticking.

---

27. See the discussion of this uncertain verb in Bruce Waltke, *The Book of Proverbs, Chapters 1–15*, NICOT (Grand Rapids: Eerdmans, 2004), 411.

28. Waltke, *Book of Proverbs, Chapters 1–15*, 409. Waltke thinks that the Reformers wrongly equated Wisdom as a hypostasis of YHWH with Jesus, the eternally begotten Son. Fox takes Waltke's reading even further with: "She did not exist from eternity. Wisdom is therefore an accidental attribute of godhead, not an essential or inherent one" (Michael V. Fox, *Proverbs 1–9: A New Translation with Introduction and Commentary*, AB 18A [New York: Doubleday, 2000], 279).

29. Waltke, *Book of Proverbs, Chapters 1–15*, 409.

The Christ hymn of Colossians recalls vocabulary from the Wisdom poem: Jesus is introduced as the "firstborn over all creation" (Col 1:15; cf. Rom 8:29) who exists "before all things" (Col 1:17; cf. Sir 1:4). The language of the "firstborn" is distributed across the Old Testament. For example, Israel is God's "firstborn" (Exod 4:22; Jer 31:9). It is a descriptor regularly used in the Hebrew Bible and the LXX to indicate not simply temporal priority but "sovereignty of rank."[30] Thus, it is said of David: "I will make him a firstborn, high among the kings of the earth" (Ps 89:27). Are we to infer, then, as the Jehovah's Witnesses seem to have done, that Jesus is a created being?

The opening declaration of the Christ hymn is that this "Son is the image [eikōn] of the invisible God" (Col 1:15). While this language may be backlit by the creation of humankind (Gen 1:26–27), it may be more illuminating to understand "image" within the conceptual world of Hellenistic Judaism and be guided by the Platonic idea of the cosmos as the "image" of God. The understanding is that "the natural order properly guides our imagination about God's identity."[31] This throws light on Christ as "firstborn": Jesus is "God's true template."[32] A cue to this comes from the deuterocanonical book Wisdom of Solomon, where, intriguingly, "[Wisdom] is a breath of the power of God, a pure emanation of the glory of the Almighty . . . a reflection of eternal light, a spotless mirror of the working of God, and an image of his goodness" (Wis 7:25–26). It's not difficult to recognize here the lode that the church fathers mined to construct the theology of Jesus as the Wisdom/Logos of God the Father as presented in John's prologue (John 1:1–3)— where Jesus is not simply preexistent, as Wisdom claims to have been, but coeternal with God the Father. Indeed, the apostle Paul formulates the deity of Christ by establishing his lordship.[33] Here, the poem does just that, setting out Jesus as the cosmic Christ with the claim that he is the Lord over all creation.

The second item of conversation between the Wisdom poem and

---

30. Raymond C. Van Leeuwen, "Proverbs," in *New Interpreter's Bible*, vol. 5, ed. Leander E. Keck (Nashville: Abingdon, 1997), 597.

31. Robert W. Wall, *Colossians and Philemon*, IVP New Testament Commentary 10 (Downers Grove, IL: InterVarsity Press, 1993), 66.

32. Wall, *Colossians and Philemon*, 67–68.

33. Wall, *Colossians and Philemon*, 65.

the Christ hymn is the scope of the preeminence of the one celebrated. The Proverbs poem defines the jurisdiction of Wisdom starting from the deepest depths and then soaring up through the layers of the world that is coming into existence: the fathomless bottom of the subterranean ocean; the dark channels of water hissing their way up to burst into springs of fresh water on the land above; the land with its hills and mountains thrusting skyward; and then up, up into the heavens (Prov 8:24–27). Then the poem turns around and swoops down: from the heavens it glides downward through the clouds, the horizon a passing blur, and now we are plunging into the watery deep, till we come smack up against the very foundations of the earth—the pillars of the earth into which are bound the roots of the mountains (Prov 8:27–29). In one uninterrupted arc, the poem encircles the three realms known to man—the heavens where God dwells, the earth where humans reside, and the underworld reserved for afterlife. There is not a nook or cranny in the cosmos that Wisdom does not know of.

In the Christ hymn, Jesus's participation in the making of the cosmos covers two ages. While the first stanza (Col 1:15–17) affirms his role in creation, the second stanza (1:18–20) declares his role in the new order of creation he has just inaugurated. Unlike Wisdom, who can at best claim that she "was there" at the creation of the universe, here Jesus is presented in no uncertain terms of lordship. What is more, he is sovereign over not one but two domains. These are set out in parallel:

> The Son is the image of the invisible God
>> the firstborn over all creation (1:15)
> He is the beginning
>> the firstborn from among the dead (1:18)
> So that in everything he might have supremacy (1:18)

The Greek word *archē* ("beginning") belongs to the word family of "rulers" and similarly, the word rendered "have supremacy" (*prōteuō*) comes from the word family of "first," as in "firstborn" (*prōtotokos*).[34] Thus, the two parallel lines are intermeshed with an impressive lexical

---

34. Wall, 71–72. See Peter T. O'Brien, *Colossians, Philemon*, WBC 44 (Waco, TX: Word, 1982), 44–45.

redundancy pointing to Jesus's firstborn-ness—his exalted rank over two orders of creation: the first creation that the Wisdom poem swooped and soared through, in which humankind was central, and the restored creation inaugurated by his resurrection, in which the church is central.

The boundaries of Jesus's dominion are sketched in an *inclusio* that frames the hymn. What is created "in him" are "things in heaven and on earth" (Col 1:16). What is restored "through him" are "things on earth" and "things in heaven" (v. 20). Within this pair of grand merisms, in the old order are listed "thrones or powers or rulers or authorities" (v. 16). One set of "thrones or powers or rulers or authorities" is for the visible world. A parallel set is for the invisible world, such as the string of authorities mentioned in 2 Enoch 20–22, where in the seventh heaven the angels are installed into ranks.[35] In the environment of this Christ hymn—as in South Asia—the two worlds, visible and invisible are inextricably enmeshed. Meanwhile, in the new order, Christ's dominion is explicitly "the church" (Col 1:18). More implicitly, his control extends over the authority figures mentioned in the old order: "in everything" he has "supremacy" (v. 18). As Andrew Lincoln observes, in the first stanza these thrones and powers, rulers and authorities are benign, but in the second, they are hostile forces, part of the "all things" needing to be reconciled.[36]

A third point of resonance across the intertexts is the work done by the one being celebrated. Wisdom concludes her poem with the claim: "Then [in that remote past], I was *'amon* by [YHWH's] side" (Prov 8:30). Who or what is *'amon*?[37] For most English translations and most scholars, Wisdom is the architect through whom the world comes to be. *'Amon* is rendered "master workman" (ESV, NASB), "master craftsman" (NET, NKJV), or "architect" (NLT, GNT). Wisdom claims her contribution to the work of creation with: "I was the architect at [YHWH's] side." This rendering is buttressed by grammatical considerations,[38] and

---

35. Andrew T. Lincoln, "Colossians," in *New Interpreter's Bible*, vol. 11 (Nashville: Abingdon, 2000), 598.

36. Lincoln, "Colossians," 598.

37. See R. B. Y. Scott, "Wisdom in Creation: The *'Āmôn* of Proverbs viii.30," *VT* 10 (1960): 213–23.

38. See Van Leeuwen, "Proverbs," 94–95. There are two significantly variant readings: (1) Fox renders 'amon as "nursling" or "ward," *Proverbs 1–9*, 286–87; (2) Waltke reads 'amon adverbially as "constantly" or "faithfully," *Proverbs*, 417–20.

further by the Akkadian cousin-word *ummanu* by which a counselor, adviser, or scribe is known—generally someone with "a wide range of wisdom, practical skill, and expertise."[39] This role of Wisdom is also seen in the deuterocanonical book Wisdom of Solomon, in which she is "the fashioner of all things" (Wis 7:22; 8:6) and the one who "was present when you made the world" (Wis 9:9). Is Wisdom an agent in creation? Or is she an enthusiastic spectator? Scholarship remains divided on the answer.[40]

In the Colossians hymn, Christ is the "image" (*eikōn*) of God, but not as a human, who is the "image" (*eikōn*) of God, might be (Gen 1:26–27 LXX).[41] Humankind merely represents God in its care of creation. Wisdom might be either an instrument or an agent in the forming of the universe. Jesus is a whole cosmic leap beyond both humankind and proverbial Wisdom.

As for the first creation, Christ is undisputedly the agent—all things were created "in him" and "through him" (cf. Heb 1:2–3; 1 Cor 8:6). But surprisingly there is more—all creation exists "for him" (Col 1:16). That Christ is the very goal of creation is beyond anything Wisdom can claim for herself. As for the second creation, it is reconciled to God "through him [Jesus]" (Col 1:20). Using formulations familiar to Hellenized Judaism, the hymn uses the head-body idea to conceptualize Jesus's function in the new creation. Zeus was thought to be the head of the cosmos, the body, with his authority governing it. If this metaphor is simply being redirected, then Jesus's rule resounds across the reconciled cosmos.[42] He is Lord over the first order by his preexistence and over the second because of his resurrection.[43] Nothing in either order stands outside his dominion—the phrase "all things" reverberates across the two halves of the hymn,[44] straddling both the former and the latter creations (Col 1:16 [×2], 17 [×2], 20). In sum, both the old and fallen,

---

39. Van Leeuwen, 94.

40. For example, Van Leeuwen, 94–95 for agent ("architect associate of Yahweh"); Waltke, *Proverbs*, 420–22 for spectator.

41. See O'Brien, *Colossians*, 43–44, for Old Testament, Hellenistic, and Wisdom associations with *eikōn*.

42. The alternate view argues for the "body" of Christ to be the church, with Christ as its "head." Lincoln, "Colossians," 598–99; O'Brien, *Colossians*, 48–50.

43. Wall, *Colossians*, 73.

44. Wall, 72.

and the new and restored orders of creation "hold together" in Jesus (Col 1:17; cf. the Logos in Sir 43:26), the center, the one supreme over all.

What is the effect of the conversation between these intertexts (T3)? We understand how each text (T1 and T2) draws its language and imagery from ideas current in its historical-cultural context. While the Christ hymn expresses the scope of Jesus's dominion with its insistent repetition of "all things," the Wisdom poem opens up the camera into panorama mode. Drawing one great circle around the height and depth of the three worlds, the Proverbs poem helps the Common Reader grasp the extent of the reconciliation Jesus makes on the cross. Jesus's work does not simply restore humankind but everything that exists from the heights of the heavens to the depths of the watery deep.

If Wisdom is the instrument, or even agent, of the first creation, Jesus is not simply the agent who brings into being the first creation and then heals sin's rupture of it to inaugurate a second one but is the end goal of both. If Wisdom "is the prior condition for the existence and functioning of all things,"[45] Jesus is the purpose for the existence and functioning of all things. As Ralph Martin puts it, "No Jewish thinker ever rose to these heights in daring to predict that Wisdom was the ultimate goal of all creation."[46] Indeed, at best Wisdom can boast that her "treasures" are intrinsic to Christ (Col 2:3).

In self-evaluation, I submit that my reading of each text has respected the rules of sound exegesis. As for the validity of the pairing of texts, the effect of the intertextual conversation (T3) is the adoration of Jesus. One greater than Wisdom is here! A collateral gain is that the Common Reader, unsettled by Jehovah's Witnesses' errant claims, now has firm biblical-theological grounds for maintaining and defending historic Christian orthodoxy.

Case 3: The Servant of YHWH: Isaiah 42:1-4

For the third case, we construct a Common Reader whose location is more generic than in the previous two studies. This person is fairly familiar with the figure of the servant of the Lord in Isaiah. As for public meaning, they have met the "suffering servant" of Isaiah 53 in

---

45. Van Leeuwen, "Proverbs," 92.
46. Ralph P. Martin, *Colossians and Philemon*, New Century Bible Commentary (Grand Rapids: Eerdmans, 1973), 58.

church services over Passion Week, especially on Good Friday. Though the Common Reader has experienced through their public setting that the servant is a figuration of Christ, they are not too familiar with the Servant Song for this case study, Isaiah 42:1–4. So, in this case, they conduct a preliminary study on the text to see what icon might emerge.

Most scholars agree[47] that in Isaiah 42:1–4 the servant is being installed into high office.[48] The introduction, "Here is my servant . . . ," or literally, "Behold, my servant . . . ," is typical of a coronation scene in which the heir to the throne is being presented to the audience,[49] perhaps the heavenly council. It even sounds like a commissioning, where this is "the public designation of the one chosen by God to perform the task he wishes carried out."[50]

God presents Saul to Samuel with the same introduction: "Behold the man . . ." (1 Sam 9:17 KJV). The Cyrus Cylinder has the high god Marduk calling Cyrus by name and being well pleased by him.[51] Similarly, God declares that this servant is "my chosen one in whom I delight" (Isa 42:1). Why is this servant chosen and not some other? The reason "rests with God alone."[52] God's pleasure in him is reason enough. What is more, God declares to the heavenly court that God will "put [his] Spirit on him, and he will bring justice to the nations" (v. 1). Since kings are commissioned by Spirit endowment and expected to promote justice (cf. 1 Sam 16:13; 2 Sam 8:15; Isa 11:2–4), the Common Reader selects this icon for the Isaianic text: the servant as a royal figure.

Casting about for a New Testament christological text, the Common Reader sees that the Isaianic text is explicitly quoted in Matthew 12:17–21, but the icon of a kingly Jesus appears absent. From the Common

47. Christopher R. Seitz, "The Book of Isaiah 40–66," in *New Interpreter's Bible*, vol. 6, ed. Leander E. Keck (Nashville: Abingdon, 2001), 362.

48. There is long-standing debate on the identity of the Isaianic "servant": is he an individual? If so, could this be the prophet himself, a king such as Cyrus, or a messianic figure? If he represents a group, might this be Israel, or more specifically, the faithful remnant of Israel? Is it several or none of these? Is Jesus the only one who is a perfect fit for Isaiah's servant? The reception-centered intertextual method, as we are using it in this endeavor, does not require a position on this debate, and so the question will not be treated here.

49. Seitz, "Isaiah 40–66," 362; Joseph Blenkinsopp, *Isaiah 40–55: A New Translation with Introduction and Commentary*, AB 19A (New York: Doubleday, 2002), 209.

50. Claus Westermann, *Isaiah 40–66*, trans. David Stalker, OTL (Philadelphia: Westminster John Knox, 1969), 94.

51. Blenkinsopp, *Isaiah 40–55*, 209.

52. Westermann, *Isaiah 40–66*, 94.

Reader's experience, Revelation 19:11–16 more readily portrays Jesus as King. The public meaning of that text is well demonstrated in hymns such as Edward Perronet's "All Hail the Power of Jesus' Name" with its rousing chorus of "Crown him!" (1780; Rev 19:12), and in classics such as Julia Ward Howe's "Battle Hymn of the Republic" (1862):

> Mine eyes have seen the glory of the coming of the Lord:
> He is trampling out the vintage where the grapes of
>   wrath are stored;
> He hath loosed the fateful lightning of His terrible
>   swift sword:
> His truth is marching on. (cf. Rev 19:15)

The Common Reader now studies the presentation of the warrior-king in Revelation 19 (T2) in dialogue with the description of the royal servant in Isaiah 42 (T1).

The divine man of war has "eyes . . . like blazing fire" (Rev 19:12), matching the description of Christ in the book's opening vision (1:14).[53] Further, this warrior-king is "called Faithful and True" (19:11) and bears the name, "the Word of God" (19:13). Scholars regularly cite Wisdom of Solomon as a parallel. This text personifies death as it descended on Egypt the night of the Passover: "While . . . night was in the middle of its own swift course, from heaven, from the royal throne, your own all-powerful word leapt as a stern warrior . . . standing, it filled all things with death, and while it touched heaven, it stood on the earth" (Wis 18:14–16).

A third name is written on the clothes and person of the mounted warrior: the much-sung "King of Kings and Lord of Lords" (Rev 19:16). Significantly, while this is a title the New Testament uses for Jesus (Rev 17:14; cf. 1 Cor 8:6; 1 Tim 6:15), in the Old Testament, this is a title that is applied to YHWH.[54] On his head, this mounted warrior wears "many crowns" or diadems (Rev 19:12). Earlier in the book, seven crowns had rested, one each, on the seven heads of the Dragon (12:3). In ironic con-

---

53. J. Ramsey Michaels, *Revelation*, IVP New Testament Commentary 20 (Downers Grove, IL: InterVarsity Press, 1997), 215.

54. See G. K. Beale, "The Origin of the Title 'King of Kings and Lord of Lords' in Revelation 17.14," *NTS* 31 (1985): 618–20.

trast, many crowns now rest on a single head![55] The warrior is monarch over as many nations as he has crowns on his head.[56]

In addition, there is a fourth name: "a name written on him that no one knows but he himself" (Rev 19:12). This immediately suggests that the rider is either divine (cf. Gen 32:29) or heavenly (Judg 13:17–18). A feature of Greco-Roman mythology is that such beings have, in addition to the name by which humankind knows them, a secret name that only the gods know.[57] This is Jesus, the divine warrior-king who bears four names.

The Common Reader is now confident that Isaiah 42 (T1) and Revelation 19 (T2) are a potential pair of intertexts for a dialogue on the icon: the kingly protagonist. Two topics of conversation arise. First, we ask, What is the task of the protagonist? That is easy to answer from the Servant Song in Isaiah, for the task iterates itself thrice over:

v. 1c: he is to bring forth justice to the nations
v. 3c: he brings forth justice in truth
v. 4b: till he establishes justice in the earth.[58]

Executing justice (*mishpat*) was an expected kingly function in ancient West Asia (Isa 9:7; 11:3–4). The monarch was "particularly commissioned to establish judicial order"[59] over their dominions (Ps 72:1–4; Prov 29:4).[60] Here the servant's jurisdiction stretches extravagantly over the whole earth, even to the utmost islands. What exactly does "justice" mean? It appears to go beyond judicial equity to a society that does not simply serve the rich minority, but in which the common good prevails.[61] The emphasis is on the servant as one who inaugurates a world order, the hallmark of which is justice.

55. Michaels, *Revelation*, 217.

56. David E. Aune, *Revelation 17–22*, WBC 52C (Nashville: Thomas Nelson, 1998), 1054.

57. Homer, *Iliad* 1.403–4. For information on the secret names of divinities in literature of the times, see Aune, *Revelation 17–22*, 1055–56. The Common Reader will be interested that he also cites the fairy tale "Rumpelstiltskin" in this regard.

58. Westermann, *Isaiah 40–66*, 95.

59. John N. Oswalt, *Isaiah 40–66*, NICOT (Grand Rapids: Eerdmans, 1998), 108.

60. James R. Pritchard, *ANET*, 164, 165, 178.

61. Oswalt, *Isaiah 40–66*, 109. See W. A. M. Beuken, "*Mišpāṭ:* The First Servant Song and Its Content," *VT* 22 (1972): 1–30.

Justice also features in Revelation 19. The vision begins like this: "I saw heaven standing open" (v. 11). This typically is the start of a judgment scenario (cf. Isa 64:1–3; 3 Macc 6:18–19).[62] So the 1812 hymn of Reginald Heber "The Son of God Goes Forth to War" is perhaps not quite correct in the second line: "The Son of God goes forth to war / a kingly crown to gain." The warrior-king already has many crowns. But now "with justice [or righteousness] he judges [*en dikaiosynē krinei*] and wages war." The Greek phrase appears in a parallel Isaianic text heavy with messianic freight: "With righteousness he will judge the needy, with justice he will give decisions for the poor of the earth" (Isa 11:4). He goes on to wage war as well, striking the earth and slaying the wicked (v. 4). In the Old Testament, YHWH judging justly had two edges to it: he vindicated the oppressed and punished the oppressor. This is the messianic expectation in Jewish literature of the Second Temple period.[63] Perhaps the task of the warrior-king is drawn from these various traditions. Certainly, by the end of the section, the oppressor—here, the beast and his coalition—is decisively judged through the instrument of war.

Next we ask, How will the protagonist execute his set task of ordering the world through justice? In the ancient world, kings set about establishing justice "through a gleeful use of their power to smash and rebuild."[64] The Isaianic servant stands in astonishing contrast:

> He will not shout or cry out,
>   or raise his voice in the streets.
> A bruised reed he will not break,
>   and a smoldering wick he will not snuff out.
>   (Isa 42:2–3)

The negatives repeated four times emphasize the servant's surprising subversion of the expected. There will be no heralds or street criers to call out his promulgations. He treats the vulnerable with a gentleness that contradicts how the world operated, in which "what is broken and burns

---

62. Aune, *Revelation 17–22*, 1052.
63. See Aune, *Revelation 17–22*, 1053–54.
64. Oswalt, *Isaiah 40–66*, 111.

dimly inevitably perishes."[65] John Oswalt says it well: "God's answer to the oppressors of the world is not more oppression, nor is his answer to arrogance more arrogance."[66] Even the nations appear to respond to the servant "in something of the irenic manner of Isa 2:1–4, where peoples and nations go up to Zion" to receive God's teaching.[67] All this concord notwithstanding, there is an iron fist within the glove expressed in a pair of negatives (42:4) that recall the previous list of negatives (42:2–3). The servant is the opposite of bruised reeds and smoldering wicks. He will not be extinguished (CEB); he will not be broken (CEB) till his commission is fully discharged (42:4).

Revelation's descriptions of the warrior-king's doings invite an R rating for violence: "He treads the winepress of the fury of the wrath of God Almighty" (Rev 19:15; cf. Isa 63:3–6). The words trip over themselves in attempting to express the intensity of God's actions. The winepress is overflowing with red liquid that is not the juice of grapes. "God Almighty" sits well here, for it is the Old Testament equivalent of the "Lord of Hosts," YHWH's military title. No wonder then that the mounted warrior is arrayed "in a robe dipped in blood" (Rev 19:13). While some think the blood is the warrior-Christ's own, shed on the cross, the context of war leans toward reading this as the blood of slaughtered enemies[68]—this warrior is no novice! An Old Testament description of YHWH on the warpath nicely speaks to the description of the warrior of Revelation: "Who is this . . . with his garments stained crimson? . . . Why are your garments red . . . ?" The Lord offers a grisly answer: "I trampled [the nations] in my anger and trod them down in my wrath; their blood spattered my garments, and I stained all my clothing" (Isa 63:1–3). The Heber hymn of my childhood—with "His blood-red banner streams afar"—hasn't paid attention to the text yet again.

The warrior-king's method of adjudicating justice is to strike down the nations with the sword of his mouth[69] (cf. 2 Thess 2:8; Rev 2:12, 16; Wis 18:16) and rule them with an iron scepter (cf. Ps 2:9; Isa 11:4).

65. Westermann, *Isaiah 40–66*, 96.
66. Oswalt, *Isaiah 40–66*, 111.
67. Seitz, "Isaiah 40–66," 363.
68. Images of YHWH as Divine Warrior abound in the OT: Exodus 15; Deuteronomy 33; Habakkuk 3; Isaiah 26:20–27:1; 59:15–19; Zechariah 14:1–21.
69. See Aune, *Revelation 17–22*, 1060–61, for messianic traditions on this.

Indeed, the vision ends with the complete rout of the coalition of the beast (Rev 19:19–21).

Looking for Jesus in the Old Testament, here is the effect (T3) we gather from the conversation between the servant of Isaiah 42 (T1) and the warrior-king of Revelation 19 (T2). God presents his servant to his heavenly council as one who will have jurisdiction over the "nations," right up to the far-flung islands, covering the "earth." The warrior-king's multiple diadems are a demonstration of exactly such jurisdiction. Taken together, we have a picture of the universal scope of the authority of the one sent forth.

We know the warrior-king is backed by God because it is from an open heaven that he descends on his battle steed. The servant is more explicitly commissioned: he is emphatically "my servant, whom I uphold," he is God's chosen, he is God's pleasure, and is Spirit-endowed. The warrior-king more than executes the wrath of the Lord of Hosts—in complete identification with God, he is called by the title that only God can hold: "King of kings and Lord of lords." While the nations anticipate the servant's teaching (*torah*), the warrior-king is himself that teaching—he is the Word of God. The servant and the warrior-king together complete the picture of Jesus as God's ultimate agent—Jesus as no other than God.

What the Common Reader will find ironic is that the Old Testament's servant is tenderly irenic while the New Testament's warrior-king enacts divine ire. The servant's hands pass gently over the damaged reed and the smoldering wick. The warrior-king's feet pump brutally, "trampling out the vintage where the grapes of wrath are stored." While the warrior-king brings terror, the servant brings hope. However, each depiction echoes the other. In the Hellenized world of Revelation, the motif of the celestial rider was regularly associated with deliverance for the oppressed.[70] Meanwhile, the servant is unfaltering, as unstoppable as a juggernaut[71] in the execution of his commission. Taken together, the servant and the warrior-king complete the depiction of the dual work of

---

70. S. I. Johnston, "Riders in the Sky: Cavalier Gods and Theurgic Salvation in the Second Century A.D.," *CP* 87 (1992): 307–16.

71. This English word comes from the Hindu deity Jagannath of the temple town of Puri in Orissa, India. Every year, the deity is taken out in a procession, seated in a mammoth chariot. Once set in motion, the sixteen-wheeled chariot of Jagannath is not easily stopped.

Jesus: the deliverance of the oppressed, and the judgment of the oppressor. Thereby a justly ordered world is established—one that knows not just the word of God, the *torah*, but the Word of God, Jesus Christ.

In assessing the validity of the intertextual method in this case study, I submit that I have paid attention to the hermeneutical rules governing sound exegesis and arrived at an effect (T3) that affirms the grand hope articulated in the Nicene Creed: Jesus Christ will come again to judge the living and the dead!

Conclusion

I wrote this essay over Lent, with a deadline that ran into Passion Week. Reading Jesus across pairs of intertexts deepened my Lenten devotions in a way that reading just the New Testament text might not have done. The Akedah narrative read with Philippians 2 moved me to tears at the Son's willingness to die. The Wisdom poem read alongside the Colossians hymn prompted adoration. The Servant Song read in tandem with the warrior vision rekindled the hope that this sad mess of a world can look forward to a day when all wrongs will be set right. And, more than all these, the intertextual reading urged me toward becoming more like Jesus—to imitate his humility; to trust in his control over all things just as he trusted his Father's will; and to stand up and speak up, as possible, against injustice. When all is said and done, the imitation of Christ should be—at the very least—one outcome of finding Jesus in the Old Testament, shouldn't it?

JOHN GOLDINGAY

A first aspect of Dr. Dharamraj's paper that struck me and intrigued me was that she brings the distinctively postmodern approach to our question—whereas one could roughly say that Dr. Carter and Dr. DeRouchie are premodern, while Dr. Longman and I are modern (I don't use these adjectives with either pejorative or affirmative implications, just descriptively). It means that her approach raised a wide-ranging set of fresh and interesting questions, and in the main part of my response, I seek to articulate some of them.

Reflections on the Reception-Centered, Intertextual Approach

First, some questions about intertextuality. I like the idea that a "reception-centered intertextuality begins with the presupposition that the sixty-six books of the Protestant canon are in conversation with each other" (130). But what difference does it make to relate intertextuality to the canon, as opposed to setting Genesis 22 or Isaiah 42 alongside Jewish texts that interpret these passages? Does setting the passage in conversation with canonical texts give the results extra authority? Does it imply extra expectations, since both passages are canonical? Conversely, what does the intertextuality framework add to an intra-canonical interpretation of passages that does not assume this framework?

Within the canon, "intertexts abound, both within each Testament and across the Testaments. Our endeavor is to identify them and get them talking to each other" (130). This makes it sound as if there is a finite number of intertextual connections to be identified. Is that what the statement implies? What would be the reason for making this assumption? Or does it just mean that we are involved in identifying the connections that are significant for us in our context? This question relates to the comment that "the openness of reception-centered intertextuality may appear to encourage the Common Reader down the slippery slope of associating a given text with just about any other text" (131). Why is it a problem to associate any text with any other text within the context of the canon?

Second, some further questions about the Common Reader. "The critic reads to evaluate, the scholar reads for knowledge, and the Common Reader reads for pleasure" (128). Surely our Common Reader isn't reading merely for any of those reasons. What difference might that make? Is the Common Reader important for a theological reason, that the Common Reader's importance links with the presence of the Holy Spirit in the church? And is the Common Reader really uninterested in the text's authorial intention? In the United Kingdom and the United States, the common Christian reader is often instinctively interested in authorial intention and is often troubled by New Testament references to the First Testament that ignore what the author would have meant. Is it different in India? Does this reflect ways in which Common Readers in the West have been shaped by pastors, and pastors by professors?! That suggests another question about the Common Reader. The Common Reader isn't going to think of Isaiah 53 and the crucifixion story as simply texts paired by a common theme—and rightly so. Doesn't one need to allow for the Common Reader's perspective here?

Third, I'm surprised at the comment that "production-centered" intertextual study is more traditional than "reception-centered" study. Indeed, the word "traditionally" applied to intertextuality is striking, given that the approach was articulated only in the 1960s, but perhaps Dr. Dharamraj has in mind that it had long been practiced in biblical study without being given that name. I think it's probably correct that a production-centered approach is more common in the world of biblical scholarship than in other contexts where the Scriptures are studied. One reason will be that it commonly involves juxtaposing texts from the First Testament and texts from the New Testament, and there is no dispute over whether First Testament texts are older than New Testament ones. So no chronological hazards attach to a production-centered approach. Within the First Testament, reception-centered approaches are safer because we don't know much about the relative or absolute dating of many First Testament texts. The examples from Genesis and Judges illustrate the point, and Ellen van Wolde in her study[1] wisely sidesteps the question of any direction of allusion in order to see what happens when one simply juxtaposes the stories. Now, one could have studied all of our three texts with a production-centered approach. So my question is, does Dr. Dharamraj think that theologically (or for other reasons) the reception-centered approach is preferable?

Fourth, some questions about public meaning. "As a literary work 'moves through time and space it accrues meaning, sheds meaning, provokes meaning.' It 'creates *public meaning.*'"[2] Put like this, does such a statement not give too much away, as if the literary work itself did not have its own inherent meaning? When Shakespeare wrote *Macbeth*, it meant something as an expression by the dramatist and an act of communication between dramatist and audience. Possibly there were aspects of its meaning that he himself didn't get, so that one could have said to him, "What you wrote here implies x, doesn't it?" and he could have replied, "Yes, I didn't see that, but I do now." Or he could have said, "No, I don't see that as implicit in what I wrote." And subsequently the work does not shed meaning, though aspects of its meaning may be forgotten. Nor does it accrue meaning, though its meaning might become clearer. I would rather say it accrues new significance in new contexts. And it does provoke meaning in the sense that it generates a new "text." Does Dr. Dharamraj think that it is actually possible or meaningful to think in terms of a work having its own meaning in its context as an exercise in expression and communication by someone? Doesn't some theological and ethical significance attach to the idea that the text had meaning as a communication between a human and a divine author on one hand and an audience on the other? Further, the "public meaning" of the Scriptures has often been the embodiment of a false apprehension of the Scriptures. How do we take that into account? Dr. Dharamraj's fifth interpretive step does link with this question in

---

1. Ellen van Wolde, "Texts in Dialogue with Texts: Intertextuality in the Ruth and Tamar Narratives," *BibInt* 5 (1997): 1–28.

2. Michael Lucey, "A Literary Object's Contextual Life," in *A Companion to Comparative Literature*, ed. Ali Behdad and Dominic Thomas (Chichester: Wiley-Blackwell, 2011), 121, 128.

referring to Christian faith and practice, though I'm not sure it means that one escapes from too confined a hermeneutical circle—a circle that has no way of breaking out from the assumptions and understandings from which the Common Reader starts.

Reflections on the Three Case Studies

Genesis 22:1–19. The result of the study is to agree with Jewish interpreters that the story is really about Isaac. Isaac is the protagonist. In this connection, isn't the Jewish tradition of interpretation more important than the Common Reader to Dr. Dharamraj's interpretation of the passage? Does she really take the Common Reader into account? In itself, the story is surely about God and Abraham. It's about how "God tested Abraham" (Gen 22:1). Dr. Dharamraj includes the quotation "You have done this and have not withheld your son, your only son" (Gen 22:16) and adds, "implicitly nested into this affirmation is Isaac's willing cooperation with Abraham's act" (137). What is the basis for saying that this is implicitly nested? To go in a different direction, taking Isaac as the protagonist in the story follows from the choice of intertext, and one might then note that intertextual study can usefully draw attention to differences between texts as well as to similarities. In this case, it might enable one to reflect on the similarity and difference between the Father's self-sacrifice and the Son's self-sacrifice.

Proverbs 8:22–31. Using intertextuality to reflect on similarity and difference does prove illuminating in connection with Proverbs 8, as it brings out the difference where Jesus is "Lord." I appreciated the point about Wisdom not being coeternal and thus about Colossians not implying that Jesus was coeternal, which I confess I had never thought about because I have focused more on the meaning of *qanah*. But the problem is that seeing how these texts justify the conviction that Jesus is preexistent but not coeternal subverts the conclusion that "the Common Reader unsettled by Jehovah's Witnesses' errant claims now has firm biblical-theological grounds for maintaining and defending historic Christian orthodoxy" (144). I also had forgotten that Athanasius relates Proverbs 8 to the human nature of Jesus, and if Proverbs 8 doesn't imply coeternity, Athanasius's interpretation is a useful argument to have for the Jehovah's Witnesses. John 1 comes closer than Colossians to undergirding orthodoxy in declaring that Jesus/Wisdom/the Word/the message goes back to the very beginning, and John 1 directly takes up Proverbs's language. Here a production-centered approach would have been possible and would have advantages for Dr. Dharamraj's Common Reader in connection with the Jehovah's Witnesses issue.

Isaiah 42:1–4. The link with Revelation 19 is creative. There is a problem with Dr. Dharamraj's understanding of not shouting or crying out, because "cry out" (*tsaʿaq*) denotes a cry of pain or protest (the other Isaiah occurrences are 19:20; 33:7; 46:7; 65:14; the noun *tseʿaqah* in 5:7 is also significant in this context). It links with the point about not being broken or extinguished. Actually, there's nothing gentle or tenderly ironic about this servant. So Isaiah and Revelation are alike here.

Some Concluding Comments or Questions

I have one or two concluding reflections arising from Dr. Dharamraj's study of the passages. One is that the collocations of the passages generate a new text and thus a new meaning. And it may also clarify the meaning of the existent texts, though it may also obscure them. Yes, Christ is in Philippians 2, Colossians 1, and Revelation 19. But it doesn't mean that he is in Genesis 22, Proverbs 8, or Isaiah 42. I have suggested that the intertextual approach obscures the meaning of Genesis 22, and it doesn't clarify Proverbs 8. It does have more potential to clarify the meaning of Isaiah 42.

The other is that Dr. Dharamraj doesn't take any account of the passages' context in the works they come from, in Genesis, Proverbs, or Isaiah. With Genesis 22, the context reinforces the impression I get from the chapter itself that the story concerns God and Abraham, as the Common Reader might know from the New Testament. With Proverbs 8, the context indicates that the concern in Proverbs is with people taking wisdom seriously, which doesn't imperil her interpretation of the passage but could point a reader in a different direction—for instance, to Jesus in the Gospels talking about wisdom and his being an embodiment of wisdom, which again the Common Reader might know about. With Isaiah 42, the context sets the description of the servant against the background of the identification of the servant in Isaiah 41, which has illuminating implications for the meaning of Isaiah 42, though Dr. Dharamraj's Common Reader probably wouldn't know about that. In this example, the context is the so-called Servant Songs, which is a scholarly construct rather than something in the text. Maybe my question is, does she think that reading passages in their context in their own books fades into insignificance compared with reading them in the context of the Common Reader's knowledge and of the intertext she identifies? Is that part of the shedding of meaning?

A related comment: Is Dr. Dharamraj sure she wants to appeal to the consideration "most scholars agree"? To start with, anything that most scholars agree about now they will not agree about in a couple of decades. And replacing the pope with scholars as an interpretive authority isn't much of an improvement, is it? What one surely needs is not appeals to authority but arguments, which she does go on to provide!

TREMPER LONGMAN III

I would like to thank Dr. Dharamraj for her thoughtful, clear, and spiritually inspiring essay. As my following comments indicate, I do have some questions and reservations about her approach (that's why they call it five views—we have our differences), but I want to begin with a note of appreciation. I learned much from her essay. I will return to specific points of appreciation, but I will begin with some questions and hesitations about her approach to seeing Christ in the Old Testament.

The first area around which I want to raise questions concerns her use of "the Common Reader" as well as her understanding of "public meaning." As Dharamraj points out, the concept of the Common Reader comes from Virginia Woolf's book by that title. Common Readers are those who read for enjoyment rather than analysis or criticism. Common Readers, according to Woolf, do not have any "literary prejudice," which I understand to mean a disciplined interpretive method (Dharamraj's examples bear this out), but rather they make associations between texts that come to them intuitively. On one level, the Common Reader is a naive reader. That is not to say the Common Reader is unintelligent, but it does mean the Common Reader is undisciplined and apparently free to make any connections that come to mind. Now it is true that Dharamraj wants to put guardrails on the Common Reader by saying that the Common Reader's conclusions must come to an understanding of the two texts that "offer a reading of Jesus that honors both the texts and the reception of these texts across the centuries within the communities of faith that have been shaped by them" (132).[1]

At this point, though, Dharamraj's Common Reader becomes a kind of Ideal Reader, at least ideal to her conception of how people should think about these texts. Interestingly, she begins her discussion of the Common Reader by saying, "This could be you" (127). In response, I would say this is doubtful because most of the people reading this book will already be formed by some kind of "literary prejudice." But when we later hear Dharamraj's examples of Common Readers interacting with biblical texts, I am tempted to say "the Common Reader" is Dharamraj herself. And of course, in a very real sense, this is true, since the fictional Common Readers are created by Dharamraj and think like her. By the way, I believe that is a good thing, since Dharamraj is a very insightful reader, bringing together texts in fruitful ways. More about that later.

Still, the danger of using the literary conceit of the Common Reader that may actually be Dharamraj herself is that it gives the impression that if everyone would just lean into reading for pleasure and without method, they would make the same interpretive moves that her Common Reader makes. However, I seriously doubt the Common Reader understood as the naive reader would, for example, naturally connect Genesis 22 with Philippians 2. That is not to say it is a bad textual relationship on which to reflect. In fact, it is a rather sophisticated and unexpected connection that the interpreter without "literary prejudice" is unlikely to stumble upon. I guess my point is that by creating the Common Reader, Dharamraj gives the impression that if we would just let people read for enjoyment, they would make all these rich interpretive moves. I think it would be more transparent for Dharamraj to say that these are her readings, not some third party, and we can learn from her and occasionally question her.

I also have questions about Dharamraj's use of the concept of "public meaning," defined as "the corpus of meaning(s) of the text generated by a collective or a community" (129). In the first place, even within a community or collective, interpretations are almost always contested.

---

1. But as I will point out below, readers must approach the text in a way that shows awareness of their original setting and thus requires a disciplined reading in order to truly honor the text.

At least that has been my experience of, say, church Bible studies where Common Readers (in the sense of naive readers) feel comfortable sharing their views and politely disagreeing with one another.

And then there is the question of different collectives and communities. What do we do when different communities through time or different theological traditions or different groups defined by ethnicity, gender, or socioeconomics have different "public meanings" (and they often do). As I will explain later, this is why I think we need to develop "literary prejudices." In other words, we need to be self-conscious and intentional in our interpretive approach.

While talking about communities of "public meaning," let me applaud Dr. Dharamraj's sensitivity to how we read through lenses shaped by who we are and where we are. Readers absolutely bring "to the reading inputs from a variety of locations—socioeconomic, cultural, political, religious, and denominational" (131). Dharamraj seems to leave it there. But if we stay there, we all stay siloed in our different interpretive communities. That is why I have long advocated "reading in community," meaning a community of diverse voices, so we can learn and be challenged in our own readings by people who come from different locations. That was the case for me as I read Dharamraj's helpful reflections on Genesis 22 and Philippians 2, Proverbs 8 and Colossians 1 (though that one was not entirely new to me), and Isaiah 42 and Revelation 19.

Thus, I am suggesting that the Common Reader (in the sense of the naive reader) needs a lesson in hermeneutics. What I find missing in Dharamraj's examples, as well as her interpretive steps for readers, is any regard for the original meaning of the text or what in my article I call the discrete meaning of the Old Testament text. There is a slight gesture toward the original meaning of the Old Testament text in her fourth step, where she says that the Common Reader needs to have "sufficient background information, whether ancient West Asian or Greco-Roman" (132). If this includes considerations like genre, narrative and poetic style, historically contextual understanding of metaphors, and so on, then I wish she had spelled it out and made it step one. But if this is the right understanding of her gesture, then the Common Reader has developed a form of "literary prejudice" and is no longer the naive reader. In this way, the Common Reader is no longer engaged in interpretation that is based solely on their own readerly intuitions but must "honor" the text by being responsible to listen for the author's intended meaning.[2]

Let me create a Common Reader to illustrate what I believe is a problem with ignoring the original meaning of an Old Testament text. My Common Reader is an American evangelical and a regular church-goer, but his pastor does not preach from the Old Testament much (an altogether too common trend these days). He has never read the Song of Songs before or at least he hasn't in a long time. Now, my guess is that this Common Reader, never having encountered the Song before, would first react by saying, "What in the world is this doing in the Bible?" But if told to think of passages in the New Testament that relate to Christ and resonate with the Song, he might, and I emphasize *might* (though now the Common Reader might segue from the naive reader to Longman's Ideal Reader), think of Ephesians 5, where the relationship between Jesus and the church is likened to a marriage.

This textual connection is a good one, a nice Christotelic move. But what has the Common Reader missed by not attending seriously to the Song of Songs's discrete message as love poetry, in which an unnamed woman and an unnamed man express their desires for physical intimacy with each other? Well, he's missed much, but here I will only name that God delights in human sexuality, a gift he gave them at creation, a gift marred by human sin but redeemed in an already-not yet sense.

But let me end by again thanking Dr. Dharamraj for her insight-ful Christotelic readings of our three test case passages. I thought it was particularly interesting how she used Isaac's role in the passage in relationship to Philippians 2. Now, the first reading (see my chapter) would want to say that a careful reading of the Genesis passage shows that the focus of the text itself is not on Isaac, and to honor the text we should acknowledge that. There is no emphasis on Isaac's obedience in Genesis 22, but there is a laser-sharp focus on Abraham's. After God stayed Abraham's hand, the angel said, "Because you have done

---

2. As I will explain in a forthcoming book on literary theory and the Old Testament, this statement does not imply we can get into the mind of the author, but rather we look at the text itself (what the author produced) and through historical-grammatical exegesis (genre analysis, etc.) create hypotheses of varying probability (some quite high and some low) as to what message the author intended to communicate to his audience; see Kevin J. Vanhoozer, *Is There a Meaning in This Text? The Bible, the Reader, and the Morality of Literary Knowledge* (Grand Rapids: Zondervan, 1998).

this . . . ," the "you" being Abraham, not Isaac. In other words, Hebrew narrative does create gaps but (in my opinion) also puts the focus where the author wants the reader to focus, and that is on Abraham; nevertheless, a little speculative reading still produces some interesting connections. That does not invalidate the connection between these two texts (indeed, I wish I had been introduced to it before I wrote my Genesis commentary!), but in my opinion it is not the most natural or obvious connection. I would argue that the more obvious Christotelic connections surround Abraham, and apparently the New Testament authors thought so as well (e.g., Gal 3:15–29).

So, yes, I have my questions and hesitations about Dharamraj's approach, the most serious of which is what appears to be ignoring the original meaning or failing to encourage what I call a first reading of an Old Testament text. But I want to end by once again thanking her for her provocative and largely persuasive Christotelic interpretation. Thanks for inventing such insightful Common Readers.

RESPONSE TO HAVILAH DHARAMRAJ
(THE REDEMPTIVE-HISTORICAL, CHRISTOCENTRIC APPROACH)

JASON S. DEROUCHIE

I commend much in Dr. Dharamraj's exegesis and intertextual appraisals, for her case studies exemplify that she observes carefully, understands rightly, and evaluates fairly much of what is in the compared texts. This is so because Dharamraj typically affirms that the Common Reader should maintain the normal author-centered "hermeneutical rules governing sound exegesis" (151) when assessing passages independently of one another. She also celebrates interpretations that are not "theologically problematic" (138) and that align with "historic Christian orthodoxy" (144).

Nevertheless, when attempting to "correlate [the OT] with Jesus" by placing "Old and New Testament texts in conversation with each other," Dharamraj thinks that the Common Reader must follow a "Reception-Centered, Intertextual Approach" that seeks to discover the interrelationship's "effect" and "christological resonance" (131). This "largely reader-centered, literary" approach "resists speculating about how one text is dependent on another" (128–29); instead, the Common Reader draws on their intuition and the "public meaning" from their "particular social universe" to "create for himself, out of whatever odds and ends he can come by, some kind of whole" (128).[1]

I agree that readers play fundamental roles in biblical interpretation, and that the social contexts from which we arise (e.g., "socioeconomic, cultural, political, religious, and denominational" [131]) influence the

---

1. Here Dharamraj cites Virginia Woolf, *The Common Reader* (New York: Harcourt, 1953), 2–3.

perspectives we bring to the Bible. Such preunderstandings are not bad in themselves; indeed, recognizing our presuppositions allows us to evaluate them in the light of Scripture and increasingly conform them to it. The challenge comes when we allow our presuppositions to become prejudices that produce meaning, and this results in the reader of Scripture assuming a higher authority than the divine author himself.[2] Dharamraj's approach to intertextual interpretation fails at just this point.

Evaluating Dharamraj's Presuppositions

To begin, I will evaluate Dharamraj's four presuppositions. First, she states that, as a "canon," the sixty-six books of the Old and New Testaments are "in conversation with each other" (130), and it is this conversation that allows one to relate "icons" (i.e., dominant themes) and identify christological Old Testament texts. I would go further and note that biblical texts can be mutually interpreting because God ultimately authored the Bible and inspired the Scriptures by his Spirit, guiding the prophets' interpretations (2 Pet 1:20–21; cf. Luke 24:27; 1 Cor 2:13) as they "searched and inquired carefully" (1 Pet 1:10 ESV) into previous Scripture and God's new revelations. Moreover, biblical texts often include "essential interpretive links" with previous texts— truths from other Scriptures that the author expects the reader to import into the present text in order to fully grasp his meaning.[3] Such an example is found in the third case study with the use of Isaiah 42:1–3 in Matthew 12:18–21. In such instances, the interpreter must perform inner-canonical exegesis to rightly understand the later passage, yet Dharamraj's model has no room for this approach (see below). Finally, the concept of canon as *rule* (i.e., *God's* authoritative word) requires that an "author-centered" approach govern all biblical interpretation, including wrestling with inner-biblical relationships, and Dharamraj's intertextual interpretive strategy misses this fact.

Second, a "corpus of meaning(s) of the text generated by a collective

---

2. I draw the distinction between "presuppositions" and "prejudices" from Grant R. Osborne, *The Hermeneutical Spiral: A Comprehensive Introduction to Biblical Interpretation* (Downers Grove, IL: InterVarsity Press, 1991), 412–13.

3. For this concept, see Christopher A. Beetham, *Echoes of Scripture in the Letter of Paul to the Colossians*, BibInt 96 (Leiden: Brill, 2008), 30–31.

or a community" influences every Common Reader and guides them as they look for "icons" (i.e., dominant themes) in a text. I concur that everyone brings to the task of biblical interpretation a web of interconnected beliefs about what is true. Yet the Bible itself needs to confirm or correct these views, and this necessitates that the interpreter allow questions of "causality and purpose" and authorial intent to guide which texts they place in conversation and how they assess their collective meaning. Through their own predictions, exegesis, and redemptive-historical themes, the biblical authors themselves must direct and arbitrate the meaning we see in intertextual relationships. How would the Jews in Berea have "examined the Scriptures . . . to see if what Paul said was true" (Acts 17:11) if they could not consider questions of intent, cause, and purpose when comparing the Old Testament text with Paul's words?

Third, Dharamraj believes that authorial intent does not significantly influence Common Readers when they build textual connections. I question this perspective, for even the Common Reader reflects on authorial intent when relating a textbook's various claims, when reading a friend's account of a conversation, or when receiving parental instruction through a sibling. This type of *personal* communication shapes Scripture, and it demands a production / author-centered approach to interpretation. Yet even if most Common Readers give little thought to an author's intent, the interpreter's role at any level is not to be a Common Reader but an Ideal Reader.[4] The Ideal Reader is one who actively seeks to become the author's implied reader—one who aligns with the author's expectations of being a disciple of Christ who approaches Scripture as authoritative and seeks to align with its teachings.[5] The goal as a reader should never be the lowest common denominator among many. Rather, the biblical interpreter must move "beyond the elementary teachings about Christ" and be "taken forward to maturity" (Heb 6:1) by training

4. I thank my doctoral fellow Brian Verrett for reminding me of the following resource. For more on "Identifying and Becoming the Ideal Reader of the Biblical Canon," see Ched Spellman, *Toward a Canon-Conscious Reading of the Bible: Exploring the History and Hermeneutics of the Canon*, New Testament Monographs 34 (Sheffield: Sheffield Phoenix, 2014), 184–215. Cf. Ched Spellman, "The Scribe Who Has Become a Disciple: Identifying and Becoming the Ideal Reader of the Biblical Canon," *Them* 41 (2016): 37–51.

5. Cf. Markus Bockmuehl, *Seeing the Word: Refocusing New Testament Study*, STI (Grand Rapids: Baker Academic, 2006), 69–72, 92; Spellman, *Toward a Canon-Conscious Reading of the Bible*, 197–215.

oneself "to distinguish good from evil" as defined by God (Heb 5:14; cf. 2 Tim 2:7, 15).

Fourth, "certainty that one text has influenced the composition of another is not always easy to nail down" (131). In response, epistemological humility accompanies our biblical interpretation not when we replace our pursuit of biblical truth with our own created meaning but when we seek to justify our claims to the Bible's meaning by the biblical text itself. Recognizably, "[Paul's] letters contain some things that are hard to understand," but it is such letters that "ignorant and unstable people distort, as they do the other Scriptures, to their own destruction" (2 Pet 3:16). Anytime we allow our own presuppositions to prejudice our biblical study, we put ourselves and those following us in grave danger. A complete approach to *exegesis* ("to bring out") and *theology* ("study of God") requires that we maintain an author-centered approach at all times, including when we assess intertextual relationships. Meaning is fixed by the biblical author(s), and our goal should be to rightly grasp not only what the Bible says but why it says it that way (including why biblical authors use other Scriptures).

Evaluating Dharamraj's Interpretive Steps and Case Studies

Because different Common Readers will pair up different texts and identify different icons, Dharamraj identifies "a measure of subjectivity" in every reader-response method (130). She claims to curb this arbitrariness with "inbuilt hermeneutical checks and balances," including these (131):

1. Probing "sufficient background information" enough to properly understand the proposed icon (i.e., dominant theme).
2. Considering "whether the icon being pursued is a significant one in both the texts" (T1 and T2).
3. Evaluating "whether the intertextual conversation (T3) emerging out of the study appears forced or flows naturally."
4. Assessing whether T3 actually deepens "the reading of each text (T1 and T2) toward orthodox Christian faith and practice." This is done by assessing T3, the transcript of the intertextual dialogue.

While Dharamraj's approach allows a given text's meaning to measure the significance of a proposed icon, it appears that intuition, public meaning, and orthodoxy supply the only measures for evaluating "whether the textual conversation (T3) . . . appears forced or flows naturally" (132). This strategy allows one to stay within the bounds of Christian orthodoxy, but it neither allows one to justify claims from Scripture nor guards one from embracing right doctrine from the wrong texts.

In Dharamraj's comparison of Genesis 22:1–19 and Philippians 2:6–11, she chooses the icon of "the willing son" (134). At no point does she wrestle with whether the narrator intended such a focus in Genesis 22:1–19; nor does she consider it significant that Paul never tags Christ the divine "Son" within Philippians. Many of her comparisons between the two texts were both valid and insightful, but I believe this is because Genesis 22:1–19 itself points ahead to Christ, both typologically and directly. Moses's conscious foresight justifies a potential theological link, even conceptually, between Genesis and Philippians, yet Dharamraj never attempts to establish such an intentional connection.

In the second case study, Dharamraj considers "the relationship between God and the one celebrated" in Proverbs 8:22–31 and Colossians 1:15–20 (138). In alignment with her method, she never considers whether Paul intentionally shaped Colossians to reflect Proverbs' wisdom tradition. In contrast to the first case study, Dharamraj identifies greater dissonance between how Proverbs portrays Wisdom and how Paul depicts Jesus. While I appreciate that "the effect of the intertextual conversation (T3) is the adoration of Jesus" (144), she unjustifiably pits Christ against Wisdom. Paul uses language that intentionally invites the reader to think of Christ as the Wisdom of Proverbs 3, 8, and 30 (cf. 1 Cor 1:24, 27, 30). When read within its close context, Proverbs teaches that Wisdom is both the preexistent Son and coeternal with God (8:22; 30:3–4), that Wisdom was God's appointed representative by whom he originally created the world (3:19–20; 8:23), and that Wisdom's joy was one of the great ends for which God made all things (8:30–31). These align with Paul's portrait of Christ in Colossians 1:15–20. Jesus did not say, "Something greater than Wisdom is here," but "Something greater than Solomon is here" (Matt 12:42; Luke 11:31). Thus, he was not contrasting himself with Wisdom but was identifying himself as both the embodiment and resulting source of all Wisdom.

The last case study clearly identifies the inherent problem with Dharamraj's reader-response approach to intertextuality. When faced with the opportunity to compare Isaiah 42:1–4 with Matthew 12:17–21, which cites it and relates it to Christ, she dismisses the possibility because "a kingly Jesus appears absent" (146). Instead, she parallels the Isaiah text with Revelation 19:11–16—a connection that is not bad and in fact opens the door for helpful insights. Nevertheless, such a move does differentiate the Common Reader from the Ideal Reader, for the latter would allow God's intentionally and clearly designated inner-biblical correspondences to initially guide all theological wrestling.

Specifically, the Ideal Reader would recognize that the kingly servant in Isaiah 42 is meek (v. 2), cares for the broken (v. 3), opens blind eyes (v. 7), and frees the captives (v. 7), and this is the very point in Matthew's identifying Jesus with this servant. Indeed, Matthew frames his whole narrative by highlighting the royal identity of Jesus (1:1; 2:2; 28:18), alludes to Isaiah 42:1 earlier at Jesus's baptism (3:16–17), and synthesizes Jesus's primary message as "proclaiming the gospel of the kingdom" (4:23). Furthermore, Matthew's citation of Isaiah 42 is preceded by the declaration that he is "Lord of the Sabbath" (12:8) and followed by the fact that his Spirit-empowered exorcisms identify that "the kingdom of God has come upon you" (12:28). To say that Jesus's healing ministry does not fulfill the portrait of the royal figure in Isaiah 42 fails to read the close context of both Isaiah and Matthew. It does not matter whether the Common Reader associates the royal servant of Isaiah with the portrait of Jesus in the Gospel. What matters is that Matthew did just this, and the evangelist's purpose aligns with God's purpose.

Lastly, following the rules of traditional exegesis would require that one seek to identify Yahweh's servant in Isaiah 42:1–4. If Isaiah's servant is not Jesus, how does the Common Reader know that their growing view and appreciation of Jesus in these two texts is indeed biblically grounded? Once again, Dharamraj's reception-centered approach to intertextuality locates authority in the reader rather than in God as Scripture's author.

Conclusion

Dharamraj's essay leaves many questions regarding Christ in the Old Testament. She identifies Isaiah's servant as "a figuration of Christ" (145), which appears to mean a pointer to but not identical with him in some way. Old Testament texts are only "potentially christological," yet one identifies "christological resonance" both through personal study and through the text's "public meaning . . . as they have experienced it" (132). Dharamraj is not clear as to whether the Old Testament even includes direct messianic predictions, let alone whether there are God-intended christological types. If one can meet Jesus only by comparing Old Testament and New Testament texts, what did Jesus mean when he claimed, "These are the very Scriptures that testify about me" (John 5:39)? And if Old Testament texts are only christological because of their (subjective) intertextual relationship with New Testament text, then it necessarily follows that none of the Old Testament authors intended to write about Jesus. Yet if this is so, how can Dharamraj justifiably speak of encountering Jesus in these texts?

Resisting questions of dependence, causality, purpose, and intention when assessing inter-biblical relationships fails to treat the scriptural canon as rule, wherein it gets to make its own claims regarding textual correspondences and an author's meaning and intent. In my view, when "the corpus of meaning(s) of the text generated by a collective or a community" becomes the a priori framework for our understanding the meaning of textual correspondences within the biblical text even before we start reading Scripture, we have undermined the Bible's authority with our own, placing ourselves over the text rather than as servants of it.

CRAIG A. CARTER

Central to Dr. Dharamraj's chapter is a distinction between two types of intertextual approaches to reading Scripture. What she terms a "production-centered intertextual approach" is a reading technique that is almost as old as the biblical tradition itself, the act of reading texts side by side to allow them to shed light on one another. As her example of Judges 19:22–26 and Genesis 19:4–8 demonstrates, biblical writers often intended their texts to be read alongside earlier biblical texts. Interest in such parallel texts has persisted throughout the history of biblical interpretation because, as she notes, one text often is thought to have influenced the other. This is one of the most important ways of reading Scripture, and it is central to biblical theology. The focus in this chapter, however, is not on this approach, but rather on a "Reception-Centered, Intertextual Approach," which is not about how one text influences another but how today's readers see connections between different texts. It is not a matter of looking for how the Scriptures hang together as a unity, but more a matter of imaginatively utilizing texts to spark thoughts about other texts. The Reception-Centered, Intertextual Approach is a postmodern (or I would say "late modern") one that may seem similar to the production-centered approach but is quite different. While the latter is compatible with a premodern approach to interpretation, the former is not.

In the postmodern context, the Reception-Centered, Intertextual Approach is to be distinguished both from a production-centered intertextual approach, as defined in this chapter, and from a related but different endeavor known as the history of reception studies. The history of how the text has been interpreted in various contexts, including liturgical, ethical, and literary contexts, as well as scholarly commentaries and theological systems, is a viable intellectual enterprise in and of itself. But it is not what Dharamraj is doing in this chapter. What she is doing is describing a method of reading any reader can employ, whether in private devotions, sermon preparation, or scholarly exegesis. While this method is very old in some ways, it is very modern in other ways. When such a method is used within a Christian metaphysical framework, such as the one I describe in my chapter, it functions very differently from when it is used in the framework of late modern naturalism. In the former case, it can lead to very orthodox conclusions, but in the latter, it becomes highly subjective and can lead to wildly varying conclusions.

The key question I have for Dharamraj is this: Does she understand reception-centered intertextuality to be exegesis? Exegesis is the uncovering or extraction of meaning from a text, as opposed to reading meaning into a text. Of course, the subjective disposition and presuppositions of the reader may either help or hinder one from seeing the meaning in the text. But in exegesis the meaning is found in the text, not brought to the text. Naturally, everyone agrees that readers often fail to reach this goal by importing meaning into the text that is not really there. We call that "bad exegesis." But the exegetical ideal remains the extraction of meaning from the text whether it is achieved totally or partially in any given instance. The simplest definition of biblical interpretation is to state the meaning of the text in other words. As the interpreter, I try to put the meaning of the text into my own words in hopes of grasping and conveying to others as much of that meaning as possible.

I can see how a production-centered intertextual method can be helpful to exegesis. However, the reception-centered intertextual method is a bit trickier. It can be a useful tool, or it can result in the reader dominating the text in such a way that the text's meaning remains opaque. This is true in general terms of all texts, but it becomes more important in biblical interpretation where the goal is to hear the word of God.

One of the problems with this chapter is that it does not set this particular reading technique within a theological or metaphysical context. Who is the author? What kind of text are we reading?

What is the relationship between the two Testaments? Who is the reader? What is at stake? These questions are left hanging. Several theological presuppositions are crucial for a successful implementation of a Reception-Centered, Intertextual Approach.

Theological Framework

First, the inspiration of Scripture is a necessary theological presupposition for the successful employment of a Reception-Centered, Intertextual Approach. Why? Dharamraj pairs texts drawn from the Old and New Testaments in her intertextual readings. It is necessary to suppose that both Testaments are inspired by God and carry authority. In short, both Testaments are part of the canon of Scripture for the Christian church. For this reason, the canonical context becomes the most important context for the interpretation of any given text.

In quoting texts from outside the canon, such as hymns, Dharamraj invites the question of why choose this text rather than some other one to pair with the text being considered? Why not use a text from the Book of Mormon or a poem by a Muslim or a novel by a modern agnostic? Such texts are not part of the canon of Scripture, and therefore they might or might not be useful to shed light on a biblical text. If one compares such a text to a biblical one and finds outright contradiction, that is fine because it is to be taken for granted that the Bible does not agree with every text ever produced by human beings. But if one biblical text seemed to contradict another, that would be a theological problem calling for more contemplation and crying out for some sort of resolution. In other words, canonical texts have a relationship to each other that makes it possible to presume they fit together in some coherent way and helps restrain interpretive anarchy.

Second, the concept of divine authorial intent is required in thinking carefully about the meaning of biblical texts. Human authorial intent only gets us so far, and ultimately we need to ask what God is saying through the text. If a Reception-Centered, Intertextual Approach helps us make progress toward determining the divine authorial intent, it can be useful and potentially illuminating. However, if a Reception-Centered, Intertextual Approach is done for its own sake with the reader's own ideas at the center, then it will not be helpful. If a premodern approach sees divine authorial intent as decisive for determining the meaning of the text, and a modern, historical approach sees human authorial intent as central to determining the meaning of the text, the reception-centered approach sees the human reader's intent as central to determining the meaning of the text. Therefore, the premodern critique of both modern and postmodern approaches is the decentering of divine authorial intent as decisive for determining the meaning of the text.

In Dharamraj's chapter, there is an ambiguity in the fourth of the five interpretive steps for readers. She says that the two texts are "in conversation with each other" (130). She uses standard historical-critical methodology in the examples of exegesis at the end of the chapter, which tends to emphasize the text as a product of its natural environment, that is, its historical situation. The problem is that this approach seems to leave out the question of what the divine author means to say through both texts. The ambiguity is centered on the question of whether the omission of the divine author's meaning is circumstantial or ideological. Is it being presumed here that after one has utilized this reading technique, one would naturally need to go on to a biblical theological synthesis of the texts to describe what God is saying through both and other texts as well? Or is this interpretive approach an alternative to such a biblical theological synthesis? I would say that a method that does not seek the divine authorial intent would be inadequate as an exegetical method. It might be adequate for other purposes, such as meditative prayer, but not for exegesis.

Implementing the Approach

In the rest of this response, I would like to focus on the three texts and point out where I see ambiguity in this approach before drawing some conclusions.

First, regarding Genesis 22, Dharamraj focuses her reflection on Isaac as a result of the decision to read this text in conversation with Philippians 2. She explains, "For a story that is often overpowered by Abraham, the father of faith, the Christ hymn throws Isaac into relief." The focus of the comparison becomes the inner psychological state of Isaac, which the narrator of Genesis 22 ignores, as a reading of the passage will confirm. The narrative focuses on who did what, not on how the various characters felt about God's strange command. If Hebrews 11:17–20 or Romans 4 had been chosen instead of Philippians 2, then the focus would have been on the obedient faith of Abraham instead of the willingness of Isaac. This shows how the choice of which passage to pair with the Old Testament passage largely shapes the reflection on the Old Testament passage.

The Reception-Centered, Intertextual Approach is highly ambiguous in that the choice of parallel passages is very subjective. Since Romans 4 and Hebrews 11 are canonical texts that engage with Genesis 22, to choose one or both would seem to reduce the subjectivism of the approach. These are canonical texts bearing apostolic warrant for engaging the narrative in Genesis 22, so it would seem that there is good reason for choosing to engage with them. In her discussion of Isaac's and Abraham's inner psychological states, Dharamraj draws from early Jewish tradition and the history of art for material on which to expand her reflections. This is understandable since such material is scarce in Genesis 22 itself.

This brings me back to the fundamental question: Is this exegesis? If the text itself and the treatment of the text in later canonical reflections on the text do not exert control on the choice of a parallel text or the reflections on how the two texts can be compared, what is driving the process? Is there a hidden agenda at work? It seems that what is happening in this example is not exegesis.

Second, regarding Proverbs 8:22–31, the parallel passage chosen is Colossians 1:15–17. The church fathers and commentators ever since have noted that Christ is called "the power of God and the wisdom of God" in 1 Corinthians 1:24. Unlike most premodern commentators, Dharamraj argues that the Wisdom figure of Proverbs 8 is not Christ. She notes that the Jehovah's Witness Christology sees Christ as the first created being and the one through whom God created the rest of creation. The ancient Arians did the same thing. Dharamraj "saves" the full deity of Christ by not seeing Christ in Proverbs 8. She writes, "One greater than Wisdom is here!" (144). This leaves the identity of Wisdom in the Old Testament ambiguous.

Third, regarding Isaiah 42:1–4, Dharamraj seems to take a similar approach as Tremper Longman does in his chapter. She starts with the Christian understanding of Christ as the suffering servant of Isaiah 53 and on that basis sees Christ in the Isaiah passage. Inexplicably, however, she sets aside the obvious passage to consider as a parallel Matthew

12:17–21, where Isaiah 42:1–4 is quoted, and chooses Revelation 19 instead. The problem is that Revelation 19 is about the second coming of Christ and fits well with Isaiah 63, whereas Matthew 12 is about Christ's first coming and relates to his rejection by Israel. She has difficulty explaining how the weakness and passivity of the servant in Isaiah 42:2–3 fit with the triumphalism of Revelation 19. In her exegesis, the mission of the servant revolves around saving the oppressed and judging the oppressor rather than dealing with the problem of Israel's sin. The message of Revelation 19 replaces Isaiah 40–53 as the context in which Isaiah 42:1–4 is read. Again, the approach seems quite subjective.

Conclusion

What seems to be going on in the discussion of these three passages is that particular New Testament passages are being chosen arbitrarily and the resulting "conversation" between the texts is under reader control rather than canonical control. This is reflection on Scripture, but it is not really exegesis. But if this is not exegesis, then what does it tell us about how we can see Christ in the Old Testament? It seems to me that it tells us little beyond the subjective opinions of the person using the Reception-Centered, Intertextual Approach.

HAVILAH DHARAMRAJ

It is wonderfully agreeable that the five views in this book spread out across premodern, modern, and postmodern approaches (152). Together they give us insights into ways of discovering Christ through the Old Testament that range from the familiar to the unfamiliar, from the comfortable to the stimulating.

Responses to the reception-centered intertextual method largely bring up the matter of the reader deciding which text may speak to which. I find it baffling when others insist that only production-centered intertextuality—that is, where a later biblical author refers to an earlier biblical author—constitutes valid exegesis. For one thing, these references may take the form of direct quotations, but more often they are "allusions" or "echoes." In the latter case, the dependence of the latter text on the earlier becomes an investigation fueled largely by hopeful speculation and intelligent guesswork, and not everyone agrees with the results. To limit intertextual conversation partners in this manner is terribly restrictive. What is more, this is not the only way the church, over the millennia and to the present day, has chosen its intertexts.

Augustine held "the firm conviction that the Two Testaments and all their parts formed a unity due to the fact the one principal author, namely God, inspired the sacred book."[1] Note the pair of intertexts in his sermon on Jacob wrestling with God: "I am speaking as far as the Lord suggests to me . . . what does this mean: *Look, morning has already*

---

1. Cardinal Michele Pellegrino, "General Introduction," in *Sermons*, Works of Saint Augustine III/1 (New York: New City Press, 1990), 44.

come, let me go? This is what the Lord says after his passion to the woman who wanted to hold on to his feet: *Do not touch me, for I have not yet ascended to the Father* (John 20:17)."[2]

In our times, Billy Graham—among the models evangelical preachers look to—launched his classic sermon "Jesus, the Hope of the World" with Ezekiel 22:30: "I looked for someone . . . who would . . . stand before me in the gap."[3] The well-known evangelist Glen Scrivener explains Psalm 88 as a "pencil sketch" of Jesus and engages the psalm with the Gospels' accounts of Jesus on the eve of his crucifixion.[4] The church, it appears, is not waiting for academia to issue a list of (production-centered) intertexts.

Would we conclude that Augustine's reading strategy was "not really exegesis" (175)? No. We accept patristic exegesis with all its idiosyncrasies. We allow that Graham and Scrivener and many other preachers are choosing their (reception-centered) intertexts impelled by the Holy Spirit, not despite him. The pairing of texts is subjective, but is that necessarily inferior to the modernist's preoccupation with "objectivity"? Certainly not, if these supposedly subjective postmodern (and premodern) intertextual conversations reinforce the historical faith and practice of the church.

Of course, a reader-centered hermeneutical method can be misused—think of the erstwhile white South African claiming biblical support for apartheid. But so also can author-centered study of biblical texts be misused—think of the extremes of "objective" source criticism of the century past. On the other hand, some of the most transformative phenomena in our sad world have resulted from appropriating the Bible through perspectival, reader-centered readings: think of black theology in America or *dalit* theology in India. These cannot be dismissed as readings that are "adequate for other purposes, such as meditative prayer, but not for exegesis" (173). One wonders if there is value in prescribing one over the other when there is a place for the author (historical-critical methods), the text (literary methods), *and* the reader (perspectival

---

2. Augustine, *Sermons* 5.7, Works of Saint Augustine III/1, 222.
3. Billy Graham, "Jesus, the Hope of the World," YouTube, www.youtube.com/watch?v=duJdk-rrl40.
4. Glen Scrivener, "Psalm 88: Worship, Lament and the Hope of Christ," YouTube, www.youtube.com/watch?v=HvOR-Zgz7o&t=167s.

approaches) in mainstream hermeneutics. "The idea that meaning occurs in the interplay of text and reader is now a standard one in hermeneutics," whether one uses the concept of Heidegger's hermeneutical circle or Gadamer's fusion of the horizons.[5] Indeed, the interpretation of any biblical text calls for a sophisticated and text-specific balancing of all three approaches. Thus, in my readings of Genesis 22, Proverbs 8, and Isaiah 42, the choice of intertexts is reader-centered, while I draw from text-centered and author-centered methods when examining each text.

As for the question of which text may be paired with which (152–53), texts cannot enter into meaningful conversation unless they share a topic, an icon. Thus, putting Genesis 22 (the ordeal of Isaac) into dialogue with, say, 1 Corinthians 6:12–20 (matters of sexual immorality) is hardly likely to engender a rich outcome. On the other hand, we could pair the Isaianic text with Matthew 12:18–21, which cites it (a production-centered choice), after identifying an icon common to the two. Church liturgy, lectionary groupings of intertexts, and hymns are precious repositories of public meaning passed down across the centuries by the church. As such, they are to be received with humility and re-appreciated. Scholars who are persuaded that reception-centered intertextuality as an interpretive method elevates the reader over the text (172–73) might fall into the trap of unduly elevating the academy over the Common Reader. (Meanwhile, the term *Ideal Reader* [163], from literary theory, perhaps applies better to single texts rather than to pairs of texts, so I prefer to stay with the standard vocabulary of the discipline of comparative literature).

Does the method ignore the larger literary context of its texts? I posit that this is more possible when we match text to text at the level of words. Identifying a (not necessarily *the*) dominant icon is less vulnerable to this pitfall since the icon is more likely to link back into its context. So, for example, the obedient faithfulness of Israel's ancestors runs across their stories (Gen 12:1–4; 17:1; 17:23; 26:5), allowing for the obedience of Isaac to be singled out for attention even in a chapter dominated by his father (161–62).

5. Jeannine K. Brown, *Scripture as Communication: Introducing Biblical Hermeneutics*, 2nd ed. (Grand Rapids: Baker Academic, 2021), 59.

All arguments and caveats considered, my hope is that the Reception-Centered, Intertextual Approach is seen as an affirmation—and even celebration!—of a reading strategy we have received through our collective Christian heritage.

REDEMPTIVE-HISTORICAL, CHRISTOCENTRIC APPROACH

JASON S. DEROUCHIE

The only Bible Jesus had was what we call the Old Testament, and he believed many of its elements concerned him (Luke 24:27).[1] Jesus opened his disciples' minds to "understand the Scriptures," and he empowered them to see a unified, overarching message in the Old Testament regarding a suffering and sovereign messiah who would spark a global mission of reconciliation with God (Luke 24:45–47). Christ's followers should aim to properly magnify Jesus where he is evident in the Scriptures. As John Owen said in 1684, "The revelation . . . of Christ . . . deserves the severest of our thoughts, the best of our meditations and our utmost diligence in them."[2] I propose the most biblically faithful way of doing this is through a multifaceted approach that accounts for the central role Jesus plays in redemptive history.

Part 1: The Nature of Scripture
Christ Is Central in God's Redemptive-Historical Purposes

The fundamental presupposition of evangelical hermeneutics is that Christian Scripture, both the Old Testament and the New Testament,

---

1. I am deeply grateful to the editors and to my research assistants, Brian Verrett and Nicholas Majors, for their help in editing this essay.

2. John Owen, "Meditations on the Glory of Christ," in *The Works of John Owen*, ed. William Goold, 23 vols. (Edinburgh: Banner of Truth Trust, 1965), 1:275.

is God's revealed word (2 Tim 3:16), which by nature implies inspiration, inerrancy, unparalleled authority, and unity amid the diversity. Redemptive history is the progressive unfolding of God's saving purposes disclosed from Genesis to Revelation, all of which grow out of and culminate in God's commitment to glorify himself in Christ. Jesus is, therefore, the beginning and end of the Bible, holding it and all else together (Col 1:16–17).

Scripture progresses through five distinct but overlapping covenants (see below) and through various events, peoples, and institutions, all of which climax in the person and work of Christ. The Old Testament's history (Matt 2:15), laws (5:17–18), prophecy (Acts 3:18), and wisdom (1 Cor 1:23–24) all point to Jesus. Indeed, in him the Old Testament's problems find their solution. All that the Old Testament anticipated is eschatologically realized as shadow gives rise to substance (Col 2:16–17), types move to antitype (e.g., Rom 5:14; 1 Cor 10:6, 11), and what God promised he now fulfills (Luke 24:44; Acts 3:18).

Christ Jesus stands as both the climax and center of God's saving purposes. This is why Jesus told the religious leaders, "You search the Scriptures because you think that in them you have eternal life; and it is they that bear witness about me, yet you refuse to come to me that you may have life" (John 5:39–40 ESV).[3] It also explains why Jesus told his disciples that we have come to "understand the Scriptures" if we see the Old Testament's message climaxing in his death and resurrection and sparking a worldwide missions movement (Luke 24:45–47; cf. Acts 26:22–23).[4]

In Christ, the new creation, new age, and new covenant overcome the old creation, old age, and old covenant as the end of history intrudes into the middle of history. Scripture's redemptive story culminates in Christ's first and second comings, and through him God fulfills all Old Testament hopes. Hence, "no matter how many promises God has made, they are 'Yes' in Christ" (2 Cor 1:20).

---

3. John 5:39 provides believers a "comprehensive hermeneutical key" for rightly interpreting the entire Old Testament, according to D. A. Carson, *The Gospel according to John*, PNTC (Grand Rapids: Eerdmans, 1991), 263.

4. For the central place of these verses in Luke-Acts's theology, see Brian J. Tabb, *After Emmaus: How the Church Fulfills the Mission of Christ* (Wheaton, IL: Crossway, 2021).

Jesus Is Central to Biblical Interpretation

In considering the relationship of the Testaments and their unity centered on the divine Son, G. K. Beale has identified five principles that are rooted in the Old Testament's own story of salvation history and that guided the New Testament authors' Old Testament interpretive conclusions:[5]

1. New Testament authors always assume *corporate solidarity*, in which one can represent the many.
2. The Messiah represented the true (remnant) Israel of the old covenant and the true (consummate) Israel, the church, of the new covenant.
3. God's wise and sovereign plan *unites salvation history* in such a way that earlier parts correspond to later parts.
4. Christ has initiated the age of eschatological fulfillment.
5. Christ stands as the climax and center of history such that his life, death, and resurrection provide *the key* for fully understanding the earlier portions of the Old Testament and its promises.

Within God's redemptive purposes, Jesus operates as the culmination of salvation history and provides both the beginning and end of Old Testament interpretation. This—Beale's last principle—is perhaps the most controversial, but it finds support from both Testaments and impacts all biblical inquiry.

The Old Testament Anticipates That God's People Will Only Understand Its Full Meaning When the Messiah Comes

Many texts in the Old Testament identify how the rebel majority in the old covenant were truly *unable* to know God's word, see his glory, or hear his voice (Deut 29:4 [29:3 MT]; Isa 29:9–12; cf. Rom 11:7–8). However, Yahweh's prophets had promised that God would overcome his people's resistance when he raised up a covenant-mediating

---

5. Summarizing G. K. Beale, *Handbook on the New Testament Use of the Old Testament: Exegesis and Interpretation* (Grand Rapids: Baker Academic, 2012), 53, 95–102.

prophet like Moses (Deut 18:15–20), the one we know of as Jesus (John 6:14–15; Acts 3:22–26). To him the restored community would listen, and they would then obey all that Moses had taught (Deut 18:15; 30:8; cf. Matt 17:5) because through this Messiah, God would have put his words in their hearts (Deut 30:14; Isa 59:20–21), taught them (Isa 54:13), and given them spiritual sight and hearing (Isa 29:18).[6] Thus, only in the latter days of the Messiah and the new covenant would God empower his people to more fully accept and understand his Old Testament word. Christ's person and work supply a necessary lens for rightly grasping all that God intended through his Old Testament prophets.

Concerning the prophets, we know that they usually understood at least most of what they were predicting, for they "searched [the Scriptures?] intently and with greatest care, trying to find out the time and circumstances to which the Spirit of Christ in them was pointing when he predicted the sufferings of the Messiah and the glories that would follow" (1 Pet 1:10–11; cf. John 1:45; 5:46; Rom 1:1–3). Most Old Testament prophets were probably like Daniel, whom God empowered to comprehend "mysteries" (Dan 2:19; 4:9) and who gained "understanding of the message" (10:1; cf. Acts 2:30–31). Nevertheless, in at least one instance, the Lord declared he would only reveal full understanding in the future "time of the end" (Dan 12:8–9).

The New Testament Identifies Jesus as the Lens for Fully Understanding the Old Testament's Meaning

The above passages disclose (1) that believers today can understand and appropriate the Old Testament better than any of the old covenant rebel majority could, and (2) that, in at least some instances, we on this side of the resurrection can understand the Old Testament mysteries more than the prophets themselves did. The New Testament affirms that unregenerate Jews could not understand how the Old Testament pointed to Christ (John 5:37; cf. Rom 11:8; 2 Cor 3:14). It also affirms how the

---

6. For this future-oriented reading of Deuteronomy 30:11–14 with Romans 10:6–9, see esp. Colin James Smothers, "In Your Mouth and in Your Heart: A Study of Deuteronomy 30:12–14 in Paul's Letter to the Romans in Canonical Context" (PhD diss., Southern Baptist Theological Seminary, 2018).

elect disciples did not even fully understand the Old Testament's meaning until Jesus's resurrection (John 2:20–22; 12:13–16)[7] but that it was
the Old Testament itself that clarified its meaning (Luke 24:27, 32; cf.
16:29–31). Indeed, it was after the resurrection that Jesus opened "their
minds to understand the Scriptures" (Luke 24:45). The Old Testament
gives necessary backdrop to Jesus's resurrection, and through Jesus's
resurrection God guides our Old Testament interpretation, revealing
the end, and by this allowing us now to arrive at the fullest meaning he
originally intended.

Thus, God has now "revealed and made known through the
prophetic writings" the full meaning of his mystery that was present
but latent in the Old Testament all along (Rom 16:25–26). Through
Christ, the veil is removed (2 Cor 3:14).[8] Additionally, only by Christ's
spiritually transforming us through his saving work does God enable
believers to accept and understand the Old Testament's ethical expectations (cf. 1 Cor 2:14).

Grasping Authorial Intent

So how should we understand authorial intent? Scripture calls us to
see both an organic unity and a progressive development between the
Testaments. Often the Old Testament authors appear to have grasped
both the shadow and the substance, the acorn and the oak tree, in relation to what they were writing (e.g., Dan 10:1; John 8:56; Acts 2:30–31).
Other times, however, while the typological nature of an event, person,
or institution was innately present from the beginning (1 Cor 10:6, 11),
the full meaning (and perhaps even the predictive recognition) of that
type may only have been understood in retrospect. In such instances,
it is as if the Old Testament gives us the start of a pattern in which we
read "2" followed by "4," but we need the New Testament to clarify what
comes next (2 → 4 → NT?). If the New Testament identifies that the
Old Testament finds its fulfillment in Christ as the digit "6," then we

---

7. D. A. Carson, "Understanding Misunderstandings in the Fourth Gospel," *TynBul* 33
(1982): 59–91; Ardel Caneday, "The Word Made Flesh as Mystery Incarnate: Revealing and
Concealing Dramatized by Jesus as Portrayed in John's Gosel," *JETS* 60 (2017): 751–65.

8. For more on the theme of mystery and the centrality of Jesus in biblical interpretation,
see Jason S. DeRouchie, "The Mystery Revealed: A Biblical Case for Christ-Centered Old
Testament Interpretation," *Them* 44 (2019): 226–48.

know not only the final answer but also that the Old Testament problem was "2 + 4." If, however, the New Testament establishes that the next digit is "8," then we know both the answer and that the Old Testament problem was "2 × 4." The coming of Christ often supplies both the answer key and the algorithm that clarify how the divine author desired all along for us to read the Old Testament and to grasp the relationship of the parts.

Part 2: Interpretive Steps for Readers
Interpret through Christ and for Christ

Though elements of discontinuity exist, we must presuppose a fundamental unity from Old to New Testaments since all Scripture comes from God. The whole Bible progresses, integrates, and climaxes in Christ, and Scripture discloses a God-intentioned unity in how the unchanging Lord is working out his purpose of exalting himself through Jesus (Eph 1:9–10, 20–21).[9]

In God's good purposes already set forth in the Old Testament, when John, Peter, and Paul met the resurrected Christ, their reading of the Old Testament was never the same. Indeed, "only in Christ" is the veil removed that allows one to read and appropriate the old covenant material as God intended (1 Cor 2:13–14; 2 Cor 3:14). By disclosing Christ as the Old Testament's goal, the Father also illuminates his intent for the earlier parts. And in turn, those earlier parts then clarify the meaning of Jesus's person and work. We may initially come to Scripture, reading it front to back. However, when God the Father has given us "the Spirit of wisdom and revelation" and "enlightened the eyes of [our hearts]" through Christ (Eph 1:17–18), we read Scripture back to front and then front to back.

The flow of God's saving purposes in history demands that Christian Old Testament exposition starts and ends with Christ. That is, our Old Testament interpretation is both redemptive-historical and Christocentric: it must flow from Jesus and point to him. The divine Son is at the heart of all exegesis and theology because he is the means

---

9. For more on the centrality of Jesus in whole Bible theology, see Jason S. DeRouchie, Oren R. Martin, and Andrew David Naselli, *40 Questions about Biblical Theology* (Grand Rapids: Kregel, 2020).

and focus of God's self-revelation through his Scriptures.[10] This is what I mean when I say that my approach is Christocentric.

Assess a Passage's Three Overlapping Contexts

Faithfully seeing and celebrating Christ in his Scriptures requires a multiform approach, because Jesus fulfills the Old Testament in various ways (Matt 5:17; Luke 24:44). Working through rigorous exegesis and theology, the Christian interpreter must follow the signals God supplies us to properly magnify the Messiah and his work.[11] Rightly identifying these signals requires that we interpret Scripture along three distinct but overlapping contexts,[12] enabling us to understand most fully what God intended a given Old Testament passage to mean and how a passage points to Jesus.

1. The "close context" (C1) focuses on a passage's immediate literary context within the whole book. Here we observe carefully what and how the text communicates, accounting for both the words and the theology that shapes those words.
2. The "continuing context" (C2) considers the passage within God's story of salvation. We examine how an Old Testament text is informed by antecedent Scripture (e.g., the OT use of the OT) and contributes to God's unfolding drama, whether by progressing the covenants or developing a biblical theme or typological pattern that culminates in Christ.
3. The "complete context" (C3) concerns a text's placement and use within the broader canon. We consider whether and how later Scripture uses or builds upon this passage and keep in mind revelation's progressive nature, the way Christ's work influences

---

10. This study approaches the question of Christ in the Old Testament in a broad rather than narrow sense by seeking to identify any legitimate means for magnifying Jesus from his Scripture.

11. Elsewhere I have summarized a twelve-step exegetical and theological process in Jason S. DeRouchie, *How to Understand and Apply the Old Testament: Twelve Steps from Exegesis to Theology* (Phillipsburg, NJ: P&R, 2017).

12. For these headings, see Trent Hunter and Stephen J. Wellum, *Christ from Beginning to End: How the Full Story of Scripture Reveals the Full Glory of Christ* (Grand Rapids: Zondervan, 2018), 42–69. My categories are similar to but not identical with the textual, epochal, and canonical "horizons" found in Richard Lints, *The Fabric of Theology: A Prolegomenon to Evangelical Theology* (Grand Rapids: Eerdmans, 1993), 293–310.

all history, and how the divine authorship of Scripture allows later passages to clarify, enhance, or deepen the meaning of earlier texts.

Principles for Seeing and Celebrating Christ in His Scriptures

My redemptive-historical, Christocentric approach identifies at least seven possible ways of faithfully magnifying Christ in the Old Testament. All seven principles assume that we are reading the Old Testament through the lens of Christ, for only in him are we empowered to see, live, and hope as God intended from the beginning.[13]

1. See and Celebrate Christ through the Old Testament's Direct Messianic Predictions (P1)

Christ fulfills the Old Testament as the specific focus or goal of direct messianic predictions and redemptive-historical hopes. The Old Testament contains many explicit and implicit predictions.[14] For example, Peter agrees that Isaiah's words directly predict the Messiah: "He himself bore our sins in his body on the tree, that we might die to sin and live to righteousness. By his wounds we have been healed" (1 Pet 2:24 ESV; cf. Isa 53:5).

2. See and Celebrate Christ through the Old Testament's Salvation-Historical Story and Trajectories (P2)

Scripture's entire story line progresses from creation to the fall to redemption to consummation and highlights the work of Jesus as the decisive turning point in salvation history (cf. Luke 16:16; Gal 3:24–26). Five major covenants guide this story line, each of which finds its terminus in Christ (Adamic/Noahic, Abrahamic, Mosaic, David, new).[15] Furthermore, various themes develop or progress as God gradually reveals more of himself and his ways, including covenant, God's

---

13. For more on these seven areas, see Jason S. DeRouchie, "Question 3: How Does Biblical Theology Help Us See Christ in the Old Testament?," in DeRouchie, Martin, and Naselli, *40 Questions about Biblical Theology*, 41–47.

14. For a few examples, see Gen 22:17–18 with Gal 3:8, 14; Ezek 34:23 with John 10:16; Micah 5:2 with Matt 2:6.

15. See Jason S. DeRouchie, "Question 22: What Is a Biblical Theology of the Covenants?," in DeRouchie, Martin, and Naselli, *40 Questions about Biblical Theology*, 215–26.

kingdom, law, temple and God's presence, atonement, and mission. Christ fulfills all of the Old Testament's salvation-historical trajectories.

3. See and Celebrate Christ through the Similarities and Contrasts of the Old and New Ages, Creations, and Covenants (P3)

Jesus's saving work creates both continuities and discontinuities between the old and new ages, creations, and covenants. For example, while both the new and old covenants contain a similar structure (i.e., God redeems and then calls his people to obey), only the new covenant supplies freedom from sin and power for obedience to *all* covenant members; the old covenant did not change hearts (Deut 29:4; Rom 8:3). Similarly, whereas Adam disobeyed and brought death to all, Christ obeys and brings life to many (Rom 5:18–19). Whereas access to Yahweh's presence in the temple was restricted to the high priest on the Day of Atonement, Christ's priestly work opens the way for all in him to enjoy God's presence (Heb 9:24–26; 10:19–22). These kinds of similarities and contrasts between the old and new ages, creations, and covenants encourage a messianic reading of the Old Testament within the redemptive-historical approach.

4. See and Celebrate Christ through the Old Testament's Typology (P4)

The author of Hebrews said the Old Testament law was "a shadow of the good things to come" (Heb 10:1), and Paul spoke similarly (Col 2:16–17). In the New Testament, these anticipations and pointers are called "types" or "examples" (Rom 5:14; 1 Cor 10:6) that in turn find their counter in Jesus as their ultimate realization. God structured the progressive development of salvation history in such a way that certain Old Testament characters (e.g., Adam, Melchizedek, Moses, David), events (e.g., the flood, the exodus, the return to the land), and institutions or objects (e.g., the Passover lamb, the temple, the priesthood) bear meanings that clarify and predictively anticipate the Messiah's life and work.

5. See and Celebrate Christ through Yahweh's Identity and Activity (P5)

When we meet Yahweh in the Old Testament, we are catching glimpses of the coming Christ. Recall that Jesus said that "no one has ever seen God" the Father except the Son (John 1:18; 6:46), but that "whoever has seen me has seen the Father" (John 14:9 ESV). Minimally, this means that those who saw God in the Old Testament enjoyed preliminary and partial glimpses of his glory (Exod 33:18–23). It also may imply that, at least in some instances where Yahweh becomes embodied in a human form in the Old Testament, we may be meeting the preincarnate Son (e.g., Gen 18:22; 32:24–30; Josh 5:13–15). Additionally, since the New Testament identifies Jesus with Yahweh (cf. Phil 2:10–11; Isa 45:23), when we hear God speaking or acting in the Old Testament as the object of people's faith, we are seeing the very one who would embody himself in the person of Jesus (see, e.g., Heb 11:26; Jude 5).

6. See and Celebrate Christ through the Ethical Ideals of Old Testament Law and Wisdom (P6)

The Old Testament's laws and wisdom provide fodder to magnify Christ's greatness. The Mosaic law pointed to the importance for Christ in the way it identified and multiplied sin (Rom 3:20; 5:20), imprisoned the sinful (Gal 3:10, 13, 22), and showed everyone's need for atonement. The law by its nature, therefore, predicted Christ as "the end of the law" (Rom 10:4 ESV).

Moreover, as God's word was made flesh, Jesus manifests in his person the essence of every ethical ideal aligned with Yahweh's revealed will, and he then imputes this perfection to believers (Rom 5:18–19; cf. Phil 3:9). When you observe how the Old Testament law and wisdom express ethical ideals, know that the justifying work of the divine Son fulfills them all.

7. See and Celebrate Christ by Using the Old Testament to Instruct or Guide Others in the Law of Love (P7)

Jesus came not "to abolish the Law or the Prophets . . . but to fulfill them" (Matt 5:17), and the way he fulfills the various precepts guides our pursuit of love. While old covenant instruction no longer bears *direct* authority in the Christian's life, it still indirectly guides us when read through the mediation of Christ (2 Tim 3:15–16). Through Christ, the very texts that used to condemn now lead us in a life of love, and God empowers such love (Rom 13:8–10) by changing our hearts and filling us with his Spirit (Ezek 36:27; Rom 2:26, 29). The Old Testament helps guide our Christian obedience, and every step of this obedience magnifies Jesus's sanctifying work.

Part 3: Applying the Approach–Three Case Studies

Having presented seven principles for seeing Christ in the Old Testament Scriptures, I now apply this redemptive-historical, Christocentric approach to Genesis 22, Proverbs 8, and Isaiah 42.

Genesis 22:1-19: Proof and Pledge That Yahweh Will Fulfill His Offspring Promise
Placing the Offspring Promise in the Context of Genesis

Before considering Genesis 22's messianic predictions, which are both typological (P4) and direct (P1), the interpreter must first place the passage within the continuing context of God's story of salvation (C2). Genesis is threaded by the promise of "offspring," which includes not only peoples but a person. Due to Adam's sin bringing both curse upon the whole world and corruption within all humanity (3:14–19; 6:5, 11–12), the Lord declared that a single male "offspring" (*zera‘*) of the first woman would, through his own personal tribulation, triumph over the evil serpent, thus reversing the curse and bringing new creation (Gen 3:15).[16] From this point forward, the world's only hope for blessing and reconciliation with God rested on Yahweh's preserving and realizing the promise of this singular offspring.

The narrator ties the offspring promise of Genesis 3:15 to the patriarchs by the book's repeated heading ("this is the account of X's family line") and the linear genealogies in 5:1–32 and 11:10–26.[17] Genesis 22:1–19 occurs within Terah's family line cycle (11:27–25:11). This cycle begins with Yahweh promising that Abra(ha)m would (1) become a great nation (12:2), (2) be the agent of curse-overcoming blessing (12:3), and

---

16. Collins rightly notes that Hebrew authors make explicit whether the collective singular noun *zera‘* ("seed, offspring") bears a singular or plural referent by including singular or plural adjectives and/or pronouns (whether independent, object, or suffix pronouns). The lexicalized singular pronoun *hu'* in 3:15 identifies that the woman's "seed" is a male individual (cf. 2 Sam 7:12–13). C. John Collins, "A Syntactical Note (Genesis 3:15): Is the Woman's Seed Singular or Plural?" *TynBul* 48 (1997): 139–48, esp. 142–44.

17. See Gen 2:4; 5:1; 6:9; 10:1; 11:10, 27; 25:12, 19; 36:1; 37:2; Jason S. DeRouchie, "The Blessing-Commission, the Promised Offspring, and the *Toledot* Structure of Genesis," *JETS* 56 (2013): 219–47.

(3) have offspring who would inherit the promised land and become numerous like the dust (13:15–16).

Genesis 15 builds on these promises by stressing that the patriarch has yet "no offspring" (v. 3 ESV) but believes (v. 6) Yahweh's promise that *one* "offspring" from his own loins will be his heir and become countless as the stars (v. 5).[18] This astronomical imagery connects directly with the singular seed of Genesis 22:17 (see below), where God promises, "I will make your offspring as numerous as the stars in the sky" (author's translation). Abraham would become the father of many nations (17:4; cf. Gen 12:2–3) in many lands (26:3–4; cf. Rom 4:13) through the promised offspring's arrival (Gen 22:17–18).

Two elements in Genesis 22:1–19 indicate that the offspring promise provides a governing backdrop for the narrative. First, the narrator stresses that the patriarch must sacrifice his "son" (22:2), frequently repeats the word "son" (22:3, 6–10, 12–13, 16), and notes Abraham's fatherhood (22:7). These elements recall God's earlier pledge, "It is through Isaac that your offspring will be reckoned" (21:12; cf. 17:19, 21), which distinguishes Isaac from the coming offspring (cf. 26:3–4). Second, Yahweh directly predicts how the individual offspring will multiply like the stars, possess the gate of his enemies, and be the instrument of blessing to the nations (22:17–18). Thus, I summarize the point of Genesis 22:1–19 as follows: God tests whether Abraham will fear him and obey the divine call to sacrifice his only son, thus proving that he truly believes that Yahweh will fulfill his promise of a singular male offspring through Isaac who will deliver and bless all nations.

Indirect/Typological Foreshadowing of Christ in Genesis 22:1-19

Genesis 22:1–19 narrates Abraham's obedient willingness to offer his son as a burnt offering, Isaac's sacrificial role and deliverance, and Yahweh's providing the ram as a substitute sacrifice. Through these features, the passage typologically foreshadows (i.e., P4) that God would not spare his own Son (Rom 8:32; cf. Isa 53:6, 12), Christ would die and rise to life (Heb 11:19), and he would serve as a substitute sacrifice for sinners (2 Cor 5:21; Gal 3:13–14; 1 Pet 2:24). Scripture suggests that

---

18. Note the singular pronoun and verbs in verse 4. For more on Genesis 15:1–6, see Jason S. DeRouchie, "Lifting the Veil: Reading and Preaching Jesus' Bible through Christ and for Christ," *SBJT* 22.3 (2018): 167–77.

the patriarch himself understood to some degree the predictive nature of his test.

The father did not spare his son. By recalling the complete context (C3), we see that the Synoptics (Mark 1:11; 9:7; Luke 20:13) and John's writings (John 3:16; 1 John 4:10) may present Jesus as the antitypical beloved son whom Isaac foreshadowed (cf. Gen 22:2, 12, 16). Romans 8:32 likely provides a more direct allusion, however: "He who *did not spare his own Son* [*idiou huiou ouk epheisato*], but *gave* [*paredōken*] him up for us all—how will he not also, along with him, graciously give us all things?" (emphasis added). Along with seeing an allusion to Isaiah 53:6, 12 (Yahweh *gave up* [*paredōken*, LXX] his servant to death for our sins), many scholars propose Paul is alluding to Genesis 22:12, 16, where the Lord declares to Abraham, "You *have not spared* your beloved *son* [*huiou . . . ouk epheisō*, LXX]."[19]

Ironically, while Father Abraham, like Father Yahweh, was willing to give up his son, God did not allow the patriarch to complete the sacrifice. The typology in this instance is therefore only partial, or perhaps better, inverted (or ironic). That is, Jesus alone as God's Son fulfills Abraham's hope that "Yahweh will see" (cf. Gen 22:14) and stands as the antitype to the substitutionary role Isaac foreshadowed but could *not* fulfill and that the ram supplied.[20]

Isaac, the potential burnt offering. Abraham's test required that he willingly "sacrifice [Isaac] . . . as a burnt offering" at Moriah (Gen 22:2–3; cf. 22:6–8, 13). Prior to the tabernacle's construction and the incorporation of the sin and guilt offerings, the burnt offering was the only atoning offering for human sin.[21] Texts like Leviticus 9:24–10:2 (C3) demonstrate that burnt offerings can consist of *substitutes* (9:24) or *sinners* (10:1–2),[22] but only the killing of the substitute allows the repentant rebel a renewed relationship with God.

19. For example, Mark A. Seifrid, "Romans," in *Commentary on the New Testament Use of the Old Testament*, ed. G. K. Beale and D. A. Carson (Grand Rapids: Baker Academic, 2007), 634; Thomas R. Schreiner, *Romans*, 2nd ed., BECNT (Grand Rapids: Baker Academic, 2018), 451.

20. For more on inverted typology, see Beale, *Handbook on the New Testament Use of the Old Testament*, 92–93.

21. Jacob Milgrom, *Leviticus 1–16: A New Translation with Introduction and Commentary*, AB (New Haven, CT: Yale University Press, 1991), 176–77.

22. Other texts identify as sacrifices the sinners Yahweh destroys at the day of his coming (e.g., Isa 34:6; Jer 46:10; Ezek 39:17; Zeph 1:7).

Was Isaac to die as a substitute or a sinner? Scripture most commonly uses the language of "burnt offering" with respect to substitution, and nothing in the close context (C1) draws attention to a wickedness in Isaac demanding immediate justice (contrast Deut 9:4–6). Hence, God likely sets Isaac forth as a vicarious sacrifice standing in for the sinner Abraham or a broader community.

However, God did not allow Isaac to stand as a substitute sacrifice, likely because he himself was a sinner. The complete biblical context (C3) informs us that burnt offerings would continue until the ultimate substitute's arrival since they functioned as an "illustration/figure" (NIV/ESV, *parabolē*) pointing to what God would accomplish in Christ during "the time of the new order" (Heb 9:9–10). Abraham, like Noah before him (Gen 8:20–22), required sustained substitutionary expressions. Isaac could not stand as the substitute, for he himself bore sin's blemish.

God supplies a curse-bearing substitute. Within the story of God's salvation (C2), the Lord had promised Abraham, "Whoever curses you I will curse" (Gen 12:3). When ratifying his covenant of land, offspring, and blessing to the patriarch, Yahweh dramatically passed between the animal parts, signaling that he would bear the curse of death if his fulfilling the covenant with Abraham was jeopardized (15:9–18; cf. Jer 34:18–20).[23] But since he also conditioned the fulfillment of the covenant promises on the obedience of Abraham's children (Gen 18:19) and because all people were innately wicked (8:21), Genesis both anticipates that God would be forced to curse them and implies that the Lord would, in turn, have to curse himself.

We now see the significance of the coming offspring and the way Genesis 22 points to the Son of God who would himself stand as humanity's substitute. At the beginning of Genesis (C1), God promised that an offspring of the woman and divine-image-bearing son would destroy the evil one and his sinful work (3:15; cf. 5:1–3). Thus, where the first man and son of God failed to provide and protect (2:15 with

---

23. On reading the covenant ratification ceremony as a self-maledictory oath sign, see Meredith G. Kline, *By Oath Consigned: A Reinterpretation of the Covenant Signs of Circumcision and Baptism* (Grand Rapids: Eerdmans, 1968), 16–17, 41–42; Peter J. Gentry and Stephen J. Wellum, *Kingdom through Covenant: A Biblical-Theological Understanding of the Covenants*, 2nd ed. (Wheaton, IL: Crossway, 2018), 286–94.

3:6), thereby bringing curse to the original creation, the logic of Genesis 3 and complete biblical context (C3) teaches that this new man and Son of God would succeed, thereby securing blessing for a new creation (cf. Rom 5:18–19; 1 Cor 15:45; 2 Cor 5:17). Nevertheless, while God would raise up this new son, his victory would be costly. The serpent would smite the man's heel (Gen 3:15), which when considered from the complete context (C3), at least implies that this son would endure a blow from the one who has been "a murderer from the beginning" (John 8:44). From the start, therefore, Genesis anticipates that the promised offspring would in some way bear the curse but overcome (smiting the serpent's head, Gen 3:15), thus reconciling the world to God.[24] Before Genesis 22, the narrator has already intimated for the reader the future curse of both the offspring and God himself. Later prophetic revelation (C3) further associates the self-sacrificing royal deliverer with Yahweh (e.g., Ps 2:1–7; Isa 7:14; 9:6) and God with his wise royal son (e.g., Ps 45:6–7 [45:7–8 MT]).

Prior to Genesis 22 (C1 and C2), the narrator has already associated Isaac with the coming offspring (Gen 15:3–5; 21:12; cf. 26:3–4), such that Isaac's arrival reinforces the certainty that the deliverer will come after (and from) him. Since Isaac's life is so bound with the offspring who is to experience tribulation unto triumph, one is not surprised that Isaac will endure suffering to foreshadow the one to come. Yet he is not sufficient for the role. In Abraham and Isaac's dramatic dialogue up the mountain, the father declared, "God himself will provide the lamb for the burnt offering, my son" (22:8). The Hebrew term rendered "lamb" is *se* (Gk. *probaton*), a generic term for any small livestock beast. After Yahweh's angel held back the patriarch's death-bringing hand, the specific type of beast God supplied was a "ram" (22:13). Perhaps to distinguish the type from its antitype, Isaiah notes that the suffering servant was "led like a lamb [Heb. *se*; Gk. *probaton*] to the slaughter" (Isa 53:7). Both Isaac and the substitute are figures for the greater substitute that Genesis itself anticipates (cf. John 1:29; Acts 8:32–35; 1 Pet 1:18–19).

24. See Alan F. Segal, "He Who Did Not Spare His Own Son . . .': Jesus, Paul, and the Aqedah," in *From Jesus to Paul: Studies in Honour of Francis Wright Beare*, ed. Peter Richardson and John C. Hurd (Waterloo, ON: Wilfrid Laurier University Press, 1984), 175–77.

Abraham rejoiced that he would see Christ's day. At least two features within Genesis 22:1–19 (close context) suggest that Abraham himself understood the predictive significance in his test. First, even after seeing the substitute ram and offering it "as a burnt offering instead of his son" (22:13), Abraham called the place "Yahweh *will see*" (*yhwh yir'eh*), not "Yahweh *has seen*" (22:14). Abraham recognized the replacement ram as a foreshadowing of how "Yahweh will see" to fulfilling the offspring promise and overcome the curse with blessing (22:18). Thus, his testimony became a perpetual statement of hope in the one we call the Christ: "At the mount of Yahweh it will be seen" (22:14, author's translation).

A second feature indicating that Abraham saw his test as predictive further supports this reading. The three-day journey from the region of Beersheba in the Philistines' land (Gen 21:33–34) to Moriah (approximately 91 kilometers, or 56.5 miles) was unnecessary if Yahweh only desired to test Abraham, for this could have been done without distant travels.[25] By means of this journey, the patriarch would have recognized something more about the promised offspring as a person and about the location, means, and timing of how God would secure his victory.

As for the *location*, God brings Abraham to a mountain in "the region of Moriah" (Gen 22:2), the future location of temple sacrifices (2 Chr 3:1) and, ultimately (C3), Christ's sacrifice (Mark 10:33; Acts 10:39). The chronicler explicitly identifies Moriah as the place of sacrifice, showing that he saw Abraham's words as prospective.

With respect to the *person*, in coming to Moriah, Abraham has returned to the region of (Jeru)Salem and the King's Valley where the priest-king Melchizedek of (Jeru)Salem blessed him (Gen 14:18–20). By this act and for Abraham's benefit, Yahweh is likely associating Melchizedek, the "king of righteousness" and "peace," with the promise of the offspring whose coming the patriarch's obedience at the mountain would secure (cf. Ps 110:1–2, 4; Heb 7:17, 21).

As for *means*, Yahweh calls a father to give up his son. Within the complete biblical context (C3), this act points to the Father's greater

25. So, too, Walter C. Kaiser Jr., "Genesis 22:2: Sacrifice Your Son?," in *Hard Sayings of the Bible*, by Walter C. Kaiser Jr. et al. (Downers Grove, IL: InterVarsity Press, 1996), 126–27.

gift in Christ (cf. John 3:16; Rom 8:32; 1 John 4:9–10). The Lord also restores this son and supplies a substitute to bear the wrath that Abraham or a broader community deserved (John 1:29; 2 Cor 5:21). Abraham knew his son would return with him, by whatever means the Lord chose. Thus, Abraham told his servants regarding him and his boy, "*We* will worship and then *we* will come back to you" (Gen 22:5, emphasis added). The author of Hebrews saw in Abraham's statement his belief that God could "even raise the dead" (Heb 11:19). Within the complete context (C3), Isaac's "resurrection" anticipates the promised offspring, who likewise would triumph through tribulation (Gen 3:15; 49:8–12; cf. Col 2:13–15).

Regarding *timing*, the narrator identifies that Abraham's test, culminating in his figuratively receiving back his son from the dead, occurred "on the third day" after he began his journey (Gen 22:4). As such, this narrative may be one of the instances where in Scripture (C3) "this is what is written: The Messiah will suffer and rise from the dead *on the third day*" (Luke 24:46, emphasis added; cf. 15:3–4).[26]

Direct Predictions of Christ in Genesis 22:1-19

In his second speech, Yahweh's messenger makes two promises, both expressed by an infinitive absolute + *yiqtol* construction in Hebrew: "I will surely bless you and will surely make your offspring as the stars of the heavens and as the sand that is on the seashore" (22:17, author's translation). Yahweh's commitment to bless recalls his words in 12:2. His mention of the stars alludes to 15:5, which identified that the offspring who would come from the son from his loins would become countless like the stars. Against the NIV, we should regard the offspring in 22:17b as singular since the verb "multiply" (*rbh*) commonly means to produce children when it governs living organisms (e.g., 1:28; 9:1, 7; 17:2, 20).[27] In light of this, it seems possible that the "offspring" in Genesis 22:17 is actually the singular deliverer who will himself multiply into a community. The masculine *singular* pronoun "his" modifying "offspring" in verse 17 further supports this conclusion. Moreover, Genesis's overall

---

26. See Jason S. DeRouchie, "Why the Third Day? The Promise of Resurrection in All of Scripture," *Midwestern Journal of Theology* 20.1 (2021): 19–34.

27. I thank my research assistant, Brian Verrett, for this observation.

plot structure witnesses a narrowing of vision that moves from the world to Israel to a royal offspring in Judah's line upon whom all the world's hopes rest (Gen 49:8–12).[28]

The offspring in Genesis 22:17–18 is singular according to C. John Collins's understanding that an adjective or pronoun's number makes explicit whether *zera'* ("seed, offspring") bears a singular or plural referent.[29] The close proximity of the three instances of *zera'* in 22:17–18 suggests that *all* are singular in this context.[30] The flow of thought is as follows:

1. The singular male offspring of the woman who will strike a death blow to the head of the serpent (3:15) and whom Yahweh will name through Isaac (21:12) will multiply like the stars (22:17).
2. The first result of this community will be that the singular offspring will possess the gate of his enemies (22:17; cf. 24:60).
3. The second result is that all the nations of the earth will regard themselves blessed in this offspring (22:18; cf. Ps 72:17; Isa 65:16; Jer 4:2).

The earth's nations counting themselves blessed (22:18) constitutes the promised great multiplication (22:17) and likely signals the eschatological shift from Abraham fathering one nation (Israel during the old covenant) to fathering many nations (the church, united to Jesus the true Israel, in the new covenant) (17:4–5). All these are in some way incorporated into the singular offspring (22:18), and through their multiplying, he claims enemy turf (22:17). This suggests that during the reign of the male deliverer, the "land" promised to Abraham will expand to "lands," which is exactly what Yahweh promised Isaac in 26:3–4. Furthermore, when considering the complete context (C3), both Peter and Paul regarded 22:18 as a messianic text (see Acts 3:13, 18, 24–26;

---

28. DeRouchie, "Blessing-Commission," 235.

29. Collins, "Syntactical Note," 142–44.

30. Contra Alexander and Steinmann, who affirm a singular referent for *zera'* in 22:17c–18 but a plural referent in 22:17b (T. Desmond Alexander, "Further Observations on the Term 'Seed' in Genesis," *TynBul* 48 [1997]: 365; Andrew E. Steinmann, "Jesus and Possessing the Enemies' Gate [Genesis 22:17–18; 24:60]," *BSac* 174 [2017]: 17).

Gal 3:8, 13–14, 16, 29). I suggest, therefore, that Genesis 22:15–19 amounts to a direct messianic prophecy (P1).

Summary

In Genesis 22:1–19 Yahweh tests Abraham to reveal whether he would fear God and obey the divine call, thus proving that he truly believed that Yahweh would fulfill his promise of a singular male offspring through Isaac (21:12). In response to the patriarch's obedience (22:18; cf. 26:5), Yahweh both typologically confirms (P4) (22:11–14) and directly predicts (P1) (22:15–19) that he will indeed realize what he has promised. He will do this by providing a penal substitutionary sacrifice for sinners (vv. 13–14) and by multiplying the male offspring into a massive community, which will result in the singular offspring overcoming his enemies' stronghold (v. 17) and in his being the one in whom some from all the earth's nations regard themselves blessed (v. 18).

Proverbs 8:22-31: Wisdom Is God's Royal Son by Whom He Creates the World
Overviewing the Poem

In the immediate context (C1) of Proverbs 8, personified Wisdom urges listeners to embrace the truth of her instruction (vv. 4–11), identifies her noble associations and the benefits she brings (vv. 12–21), notes her eternal origins and joyful involvement in creation (vv. 22–31), and charges her "sons" to heed her voice to experience life rather than death (vv. 32–36). This meditation on creation includes many semantic and conceptual links with Genesis 1:1–2:3 (C3).[31] Analyzing the discourse suggests that the unit divides into two parts (Prov 8:22, 23–31), both of which offer interpretive challenges.

Concerning the first part, Wisdom declares that Yahweh "possessed" (*qnh*) her before he did any acts (Prov 8:22 ESV). The verb *qnh* in Proverbs 8:22 means "to possess," whether by *acquisition* (e.g., Exod 15:16; Isa 11:11; Prov 1:5; 4:5, 7), *purchase* (e.g., Gen 47:22; 49:30; Lev 25:30; Jer 32:9), or *generation* (Gen 4:1; Deut 32:6; Ps 139:13). The NIV's "brought forth" derives from the verb's use in contexts of generation,

---

31. See Michael B. Shepherd, *The Text in the Middle*, StBibLit 162 (New York: Lang, 2014), 10.

but "to possess" still appears to be the base meaning of *qnh*.[32] God has always "possessed" Wisdom, which was present with him before he created anything. It was present as an underlying divine quality or function that his being generates and that is essential or organic to his nature.[33] I render Proverbs 8:22 as follows: "Yahweh possessed me, the beginning of his way, earlier than his acts from then." The phrase "the beginning of his way" stands in apposition to "me" and likely marks Wisdom as the preeminent element of his purposes (cf. Job 40:15; Col 1:15).

Second, Wisdom declares herself to be Yahweh's means for carrying out his intentions both before creation (Prov 8:23–26) and at creation (vv. 27–31). *Before creation*, Yahweh installed Wisdom as his representative (v. 23: "I was formed" [NIV] or "I was set up" [ESV]). The verb *nsk* with this meaning occurs elsewhere only in Psalm 2:6: "I have *installed* my king on Zion" (emphasis added). Solomon likely associates Wisdom's primordial exaltation in Proverbs 8:23 with the future anointed king's exaltation in Psalm 2:6 (see below). At the very least, the link probably identifies Wisdom's royal status in relation to God even before time began. Thus, the Complete Jewish Bible renders Proverbs 8:23 as "From the distant past I was enthroned."[34]

Wisdom portrays itself as God's commissioned image bearer or royal agent who has enjoyed this post "from eternity [*me'olam*] . . . from the beginning, from times before earth" (Prov 8:23, author's translation). The noun *'olam* means only "a remote time," but the close context (C1) concerns eternity past. As Seth Postell notes, "Because Wisdom precedes creation, it must be regarded as uncreated, and, as a consequence, eternal."[35]

Yahweh "brought forth" or "strengthened" (*hyl*) Wisdom before the waters, mountains, and fields (8:24–26 ESV). While interpreters debate the precise meaning of the Hebrew verb *hyl*, the text's overall flow depicts Wisdom as an eternal effect of God himself.

32. See R. B. Y. Scott, *Proverbs-Ecclesiastes*, AB 18 (Garden City, NY: Doubleday, 1965), 72; Bruce Vawter, "Prov 8:22: Wisdom and Creation," *JBL* 99 (1980): 205–16.

33. See the discussion below on Proverbs 30:4.

34. See the rendering of the Complete Jewish Bible at www.chabad.org/library/bible_cdo/aid/16379/jewish/Chapter-8.htm.

35. Seth D. Postell, "Proverbs 8—The Messiah: Personification of Divine Wisdom," in *The Moody Handbook of Messianic Prophecy: Studies and Expositions of the Messiah in the Old Testament*, ed. Michael Rydelnik and Edwin Blum (Chicago: Moody, 2019), 652.

Next, *at creation* Wisdom was Yahweh's constant companion (8:27–31)—present when he established the heavens (v. 27) and joyfully and faithfully (*'amon*) serving beside him when he made the earth (vv. 28–31). The noun *'amon* in verse 30 is likely a bi-form of the adjective *'emun* ("faithful") and noun *'emunah* ("faithfulness"). While some point to Song of Songs 7:1 [7:2 MT] and Jeremiah 52:15 to render *'amon* "artisan" or "craftsman" (CSB, ESV, NASB, NET, NKJV, NRSV), the meaning "faithful one" works fine in these contexts. The NIV's "I was *constantly* at his side" adequately captures the meaning.[36] At creation Wisdom constantly rejoiced before Yahweh, in his earth's soil, and with the sons of Adam (8:30–31).

Wisdom as God's Son in Proverbs 8:22-31

Solomon portrays Wisdom as a woman to entice his royal son(s) to desire her (cf. 1:8; 2:1; 4:10). Nevertheless, Wisdom's female persona is secondary to the book's message, for the royal son(s) should not only embrace but also embody Wisdom. Furthermore, in Proverbs 8:22–31 Wisdom is neither a feminine part of God nor his consort. Instead, the first-person speech ("I, me, my") mutes the feminine portrayal, thus allowing Wisdom to be both with God and of God.

Significantly, at the book's end (close context) a certain Agur son of Jakeh asks four rhetorical questions whose contents recall Yahweh's queries in Job 38 and echo Yahweh's creative acts that Proverbs 3:19–20 and 8:27–31 describe: "Who has gone up to heaven and come down? Whose hands have gathered up the wind? Who has wrapped up the waters in a cloak? Who has established all the ends of the earth?" (30:4). He then queries, "What is his name, and what is the name of his son? Surely you know!" John Sailhamer claims that this verse intentionally alludes to Wisdom's part in creation (8:27–31) to raise "the question of the identity of the One who is with God."[37]

More specifically, 30:1–6 is prophetic speech, making up what 30:1 terms an "inspired utterance" (NIV) or "oracle" (ESV, *massa'*). The text reinforces this through the phrase "the man's utterance"

---

36. Cf. Proverbs 3:19–20; see Bruce K. Waltke, *The Book of Proverbs: Chapters 1–15*, NICOT (Grand Rapids: Eerdmans, 2004), 417–20.

37. John Sailhamer, *NIV Compact Bible Commentary* (Grand Rapids: Zondervan, 1994), 354.

(*ne'um haggeber*), which occurs elsewhere only three times and always at the head of (messianic) predictions (see Num 24:3, 15; 2 Sam 23:1).[38] Contemporary translations consistently render 30:3b negatively, as the last of four declarations of ignorance. However, the Hebrew retains no negative in 30:3b, and the word order suggests a contrast with what precedes: "I have not learned wisdom, *but knowledge of Holy Ones I know*" (author's translation). Despite being weak and uneducated (30:2–3a), Agur received an "oracle" (30:1)—a truthful "word of God" (30:5) that supplied "knowledge of Holy Ones [*qedoshim*]" (30:3b). The plural form "Holy Ones" is unexpected as a reference to God. In Scripture its only other unambiguous use as a substantive with reference to God is in Proverbs 9:10, which captures the book's thesis at the end of the first main unit: "The beginning of wisdom is the fear of Yahweh, and knowledge of Holy Ones is understanding" (author's translation). Most interpreters view these examples as plurals of majesty, following the pattern of *'elohim* ("God"), so they give the plurals a singular referent, "Holy One."[39] However, these would be the only such examples in Scripture, and the singular forms *'el* (30:1) and *'eloah* (30:5) for "God" draw further attention to the plural *qedoshim*. Tracy McKenzie and Jonathan Shelton rightly note, "The occurrence of the duo at the end of verse 4 suggests a plurality in the holy ones here in verse 3."[40] Similarly, the Father and Son in 30:4 naturally point back to the "Holy One[s]" of 30:3. This link identifies a united holy nature in the distinct persons of the Father and his Son. Furthermore, the connection with 9:10 (cf. 1:7) strongly associates the relationship of the Father and Son in 30:4 to Yahweh and an eternally begotten Wisdom in 8:22–31. Targum Neofiti ties these texts together by rendering Genesis 1:1: "In the beginning, with wisdom, the Son of Yahweh completed the sky and the land" (cf. Jer 10:12; Ps 104:24).[41]

---

38. For these links, see Tracy J. McKenzie and Jonathan Shelton, "From Proverb to Prophecy: Textual Production and Theology in Proverbs 30:1–6," *Southeastern Theological Review* 11.1 (2020): 8–11.

39. The NRSV is an exception, rendering *qedoshim* as "holy ones" in Proverbs 30:3 but not 9:10. Nevertheless, the phrase's limited use within Proverbs suggests both instances envision the same referent.

40. McKenzie and Shelton, "From Proverb to Prophecy," 13.

41. As cited in Shepherd, *Text in the Middle*, 11.

The Wise King as God's Son in Proverbs and Beyond

Additionally, Proverbs most commonly uses the language of "sonship" with respect to the royal line, which we learn elsewhere will culminate in a king whose dominion will never end. While Proverbs never explicitly mentions the promises of 2 Samuel 7:12–16, the superscription identifies Solomon as the "son of David, king of Israel" (1:1), which places Proverbs within this historic and prophetic continuing context (C2).[42] Furthermore, Proverbs intends to train the royal "son[s]" whose wisdom is grounded in the fear of Yahweh. It is here that Solomon's allusion to Psalm 2 becomes significant. Just as Yahweh from eternity past installed his Wisdom-Son to represent him (Prov 8:23), so also Yahweh designates his messianic King his "begotten Son" (Ps 2:7, author's translation) upon his installation as King in Zion, having triumphed over his enemies (Ps 2:1–2, 6; cf. Acts 4:24–28; 13:32–33). Utilizing the complete biblical context (C3), Thomas Schreiner notes, "If Proverbs is viewed from a canonical perspective, the ideal picture of the king points to a future king—a king who fulfills the promise of the covenant with David . . . Jesus Christ."[43]

The internal witness of Proverbs suggests that those who composed and/or compiled the book portrayed Wisdom as God's eternally begotten Son and also believed that the royal son of David and of God would be Wisdom incarnate. This accords with the complete context (C3) when one considers the New Testament's description of Jesus. What "the Wisdom of God said" (Luke 11:49–51 ESV), Jesus said, thus identifying himself as Wisdom.[44] Jesus's wisdom exceeds Solomon's (Matt 12:42), and he proves it in his deeds and testifies to it in his teaching (11:2, 19; 13:54). Christ is God's wisdom who stands against foolish human speculations (Col 2:1–8) and who becomes our wisdom through his cross-victory (1 Cor 1:24, 30; cf. 2:7–8).

Other New Testament texts identify Jesus as Wisdom when they declare him to be the divine Word through whom "all things were

42. So, too, Barry R. Leventhal, "Messianism in Proverbs," in *The Moody Handbook of Messianic Prophecy: Studies and Expositions of the Messiah in the Old Testament*, ed. Michael Rydelnik and Edwin Blum (Chicago: Moody, 2019), 639–40.

43. Thomas R. Schreiner, *The King in His Beauty: A Biblical Theology of the Old and New Testaments* (Grand Rapids: Baker Academic, 2013), 294.

44. Hartmut Gese, "Wisdom, Son of Man, and the Origins of Christology: The Consistent Development of Biblical Theology," *HBT* 3 (1981): 43.

made" (John 1:1, 3, 14) and "in very nature God" who becomes human, dies a substitutionary death, and then is "exalted . . . to the highest place" (Phil 2:6–11). Perhaps the clearest parallels appear in Colossians 1:15–20. Here Paul alludes to the Wisdom-Son of Proverbs 8 and 30 when he identifies that God has brought believers "into the kingdom of the Son" (Col 1:13), who is "the image of the invisible God, the first-born over all creation" (1:15), the one who "is before all things, and in [whom] all things hold together (1:17), and the one in whom all God's "fullness" dwells (1:19).

Summary

As Yahweh's eternally begotten Son, Wisdom was the beginning of God's way, which manifests itself both in Yahweh's appointing Wisdom as his representative even before creation and by Wisdom's serving joy-fully and faithfully beside Yahweh at creation. Alongside the Father, the Wisdom-Son was one of the Holy Ones, which implies the Father and Son enjoyed a unified nature but were distinct in person. As Son, Wisdom incarnate would represent the Father by reigning as the mes-sianic King, fulfilling the promises to David and standing greater than Solomon as the bestower of wisdom on future children of God. Thus, Proverbs 8:22–31 magnifies Jesus through a blend of principles 5 (Jesus as Yahweh) and 6 (Jesus as Ethical Ideal).

Isaiah 42:1-9: The Servant-Person Will Give Justice and Bring Light to the World

An Overview of Isaiah 42:1-4

Inspecting Isaiah 42:1–9 (close context) reveals that these verses provide a direct messianic prediction (P1) in that they communicate the servant-person will faithfully give justice to the nations and be empowered by Yahweh as a covenant for the people and light for the nations. After identifying the world's folly in pursuing idolatry (41:21–29), Yahweh advances his servant as the remedy—one who will care for the wounded and the weak and faithfully give justice to the nations. Yahweh upholds and delights in his servant, who is endowed by God's Spirit (42:1). Yahweh then highlights both the nature and certainty of the justice that the servant will bring. He will give justice "to the nations" (42:1d), and he will do so "in faithfulness" (42:3c). His pattern of justice will be neither self-advancing and assertive (42:1d) nor dismissive and abusive (42:3ab). And he will persevere until his task is accomplished—establishing justice throughout the earth and satisfying the longing coastlands with his law (42:4). The Lord of creation (42:5) commits to empower his servant as a covenant for people and a light for nations (42:6–7), all for the sake of his own name and purpose (42:8–9).

Significantly, 42:10–17 rings out that Yahweh will accomplish the very things he calls his servant to fulfill: the coastlands will sing his praise (42:10, 12; cf. 42:4) as he leads the blind (42:16; cf. 42:7), shines light into darkness (42:16; cf. 42:6), and receives the worship he is due (42:17; cf. 42:8). These links suggest that the servant of 42:1–9 is closely associated with Yahweh and serves as the very means by which God fulfills his restoring work.

Isaiah's King, Servant, and Anointed Conqueror

Isaiah 42:1–9 is the first of four Servant Songs (cf. 49:1–13; 50:4–11; 52:13–53:12), which, along with many other texts from Isaiah, Christians have long believed anticipate an eschatological king, servant, and anointed conqueror who will reign in righteousness over a righteous community (11:1–9; 32:1–8), save the Lord's multiethnic people by providing them righteousness (49:6; 53:11; 54:14, 17), and effect righteousness by overcoming opposition, delivering the wounded and bound, and inaugurating the new creation (59:21; 61:1–3; 63:1–6).[45] Yahweh chooses his servant (42:1; 49:7), empowers him with his Spirit (42:1; cf. 11:2; 59:21; 61:1) and word (49:2; 50:4), and declares him righteous (50:8–9; 53:11). Bearing no guilt (50:5, 8–9; 53:9) and triumphing through struggle and abuse (42:4; 49:4, 7; 50:6–7; 53:3, 7–8), this servant will instruct and give justice to the nations (42:1, 3–4; cf. 9:7; 11:3–4), sustain the weary by his teaching (42:3; 50:4), be highly exalted and praised by kings (49:7; 52:13, 15), and restore Israel and save many from the world (49:6; 53:11). He will accomplish this by serving as a vicarious, atoning sacrifice (53:4–6, 10–12) and as a covenant for people and light for nations (42:6–7; 49:6, 8; 55:3; cf. 54:10; 60:3) in order to herald the good news (52:7; cf. 61:1), heal the disabled (42:7;

---

45. See J. Alec Motyer, *The Prophecy of Isaiah: An Introduction and Commentary* (Downers Grove, IL: InterVarsity Press, 1993), 13–16.

53:5; cf. 61:1), free captives (42:7; 49:9; cf. 61:1), generate a context of security and justice (42:3; cf. 4:6; 9:7; 11:6–9; 61:2), and create lives that evidence the new creation (53:11; cf. 4:2–4; 61:3), all for God's glory (42:8; 49:3; cf. 11:9; 61:3). At least six key conceptual connections working along all three interpretive contexts indicate that Isaiah's portraits of king, servant, and anointed conqueror throughout the book all refer to the same person:

1. Yahweh endows this figure with his Spirit and the word (Isa 11:1–2, 4; 42:1; 49:1–3; 50:4; 59:21; 61:1–3).
2. Righteousness distinguishes both the person (Isa 9:7; 50:8; 53:11; 61:10) and his work (11:4; 53:11; 54:17; 61:3).
3. The prophet equates the individual with the Davidic descendant who would be God's Son and reign forever over God's kingdom (Isa 9:6–7; 55:3; cf. 2 Sam 7:14).
4. Operating as a signal or banner to which the nations will gather (Isa 11:10, 12; 49:22; 62:10), this person will reign over and redeem a global people (Isa 11:6–12; 19:23–25), extend revelation and salvation to the ends of the earth (Isa 42:1–4; 49:6; 52:13–53:12; 55:3–5), and deliver a multiethnic remnant (Isa 56:6–8; 66:19–20)—all of whom Yahweh will centralize in a restored Zion that will stretch across the new creation (Isa 2:2–4; 11:6–9; 54:2–3; 55:5; 59:20; 60:1–22; 62:11–12; 65:17–18, 25; 66:20–22).
5. The person is human yet truly God. He is both David's descendant (Isa 11:1) and the source from which David came (11:10)—"Immanuel [God with us]" (7:14) and the "mighty God" (9:6). While bearing human form and ancestry (52:13; 53:2) and experiencing human suffering (49:7; 50:6; 52:14), he was sinless and righteous (50:5, 8–9; 53:9, 11) and the very "arm of Yahweh" (53:1), who is endowed with Yahweh's garments of salvation (11:5; 59:17; 61:10) and through whom Yahweh delivers and conquers (51:9; 52:10; 59:16; 63:5).
6. The New Testament clearly associates Jesus with the king (e.g., Matt 1:23; 4:15–16; Rom 15:12), servant (Matt 8:17; 12:18–20; Acts 8:32; 13:34; 26:22–23; 1 Pet 2:22–25), and anointed conqueror (Luke 4:18–19).

Isaiah's Messianic Hope in the Servant-Person

Recognizably, some, like the Ethiopian eunuch, have wondered whether the servant of the Servant Songs refers to Isaiah himself: "Who is the prophet talking about, himself or someone else?" (Acts 8:34). Yahweh refers to the prophet as "my servant" in Isaiah 20:3, and Isaiah may be "his servant" in 44:26 (ESV). The autobiographical, first-person speech in the second and third Servant Songs (49:1–6; 50:1–9; cf. 61:1–3, 10–11; 63:1–6) certainly could also point in this direction, but it does not explain the biographical portrayal of the servant in third person in 42:1–9 and 52:13–53:12.[46] Moreover, the prophet appears to include himself among those for whom the servant's atoning death works (53:6), and no one who is merely human has sprinkled many nations with atoning blood (52:15) and served to see God's "salvation . . . reach to the ends of the earth" (49:6).

The term "servant" occurs twenty times in Isaiah 40–53, always in the singular. Some of these instances clearly refer to the collective and rebellious nation of Israel (42:19, 22; 43:8, 10). But this chosen servant does not need to fear, for the Lord will strengthen him (41:8–10) and pour out his Spirit on his offspring, making them blossom in new creation (44:1–5). With predictive certainty, as if already accomplished, God has forgiven his servant's sins and redeemed him. He will confirm this coming redemption by raising up Cyrus to return Israel from Babylon to the land (44:21–28; 48:17–20).

Many texts, including 41:8–10, support reading the "servant" in 42:1–4 as corporate Israel. The LXX made this view explicit by including "Jacob" and "Israel" before "servant" and "chosen," respectively, thus reversing the order found in 41:8 but identifying the same referent—the nation. However, the following reasons lead me to see the eight instances of "servant" in the Servant Songs (42:1; 49:3, 5–7; 50:10; 52:13; 53:11) (C1) as direct prophecies (P1) of the singular eschatological messiah of whom the earlier and later parts of the book speak.[47]

46. G. P. Hugenberger, "The Servant of the Lord in the 'Servant Songs' of Isaiah: A Second Moses Figure," in *The Lord's Anointed: Interpretation of Old Testament Messianic Texts*, ed. Philip E. Satterthwaite, Richard S. Hess, and Gordon J. Wenham (Grand Rapids: Baker Academic, 1995), 113.

47. Cf. Hugenberger, "Servant of the Lord," 108–11; Walter C. Kaiser Jr., "The Identity and Mission of the 'Servant of the Lord,'" in *The Gospel according to Isaiah 53: Encountering*

1. The Lord gives his servant as "a covenant for the people and a light for the gentiles" (42:6; cf. 49:8). The singular "people" contrasts with the plural "gentiles" and refers to collective Israel. The servant here is not the people but represents them, and his covenant-mediating sacrifice will be for them and on behalf of the broader nations (cf. 55:3–5).

2. Isaiah 49:3 and 6 explicitly distinguish the servant-person named Israel from the servant-people also named Israel. Yahweh gives the former a mission to restore the latter and also to save peoples to the ends of the earth.

3. The chosen servant of Isaiah 49:1–13 is the one Yahweh redeems, whom kings worship, and who is "despised and abhorred by the nation" (49:7; cf. 50:6; 52:15; 53:3).

4. Unlike the nation of Israel (Isa 1:4; 42:18–25; 43:8–13; 46:12; 59:2; 64:7), within Isaiah (C1), the servant-person is righteous (50:8; 53:11) and guiltless (50:9), having not rebelled (50:5) and done no violence or deceit (53:9). Indeed, he can operate as "an offering for guilt" (53:10 ESV), which Leviticus 5:15, 18 declare had to be "without defect." None in the nation could save (Isa 59:16), so Yahweh would act by raising up the messiah who stands distinct from the nation of Israel, just like the servant from our passage in question (cf. 42:6; 53:6).

5. In Isaiah 53:1 the prophet queries, "Who has believed our message and to whom has the arm of the Lord been revealed?" (cf. John 12:38; Rom 10:16). In the close context (C1), the "arm of the Lord" is none other than the "servant" (Isa 53:10, 12), whom God reveals to an unbelieving people (53:1) and to believing outsiders (52:13; cf. Rom 15:21). Later Yahweh asserts, "All day long I have held out my hands to an obstinate people" (Isa 65:2; cf. Rom 10:20), and this people is none other than corporate Israel, whom, therefore, we cannot equate with the servant.

6. This servant was "cut off," and Yahweh "punished" him "for the transgression of my people" (Isa 53:8). The stress here is on

the *Suffering Servant in Jewish and Christian Theology*, ed. Darrell L. Bock and Mitch Glaser (Grand Rapids: Kregel Academic, 2012), 89–92.

penal substitution, with God's just wrath falling on the substitute rather than on the sinners. A collective servant does not die on behalf of itself and still live, but the servant-person does just this and brings righteousness and life to the many (53:11).[48]

7. The nation Israel was incapable of fulfilling the demands of worldwide justice and restoration for the weak within Isaiah 42:1–4. Israel's inability to accomplish such a task suggests that an individual messianic figure rather than the nation is the servant from verse 1.

The New Testament Identifies Isaiah's Servant-Person as the Christ

Matthew notes how Jesus's healing ministry fulfills Isaiah's assertion: "He took our illnesses and bore our diseases" (Matt 8:17 ESV; cf. Isa 53:4). Peter, too, after noting how "Christ suffered for you," cited Isaiah 53:7–9, stressing how Jesus never sinned or retaliated under abuse as he bore our sins and brought healing (1 Pet 2:21–25). When the Jews rejected Messiah Jesus (John 12:38; Rom 10:16) and the gentiles received him (Rom 15:21), they fulfilled Isaiah's prophecy (Isa 52:15–53:1).

More specifically with respect to Isaiah 42:1–9, Yahweh marked Jesus as his promised "chosen" one (Luke 9:35; cf. 23:35), and Jesus identifies himself with Isaiah's Spirit-empowered agent of God's good news who would give sight to the blind (Matt 11:5; Luke 4:18–19; cf. Isa 42:1, 7; 61:1–2). Matthew freely translates the Hebrew text of Isaiah 42:1–4 in its entirety, declaring that Jesus willingly healed those who followed him "to fulfill what was spoken by the prophet Isaiah" (Matt 12:17–21). While one could posit that Matthew treats Jesus as ultimate Israel (via typology or *sensus plenior*) or portrays Jesus's healings as a second fulfillment after the nation of Israel's prior acts (whatever those would be),[49] my argument above clarifies that Isaiah (and Matthew) would have seen Jesus's person and work *directly fulfilling* the earlier predictions (P1). Drawing together Isaiah's images of the hoped-for king

---

48. Thomas D. Petter, "The Meaning of Substitutionary Righteousness in Isa. 53:11: A Summary of the Evidence," *TJ* 32 (2011): 165–89.

49. For example, Craig L. Blomberg, "Matthew," in *Commentary on the New Testament Use of the Old Testament*, ed. G. K. Beale and D. A. Carson (Grand Rapids: Baker Academic, 2007), 43.

and servant (Isa 9:2; 42:7; 49:6), Zechariah highlighted how Jesus would "give light to those who sit in darkness" (Luke 1:79 ESV). Similarly, Simeon stressed that Jesus was "a light for revelation to the gentiles, and the glory of your people Israel" (Luke 2:32; cf. Isa 42:6; Acts 26:23). Jesus claimed that he was "the light of the world" (John 8:12), and Paul asserted that Jesus brought "the message of light to his own people and to the gentiles" (Acts 26:23; cf. Isa 42:7; 49:6)—a mission he continued in Christ (Acts 13:46–47; 26:18). Without exception, the New Testament identifies the individual of Isaiah's Servant Songs as Jesus.

Summary

Isaiah directly predicted a messiah who would be king, servant, and anointed conqueror (P1). Isaiah 42:1–9 speaks of a servant-person who would right every wrong, heal the hurting, proclaim God's law, and mediate a covenant that would bring saving light to many, resulting in blind eyes seeing and bound lives being freed. Jesus realizes Isaiah's hopes and ours.

Conclusion

Scripture bears an overarching unity and Christocentric framework, which we grow to appreciate only when God grants us spiritual sight and discloses to us the revealed mystery of the gospel through Jesus's saving work (Rom 16:25–26; 2 Cor 3:14; 4:6). Christian interpreters are uniquely qualified to allow the Bible to speak in accordance with its own contours, structures, language, and flow. Doing so should disclose both an overall consistent message concerning Christ and varied organic (i.e., natural, unforced) salvation-historical and literary-canonical connections between the parts, all of which directly or indirectly relate to Christ, in whom "all things hold together" (Col 1:17).

As Christians, we must approach the Old Testament through Christ and for Christ, using a multi-orbed approach that assesses Scripture's close, continuing, and complete contexts (C1–3) and considers in what way(s) the Old Testament magnifies Jesus. I propose seven possible ways: (P1) direct messianic predictions; (P2) the salvation-historical story and trajectories; (P3) similarities and contrasts between the old and new ages, creations, and covenants; (P4) typology; (P5) Yahweh's identity and activity; (P6) ethical ideals; and (P7) obedience to the law. Interpreting in the light of all three contexts, I identify Christ through typology and direct messianic prediction in Genesis 22:1–19, through Yahweh's identity and ethical ideals in Proverbs 8:22–31, and through direct messianic prediction in Isaiah 42:1–4.

JOHN GOLDINGAY

I agree with Dr. DeRouchie that we must approach the Old Testament through Christ. And I agree that Jesus is the climax to the biblical story. However, I want to suggest different implications from the ones he describes.

Christocentric or Theocentric?

My key question concerns who is central in the Scriptures. Dr. DeRouchie speaks of Christ being central. Actually, God is central. I know he recognizes that Jesus is the second person of the Trinity. But focusing on the second person risks obscuring the way God as Father, Son, and Holy Spirit appear in the Scriptures. Dr. DeRouchie says that Jesus is "the beginning and end of the Bible, holding it and all else together (Col 1:16–17)" (182). But Colossians is making a statement about creation, not about the Scriptures.

I offer two main arguments for this point about the Scriptures being theocentric. The first is that Jesus came to make it possible for us to know God, came to enable us to "become children of God," and came to make God known (John 1:12, 16).

The other argument coheres with that one. From beginning to end, the First Testament talks about God. Very occasionally it talks about a new David who will come in the future, but mostly it talks about God. That does mean it is talking about Jesus, because the God of the First Testament is the God whom the church will later recognize as Father, Son, and Holy Spirit. But it also means that the First Testament's talk about Jesus is not confined to its talk about the messiah. Throughout these Scriptures, God is relating to his people as the God of grace and truth. In due course Jesus is the visible embodiment of God as the God of grace and truth (John 1:17–18), but throughout the First Testament, God is the one who relates to his people as grace and truth. Throughout the First Testament, God had been letting himself be rejected, yet refusing to settle for that rejection, and refusing to reject his people in return. In effect, he was being crucified throughout the scriptural story, though his people couldn't see that. So eventually he does this extraordinary thing of becoming a human being, and again letting himself be rejected. He is now literally crucified, but he again refuses to accept rejection. He again refuses to reject his people in return, and declines to stay dead, so that he can then say, *Now will you believe in me?*

It is in this connection, then, that we read the Scriptures through Christ. When we read his story in the Gospels, it takes us back to the Scriptures to see the implications in the text itself regarding God. God is the center of the First Testament Scriptures, the center of the New Testament Scriptures, the focus of our worship, and the object of our service. Our challenge and invitation as we study the Scriptures is not to find Jesus hidden behind them but to see God openly there.

Pointing to Jesus?

Dr. DeRouchie's summary of Genesis 22:1–19 describes Abraham as showing that "he truly believes that Yahweh will fulfill his promise of a singular male offspring through Isaac who will deliver and bless all nations" (192). Let's imagine the story being told among the Israelites in Egypt before the exodus or being read as a synagogue lesson in the time of Ezra and Nehemiah. How might Moses or Ezra have expounded it? There is nothing there to tell expositor or people that Abraham was believing in such a promise or that Isaac was a type of a coming messiah. If that was the meaning of the story, why does the story not indicate any pointers toward that meaning? Dr. DeRouchie speaks of such stories as pointing to Christ. But where are the signposts that could be seen by someone hearing or reading the story?

Dr. DeRouchie makes a key converse point regarding his approach when commenting that "types move to antitype (e.g., Rom 5:14; 1 Cor 10:6, 11)" (182). But these texts do not say that. Romans 5 says that Adam *is* a type, not that he *was* a type. First Corinthians 10 talks about things that happened as types *for us* (more literally, "as our types"); although as types they happened to the Israelites, they were written down "for the cautioning of us to whom the end of the ages arrived." What happened in Eden and in the aftermath of the exodus did not have significance as a type for Adam and the Israelites themselves. It only came to have significance as a type when Jesus came and when Paul read the story about these events. Types do not move to antitypes. Antitypes move to types. Antitypes create types. Antitypes point to types, not the other way around.

Dr. DeRouchie similarly refers to Matthew 2:15 with its quotation from Hosea 11:1 as an indication that "the Old Testament's history" is one of its aspects that "point[s] to Jesus" (182). But in Hosea 11:1 God looks back to the exodus and recalls, "Out of Egypt I called my son." Neither Exodus nor Hosea suggests that the exodus story points forward to anyone or anything. Exodus makes clear the sort of thing that people are supposed to learn from the story—for instance, that they need to live lives of commitment to God (e.g., Exod 20:1–17). Hosea makes the same assumption: he appeals to the exodus to draw attention to the failure of God's son Israel. The exodus was important because of what it meant to Israel. It was a bonus that it also eventually helped people understand Jesus. It did not in itself point to Jesus.

In Jesus, Dr. DeRouchie comments, "the Old Testament's problems find their solution" (182). I wonder what problems does he have in mind? Romans 3:25–26 does suggest a question about whether the holy God can forgive sin, but as with types and antitypes, the "problem" emerges only in light of the "solution." The First Testament doesn't think that God has a problem about forgiving his people's sin. As the God of grace and mercy, he was quite willing to carry their sin for them, as he was doing all through their story. He was like a father who readily forgives his children's wrongdoing. Another possible problem is that many of the promises God gave through his prophets did not come true in First Testament times, though again the First Testament doesn't show much indication that it sees this as a problem. Jesus is then the fulfillment of prophecy, but we have to be wary about how we articulate that fact. Jews are inclined to point out that the Scriptures promised a reign of peace and righteousness, and that reign has not come about, so therefore Jesus is not the Messiah! It is a troublesome argument.

I'm glad Dr. DeRouchie notes the New Testament's important statement in this connection, that all God's promises find their "Yes" in Christ (2 Cor 1:20). But that comment doesn't mean they have come true yet. His coming provides us with a confirmation that God will fulfill his promises.

Seeing Things During and Seeing Things After

In Dr. DeRouchie's opening statement, he says that Jesus "empowered [the disciples] to see a unified, overarching message in the Old Testament regarding a suffering and sovereign messiah who would spark a global mission of reconciliation with God (Luke 24:45–47)" (181). Doesn't this statement go far beyond what that Scripture says? And it doesn't match the First Testament Scriptures themselves, does it?

If there might be a mismatch, we need to return to Luke and ask whether we have interpreted him correctly. He said that Jesus opened the disciples' minds to understand that it is written in the Scriptures that "the Messiah will suffer and rise from the dead on the third day, and repentance for the forgiveness of sins will be preached in his name to all nations" (24:46–47). It's quite a ways from that statement to Dr. DeRouchie's description of an overarching message.

A perspective from outside does sometimes help one understand something, but one expects then to be able to say, "Oh, yes, I can see that now." Yet when one goes back to the First Testament from Dr. DeRouchie's description of the overarching message, it doesn't have that effect, does it? One can read page after page of the First Testament and not be able to see the overall message Dr. DeRouchie describes. The same consideration emerges from the comment that "the Old Testament's . . . prophecy (Acts 3:18) . . . point[s] to Jesus" (182). Yes, Jesus brings a fulfillment of God's promises. But isn't this statement too sweeping? Acts 3:18 says that "God fulfilled what he had foretold through all the prophets, saying that his Messiah would suffer." But that is not literally true. There is nothing like talk of the Messiah suffering in, say, Joel or Obadiah or Nahum, is there? Peter surely speaks hyperbolically.

I suggest a different inference from Luke 24 and Acts 3, that these statements might point in the direction I suggested in the first part of this response (I use the metaphor of "pointing" to infer something that was not what the person said, but something that it might make us think of—this parallels Dr. DeRouchie's use of it!). One might say that all the prophets speak of a God who lets himself be rejected. And the First Testament does contain an overarching message about a God who was prepared to cope with all manner of resistance and rejection in order to take the world to its destiny. The New Testament then tells us about the way that insistence came to its climax in Jesus. But that doesn't mean the First Testament's story "points to Christ."

My wife and I once went on a walk through the countryside to get to a certain place, and the walk was more adventurous than we had expected. We had to cross a rickety bridge over a stream and climb over a five-barred gate just before we reached our destination, and my wife (who used to live in Arizona) was pretty worried about possible snakes in the grass. This past Friday we walked to the same destination, now knowing not only where we were going but also how to get there, and the walk was quite straightforward.

Even on the first occasion, the destination was clear and everything on the way actually did lead to the destination, but as we stood at the rickety bridge from which we could not see our destination, we could not have said that the bridge pointed that way. The bridge and the gate existed for their own sake, not for the sake of our journey. They were not designed to lead toward the place where we were going, and they bore no signposts. Their own importance did not lie there. But they did constitute our route to the destination so that they came to have that significance for us.

Our first walk corresponds better to the scriptural story than the second one does. God had a wide-ranging perspective (a drone's perspective?) concerning the journey on which he was taking Israel. He knew about the rickety bridges and five-barred gates (the parable is not an allegory, but I am tempted: is the rickety bridge the exile, and is the five-barred gate the Torah, and the snakes . . . ?). But they were not designed to lead toward Jesus, and they bore no signposts. There was no more indication that the exodus pointed to Jesus than indication that the bridge or the gate pointed to our destination.

We don't get to understand the meaning of the exodus or Sinai or the exile or the Second Temple by thinking too much about Jesus. The First Testament can help us understand Jesus, but it's also worth understanding in its own right without thinking too much about Jesus. After all, it's God who matters.

TREMPER LONGMAN III

I resonate with many of the assumptions of Dr. DeRouchie's chapter. I want to say a hearty "Amen!" when I read his headings:

- "Christ Is Central in God's Redemptive-Historical Purposes"
- "Jesus Is Central to Biblical Interpretation"
- "The Old Testament Anticipates That God's People Will Only Understand Its Full Meaning When the Messiah Comes"
- "The New Testament Identifies Jesus as the Lens for Fully Understanding the Old Testament's Meaning"

These principles for the most part are also key to the Christotelic approach I develop in my chapter. That said, not surprisingly, since, after all, this book presents five different views, I recognize differences in how we act on these basic ideas and maybe what we exactly mean by these statements in the final analysis.

There are two general areas where I find myself in a different place than DeRouchie. First of all, he appears to think that the Old Testament authors, readers, and even characters, like Abraham, were more aware than I think they were about the future import of their words. He does make a distinction between the "rebel majority" of Israelites who did not understand and the prophets whom he believes had an awareness, though not a full awareness (183–84). He has not convinced me this is the case.

Let's take his comments about Abraham in Genesis 22 as a case in point. He argues that there are "at least two features within Genesis

22:1–19 (close context)" that "suggest that Abraham himself understood the predictive significance in his test" (196). Before considering these two features, let's begin by saying that it is impossible to get into the mind of a character just as it is difficult to get into the mind of the author of a written text. Also, the way Hebrew narrative works is that authors of biblical stories will foreground important matters through the presentation of actions and speech. I simply find that DeRouchie reads too much into the text to make his case (others may differ). Also, his interpretation at points depends on translations that are at best contested.

DeRouchie believes that Abraham's naming of the place of the sacrifice "Yahweh will see" signals that Abraham "recognized the replacement ram as a foreshadowing of how 'Yahweh will see' to fulfilling the offspring promise and overcome the curse with blessing (22:18)" (196). He believes that this shows us that Abraham "understood [the] predictive significance in his test" (196). He also cites 22:14, where the narrator informs the reader that "at the mount of Yahweh it will be seen" (22:14, DeRouchie's translation).

In the first place, DeRouchie's understanding depends on the translation of the relevant verb as "see" rather than an alternative possibility from the verb "provide" (accepted by most modern translations). It also depends on his translation of the verb in the future tense. He is, of course, correct that the imperfect verbal aspect should not be translated in the past, but it could be translated in the present: "God provides/sees" and "it is provided/seen." My point is not that DeRouchie's translation is wrong, but it is far from certain and therefore a kind of thin platform upon which to make the bold claim that the verb indicates that Abraham understood the predictive significance of the event.

But let's assume that DeRouchie's translation is correct or that he would make the same case whether one translates with the verb *see* or *provide*. I still think it is too much to say, for instance, that "it will be seen" (22:14) is "a perpetual statement of hope in the one we call the Christ" (196). It certainly is a statement of perpetual hope that into the future God will see or provide, but to say "in Christ" is going too far at least to make the case that Abraham was himself aware of the predictive significance of the event. I agree with Victor Hamilton when he says that these statements "give the entire narrative a certain timelessness. It witnesses to the gracious provisions of God."[1]

The second feature that DeRouchie finds indicative that Abraham had a sense of the predictive nature of the event is the three-day journey to Moriah. He asks, why make him walk to Moriah? Why not ask him to sacrifice Isaac right where he lived? He believes that Abraham might have asked himself those questions.

My response is we don't know why because the text does not tell us or let us know what Abraham was thinking, so it must not be important to the story. Again, it is problematic in my opinion to speculate what a character in a narrative was thinking when the text does not spell it out as it would if the narrator thought it important. DeRouchie's comments connecting the location, the person, the means, and the timing to the future messiah may have some merit when reading backward from the New Testament, but those things could not have been divined by Abraham at the time. Thus, this feature, too, in my opinion does not support his contention that Abraham recognized the predictive significance of this event.

In conclusion, I believe DeRouchie's interpretation of this passage to make his point is overfine—that is, it depends on too many contested exegetical decisions.[2] And in the final analysis, I would like to ask, what difference does it make? What is at stake whether or not Abraham (or the author of Genesis for that matter) understood the predictive nature of the event? I am not sure *predictive* is the right word to describe Genesis 22, but I agree that the story of the binding of Isaac has a typological significance to Christ's sacrifice. Whether or not Abraham had a sense of that is not important for it to be true.

I have similar questions about DeRouchie's interpretation of Proverbs 8. He does present a close context interpretation (similar to what I call a first reading), but his understanding of the chapter in its original context cannot be derived from the close context. Indeed, I don't think anyone

---

1. Victor P. Hamilton, *The Book of Genesis: Chapters 18–50*, NICOT (Grand Rapids: Eerdmans, 1995), 114.

2. This is a problem, at least from my perspective, with some of DeRouchie's other interpretations of texts, but space does not allow me to develop all of them.

would think of interpreting the chapter the way he does except in the light of the New Testament (and even then I would disagree with it).

DeRouchie's most unexpected move is to change the gender of Woman Wisdom in order to present her as the royal son. This involves two questionable interpretive decisions. The first is the most daring when he states that "the first-person speech ('I, me, my') mutes the feminine portrayal, thus allowing Wisdom to be both with God and of God" (201). DeRouchie simply asserts this without arguing for it, and it is clearly wrong. The chapter's first verse introduces her as a female: "Does not wisdom call out? Does not understanding raise *her* voice?" (8:1, emphasis added). When this woman speaks in the first person later, it does not mute her gender. Indeed, when Wisdom appears and speaks in Proverbs 1–9, she is a woman. The fact that her gender is *not* muted in Proverbs 8 throws a serious wrench into DeRouchie's close context reading.

A second problem is his assumption that the *royal* son(s) are the addressee of the wisdom in Proverbs. Admittedly, contrary to DeRouchie's ideas about the muting of Wisdom's gender, this interpretive decision has some minority support among interpreters and can be argued for on the basis of the superscription where Solomon is named and some of the wisdom is spoken to a son or sons. But most Proverbs scholars would not come to this conclusion for the final form of the book of Proverbs since it shows clear signs of what we might call democratization, so that we would be wrong to read the book of Proverbs in its canonical Old Testament setting as addressed to Solomon's royal son(s).

In the first place, the canonical book of Proverbs does not present itself throughout as the words of Solomon. That the book was not completed by Solomon is clear first by the fact that Hezekiah's men added material approximately three hundred years after Solomon, even if that material actually had a connection to the historical Solomon (25:1). Even more telling is that the book itself names other contributors ("the wise" [22:17; 24:23], Agur [30:1], Lemuel [31:1]), leaving open the possibility that other unnamed authors may have contributed. Indeed, many have thought that Proverbs 1:8–9:18 was composed by other(s) than Solomon, explaining the necessity of the superscription naming Solomon at 10:1.

But even more important is that the canonical form of the book is not addressed to specific son(s) of anybody in particular, not to speak of Solomon's sons. The preamble to the book (1:1–7) makes this clear when it explicitly names the implicit addressee of the book not as the son, royal or not, but as essentially everyone. Verses 4–5 set forth the purpose of the book:

> for giving prudence to those who are simple,
>> knowledge and discretion to the young—
> let the wise listen and add to their learning,
>> and let the discerning get guidance.

The book's audience is not the royal son but everyone from the most immature to the wise, because everyone can grow in wisdom.

When it comes to Isaiah 42, I will simply say I find DeRouchie's reading compelling as a second reading of the book (see my chapter). However, he presents it as a first reading and thus understands the text as a direct messianic prophecy. I express my own understanding of how Isaiah 42 anticipates Christ in my own chapter, and I won't repeat it here. I will simply say that from what we read in the New Testament, it appears that no one was reading Isaiah 42 in this way at the time of Jesus. My guess is that DeRouchie would chalk this up to the people's rebellious heart—maybe so, but I think if one reads Isaiah 42 in its historical and literary context, the two readings approach that I lay out in my chapter better accounts for what we have in the text.

Let me return to the beginning of my response to say that I do really resonate with much of DeRouchie's proposal in theory. I just believe that in his implementation he moves too quickly to impose a New Testament reading on what he presents as a reading in close context. Others may be persuaded, but so far I am not.

RESPONSE TO JASON S. DEROUCHIE
(THE RECEPTION-CENTERED, INTERTEXTUAL APPROACH)

HAVILAH DHARAMRAJ

What makes the redemptive-historical method particularly attractive to me is its determination to hold the two parts of the Christian canon together, and that, in the person and work of Jesus Christ. This is because, in South Asia, where I come from, the Old Testament is sometimes considered superfluous to the Christian faith. In some quarters, it might even be considered the sacred text of another religion, Judaism, whose deity is not Jesus. Considering that in my region religions and sacred texts live side by side, such thinking comes easily: as the Bhagavad Gita is to Hinduism and the Qur'an to Islam, as the Guru Granth is to Sikhism and the Zendavesta to Zoroastrianism, the Old Testament is to Judaism. The redemptive-historical method robustly challenges this deeply erroneous idea.

Further, the method seeks to unify the message of the two Testaments by reading a given text within its close, continuing, and canonical contexts. So Dr. DeRouchie's chapter tracked themes such as creation and divine kingship, showing the reader that the various parts of the Christian canon are in meaningful conversation with each other.

There are, however, at least three aspects of the method that I continue to mull over. The first is an assumption of the method, and the next two relate to the method itself.

First, the Old Testament is, at least to some degree, a mystery. Indeed, it is a mystery not only to modern readers but to ancient readers as well. Thus, "only in the latter days of the Messiah and the new covenant would God empower his people to more fully accept and understand his Old Testament word" (184). This is said to be true not only of the people but also, at times, of the human authors: "While the typological nature of an event, person, or institution was innately present from the beginning (1 Cor 10:6, 11), the full meaning (and perhaps even the predictive recognition) of that type may only have been understood in retrospect" (185). However, the three case studies indicate that all is not as clear "in retrospect" either. The three texts have to be decoded, and DeRouchie's process of demystifying the Old Testament texts often appeals to uncommon readings.

In the case study on the ordeal of Isaac, the discussion rests on the premise that the serpent-crushing "offspring" (*zera*) of the woman (Gen 3:15) is the exact same person as the "offspring" (*zera*) promised to Abraham—namely, Jesus. This contrasts with the regular reading that the offspring promised to Abraham is Isaac, and the extended offspring as numerous as the sand and stars is the nation of Israel. Indeed, the various tables of post-flood genealogy in Genesis—from the descendants of Ham and Japheth (10:1–20) to the descendants of Lot (19:37–38) to the descendants of Ishmael (25:12–18) to the descendants of Esau (36:1–43)—seem to form the backdrop against which the narrator throws into relief the burgeoning bloodline of Abraham from one single male infant—Isaac (21:2)—to the twelve eponymous ancestors of the nation Israel (46:8–25; 49:28).

With DeRouchie's interpretation of "offspring" in Genesis 22 departing from the plain sense as in the narrative, the blessing on Abraham requires to be read like this: "Because you [Abraham] have done this and not withheld your son, your only son [Isaac], I [YHWH] will surely bless you [Abraham] and make your offspring [Jesus] as numerous as the stars in the sky and as the sand of the seashore [i.e., the church of Christ]" (22:16b–17a). It is a reading that comes not without help from the redemptive-historical expert.

Similarly, in the case study on the Proverbs poem, Wisdom is identified with Jesus through the Hebrew verb *nsk* (by linking Prov 8:23 with the "only" other instance that shares its meaning, in Ps 2:6); through a preferred reading of the noun *'amon* (Prov 8:27); and through a reading of the noun *qedoshim* ("Holy One," 30:3b), which DeRouchie concedes is not held by "most interpreters." The case study on the Isaianic text rests on the use of the noun "servant" across Isaiah 40–52, calling for differentiating between (twelve) instances in which the term "servant" is referring to the nation Israel and (eight) instances in which DeRouchie sees "servant" as a direct reference to Jesus.

With this, the Old Testament seems like a cryptic crossword in which every clue, both Across and Down, yields the one answer: JESUS. This deciphering is beyond the scope of the Common Reader and requires the services of a specialist. The method (as it is presented in this chapter) might reinforce what the Common Reader suspected all along to be the case: the Old Testament is esoteric and is best left to academics.

Second, reading the Old Testament is largely a dot-joining exercise. In this method, the close context (C1) isn't the immediate literary matrix, that is, the text immediately preceding and following. The boundaries of C1 are taken to be the book. This allows for leaps across the book in the search for associations. Genesis 22 was first linked to Genesis 3:15, based on the word "offspring" (*zera'*). Genesis 3:15 was linked to the *toledoth* formulas ("this is the account of the family line of X") and genealogies that recur across the book's telling of the ancestral narratives. These were then tied to the instances in the Abraham story in which Abraham is promised "offspring" (13:15–16; 15:5; 17:4; 22:17–18; 26:3–4). The "dots" that are being joined are the keyword ("offspring") and the key motif of genealogies and bloodlines that runs through Genesis.

If, instead, we allowed C1 to be the text on either side of Genesis 22, this is what we might see. Interwoven into the story of the "father of faith" are stories of the non-chosen "other." Right from the call of Abraham (12:1) to his death and burial (25:11), the narrator introduces other characters: Pharaoh (12:10–20); Hagar (16:1–16); Abimelek (20:1–18; 21:22–34); Hagar and Ishmael (21:8–21); the Hittites at Hebron (23:1–20); and Ishmael (25:9). In these stories, the expected black-and-white categories dissolve. Surprisingly, the chosen and the "other" both attract God's interest. Take, as a case in point, the parallel relationship between Genesis 22 and the chapter immediately prior, which tells the story of the expulsion of Hagar and her son Ishmael.

Besides the parallels that run right across the two stories, consider how they end. God provides for both the boys. "The angel of God" halts Ishmael's death cries (21:17), while "the angel of the Lord" (22:11) intervenes to save the unresisting Isaac. The angel calls Hagar by name (21:17), just as he calls Abraham by name (22:11). Both Hagar and

Abraham "see" alternatives by which to save their sons' lives (21:19; 22:13). God shows Hagar a well that she had not noticed so far. Abraham similarly sees a ram for the sacrifice. Just as Ishmael receives a life-giving drink, Isaac is literally released from death. Both Ishmael and Isaac are guaranteed a blessing, each to his own measure (21:18; 22:17–18). Ishmael receives the promise that he will become a "great nation." Isaac receives the promise that his descendants will be as numerous as the sand and stars.

It would appear, then, that the narrator "has created a sustained and serious biblical reflection on 'the other.'"[1] If this is the case, the redemptive-historical method appears to miss appreciating—and appropriating for faith and practice—the rich (theological) tapestry the narrator is weaving. Rather than pay attention to the picture of God and his world that is emerging through his skillful storytelling, the method is looking for "dots" that it can join to form another, superimposed image.

Similarly, in the case of the Wisdom poem of Proverbs 8, the most significant "close context" was found in 30:1–6, toward the end of the book. This overrides the consideration that the book is an anthology. While Proverbs 8 is in the collection of "the proverbs of Solomon son of David," Proverbs 30 is a collection of the "sayings of Agur son of Jakeh." The C1 for the Wisdom poem might be better limited to Proverbs 1–9, the unity of which is generally accepted.

Third, the world of the Old Testament text need not be factored into the reading. The method applied in this chapter proceeded more like systematic theology than biblical theology in that the reading of the text was largely ahistorical. In the study of the ordeal of Isaac, the question was asked, "Was Isaac to die as a substitute or a sinner?" The answer was arrived at like this: "Scripture most commonly uses the language of 'burnt offering' with respect to substitution, and nothing in the close context (C1) draws attention to a wickedness in Isaac demanding immediate justice (contrast Deut 9:4–6). Hence, God likely sets Isaac forth as a vicarious sacrifice standing in for the sinner Abraham or a broader community" (194).

---

1. Adriane Leveen, "Reading the Seams," *JSOT* 29 (2005): 280.

The question, "Was Isaac to die as a substitute or sinner?" might not have arisen if we had read the story informed by the ancient West Asian practice of child sacrifice. The sacrifice of a firstborn son in order to gain the favor of the patron deity is well attested. A thirteenth-century tablet from the Canaanite city of Ugarit contains a prayer to Baal promising him a firstborn child if Baal will deliver the city from a siege.[2] This is supported by a bas relief on the wall of a temple in Karnak, Egypt, of similar date, showing Egyptians storming the Canaanite city of Ashkelon. The city's desperate response is to drop children over the walls onto the heads of the Egyptian army below.[3] Depictions of a similar practice are found in Egyptian reliefs in Medinet Habu, Abu Simbel, and Beit el-Wali,[4] giving us to understand that child sacrifice was not at all uncommon. Evidence in biblical narrative is best found in 2 Kings 3:4–27, where the coalition of Israel and Judah has overrun Moab, c. 850 BC. As a last resort, its king, Mesha, "took his firstborn son, who was to succeed him as king, and offered him as a sacrifice on the city wall" (cf. 2 Kgs 16:3; 21:6). In non-war situations, Hiel appears to have protected his rebuilding of Jericho against Joshua's ancient curse (Josh 6:26) by sacrificing his oldest and youngest sons (1 Kgs 16:34). (Cases of kidnapped children offered as foundation sacrifices are not unknown even in present-day India.) The understanding in all these cases is that the sacrifice of one's child pleases deity "precisely" because "the child was treasured" as one's "most valuable possession."[5] It can be argued that in Genesis 22 Abraham understands that YHWH is demanding of him this ultimate expression of devotion.[6] What he does not (yet) know is that—unlike the bloodthirsty gods of the land—YHWH detests human sacrifice (Deut 18:9–10), and that this demand is only a test of that devotion.

---

2. Baruch Margalit, "Why Mesha King of Moab Sacrificed His Oldest Son," *BAR* 12.6 (1986): 76.

3. Frank J. Yurco, "3,200-Year-Old Picture of Israelites found in Egypt," *BAR* 16.5 (1990): 20–38.

4. Anthony Spalinger, "A Canaanite Ritual Found in Egyptian Reliefs," *JSSEA* 8 (1978): 47–60.

5. Francis Anderson and David Noel Freedman, *Micah: A New Translation with Introduction and Commentary*, AB 24E (New York: Doubleday, 2000), 524.

6. See Alice Logan, "Rehabilitating Jephthah," *JBL* 128 (2009): 678.

In summary, it appears that the method approaches the Old Testament with not so much a *key* as with a fishing net. And since the net is a large one—with seven parameters (P1 to P7)—it is bound to catch *something* every time it is lowered into the water. Once Christ has been netted out, the text is reduced to a pool of fish-less water, perhaps even of negligible theological significance. That, it seems to me, is an issue the method could attend to.

RESPONSE TO JASON S. DEROUCHIE
(THE PREMODERN APPROACH)

CRAIG A. CARTER

I agree with nearly all that Dr. DeRouchie has written in this chapter. Any potential differences that might exist between us would concern what he does not explicitly say but may well be presuming to be the case. The chapter is the mirror image of my chapter in that it is primarily a description of the way in which biblical theologians interpret Scripture, but it only briefly explains why biblical theologians are justified in interpreting Scripture as they do. My chapter focuses primarily on the rationale for christological interpretation and is light on actual exegesis. DeRouchie's exegesis of the three passages is outstanding and exactly the kind of interpretation my approach aspires to generate. However, the reader is left to speculate as to the reasons why DeRouchie feels constrained to interpret the Old Testament christologically. Of course, he stands in the mainstream of the Christian church in doing so, and I would agree that this procedure is justified. But *why* is it justified?

The question is worth raising because many biblical interpreters today would not agree with his approach. Some would see his procedure as reading a Christian interpretation into the Hebrew Bible, which unjustly appropriates the sacred Scriptures of a different religion. DeRouchie would likely respond that he is not reading Jesus into the Old Testament text but discovering that the Old Testament text is best interpreted as foreshadowing Jesus as the Messiah. And, of course, I would agree. But the non-messianic, rabbinic interpreter would likely not agree because he would be convinced of the interpretation that rejects Jesus of Nazareth as the Messiah. Such a person would see DeRouchie's approach as injection of Christian bias into the interpretation of Jewish sacred texts. We should not simply rely on the institutional dominance of the Christian church in society or the long history of this sort of interpretation to justify it as a "fact on the ground." The issue requires that we see it as justifiable in principle. Should it ever have started in the first place?

Another class of interpreter is the secular skeptic who rejects the miraculous and any theory of inspiration that could enable a miracle, such as predictive prophecy, for example. Such a person would not be inclined to accept much of what DeRouchie sees as legitimate interpretation. DeRouchie's response to such a skeptic would, undoubtedly, revolve around his confession of the church's doctrine of inspiration of Scripture. Here, unlike the previous example, DeRouchie is on stronger ground because the doctrine of inspiration is essential for biblical interpreters and a prerequisite for faithful interpretation, assuming that biblical interpreters are responsible first and foremost to the church and not to the secularized academy. I would note that this is a point where biblical studies requires and is based on systematic theology; good biblical interpretation requires a sound doctrine of Scripture. Thus, biblical interpretation and dogmatic theology need each other. It is not the case that biblical studies scholars do not need doctrine because they just interpret the text from a neutral perspective and then doctrine comes later on the basis of exegesis. The progression is not simply linear from exegesis to biblical theology to doctrine. Once we have doctrines in place, we go back to Scripture and do a "second exegesis" in which we often discover deeper meaning in the text.

I want to point out three strengths I see in this chapter and then go back to the question of how to respond to the charge of "reading Jesus into" the Old Testament.

The Strengths of DeRouchie's Approach

The first strength of this chapter is that it is thoroughly Christocentric. DeRouchie sees Jesus's teaching in Luke 24 as a basic principle of Christian discipleship that one follows Jesus by imitating his interpretation of the Old Testament Scriptures as testifying to him as the Messiah. Here we see the self-involving logic of biblical interpretation, which has been central to the church's tradition all throughout church history. In analyzing Luke 24, one realizes that one's own relationship to Jesus is determined by whether one agrees with his clear and uncompromising view of the Old Testament as testifying to him. If one rejects the view of Jesus on this point, one is no longer a neutral interpreter because one would now be operating in opposition to the expressly stated teachings of Jesus. On the other hand, if one accepts the teaching of Jesus on this point, one is no longer a neutral interpreter because one is now a disciple seeking to learn from Jesus and his apostles, which means one is now engaged in the project of faith seeking understanding. Since Jesus forces such decisions on the reader, the upshot is that neutrality in biblical interpretation is not possible. Nowhere does this become more obvious than with regard to the question of seeing Jesus in the Old Testament.

A second strength of DeRouchie's approach is that it is multifaceted. His seven "Principles for Seeing and Celebrating Christ in His Scriptures" are helpful because they account for the diversity of form in the Scriptures and encourage interpreters to avoid imposing a rigid methodological straitjacket on the text that fails to take sufficient account of the diversity of ways in which God speaks through various genres of literature. Since he begins from Luke 24, his working assumption is that Christ is there somehow in the Old Testament text, and the task is to figure out *how* he is there. This approach allows various types of reading strategies to be employed and allows the interpretive flexibility needed for the task.

There is no one right method for all texts, whether that be a literary approach, a historical approach, a prosopological approach, or a typological approach. And no set of methodological principles systematized into a set of actions to be performed on every text mechanically will ever be adequate for biblical interpretation.

A third strength of DeRouchie's approach is that he makes use of both the immediate context and also the canonical context in his interpretation of specific texts. His exegesis of Genesis 22 exemplifies this strength. He interprets the narrative in the light of Genesis 22 itself and then in the context of the flow of Old Testament redemptive history and, finally, in the context of the two-Testament, Christian Bible. The rich texture of detail makes the text brim over with meaning as it is considered within the context of the whole Bible.

However, one is left wondering whose intention is decisive in DeRouchie's interpretation of the story. He goes back and forth between talking about the narrator's intention and Abraham's intention. He also speaks of God's action in commanding Abraham and then preventing Abraham from going through with the sacrifice and providing a substitute. He writes, "Yahweh both typologically confirms . . . and directly predicts . . . that he will indeed realize what he has promised." DeRouchie takes the words of the Angel of Yahweh as Yahweh speaking in verses 15–19, which I agree with. However, this leaves open the question of who is speaking in verses 1–14: the narrator, Abraham, both the narrator and Abraham, or God through the narrator? Is the meaning of the story limited to what the human author/editor might have been able to conceive in terms of how Yahweh might fulfill his promise in the future? Or can we see a deeper, spiritual meaning as an extension of the literal sense? This brings us back to the question of divine authorial intent.

A Potential Weakness of DeRouchie's Approach

Again, it is important to begin by reminding everyone that this slender point of disagreement exists in the context of massive agreement. I wonder if DeRouchie would be willing to agree with the criticism I am about to offer. He may already implicitly accept it.

I think DeRouchie's approach would be strengthened by the explicit adoption of a metaphysical framework in which divine action of three distinct types would be comprehensible and possible. God inspires the Scriptures, God illumines the meaning of the Scriptures, and God speaks through the Scriptures. The divine authorial intent constitutes the literal sense, and this literal sense can be discerned in the viewpoint expressed by the narrator, as well as by characters in the narrative. This literal sense can have an extended or expanded sense, which must be christologically controlled in the canonical context.

The metaphysical framework is a theological account of the nature of God, the relationship of God to creation, and the nature of divine action. Early in his chapter, DeRouchie discusses authorial intent but does not distinguish between human and divine authorial intent. He says, "Scripture calls us to see both an organic unity and a progressive development between the Testaments." By distinguishing (without separating) divine and human authorial intent as layers of meaning in the text, we can account ontologically for what he is here describing phenomenologically. I want to give a couple of brief examples of how the distinction between divine and human authorial intent could help with the weakness identified above—namely, the "reading in" problem.

In his discussion of Proverbs 8, DeRouchie quite rightly notes that personified Wisdom is speaking in this poem about creation, in which Wisdom played a central role. He writes, "Wisdom portrays itself as God's commissioned image bearer or royal agent who has enjoyed this post 'from eternity'" (200). But a couple of paragraphs later, DeRouchie speaks of Solomon as the human author of Proverbs and his portrayal of Wisdom as a woman who entices the royal son to desire her. DeRouchie says that Proverbs 30:1–6 is inspired, prophetic speech and a messianic prediction. Here DeRouchie discovers a link between the Father and the Son in the Godhead. DeRouchie then builds on this idea of the Father-Son relationship to draw a typological comparison between the royal son of David and the coming Messiah:

> Just as Yahweh from eternity past installed his Wisdom-Son to represent him (Prov 8:23), so also Yahweh designates his messianic king his "begotten Son" (Ps 2:7, author's translation) upon his installation as king in Zion having triumphed over his enemies (Ps 2:1–2, 6; cf. Acts 4:24–28; 13:32–33). (203)

This is a highly compressed argument and necessarily so, given the constraints of space in this essay. But I just want to point out that several intentions are being discussed here: the intention of Solomon in Proverbs as a whole, the intention of the narrator of the poem in Proverbs 8:22–31, the intention of Yahweh in creation, the intention of the author of Psalm 2, and the intention of God in embedding the type of the messiah in Proverbs.

Without negating the role or significance of the human authors and editors, because of inspiration I think it is possible to view the divine authorial intent as the primary and literal sense of all these passages and the Bible as a whole, which provides a basis for understanding them as a unity. There is no way human intention within the historical framework of each person's own situation can possibly be reconciled into one unified perspective without it looking artificial and forced. But if we recognize that divine authorial intent represents the true meaning of the text because it is inspired Scripture, then we can expect Psalm 2 to cohere with Proverbs 8 and both of them to point forward to the New Testament revelation of God's incarnate Wisdom in the person of the Son.

Conclusion

Finally, it seems important to reiterate that if Jesus is not really in the Old Testament, which is to say, if the meaning of the Old Testament text itself is not Jesus, then the reading in of Jesus by the apostles and church fathers is not warranted. So, hermeneutics must explain how it can be that Jesus Christ is ontologically present in the Old Testament text and intended as the meaning by the author. Only if we posit the divine author as the primary author of the text and the one who determines the literal meaning of the text, can this be justified. It is not supersessionist or anti-Semitic to assert (as the Jewish apostles did) that the God of Israel has spoken of himself as Father and Son in his own Scriptures. The New Testament simply recognizes that fact and proclaims it as gospel.

REJOINDER

JASON S. DEROUCHIE

I thank my fellow contributors for thoughtfully engaging my approach to Christ in the Old Testament. The five views in this book include both substantive and less significant differences. I will briefly engage the other contributors and then synthesize my approach's key distinctions.

Goldingay asserts that focusing on Christ in the First Testament implies a perspective that God does not matter (212). In contrast, Jesus is the only way to the Father (John 14:6), and "whoever does not honor the Son does not honor the Father, who sent him" (5:23). Additionally, Goldingay's denial that Luke 24:45–47 speaks of a unified Old Testament message centering on Jesus and global missions may result more from Goldingay's own hermeneutic than Luke's meaning. Only by ignoring my arguments can Goldingay assert that I do not supply "signposts" for showing how the Old Testament points to Christ (213). Goldingay also maintains that antitypes create and point to types, not the other way around (213–14). However, Adam "was a type *of the one who was to come*" (Rom 5:14 ESV, emphasis added), indicating that the type was present before the antitype arrived. Lastly, because hyperbole illuminates truth (unlike exaggeration, which misleads), Goldingay's claim that Peter hyperbolically stated that "all the prophets" spoke of Christ (Acts 3:18) would still mean that the prophets as a whole clearly spoke of Jesus's death, which is more than Goldingay concedes. Paul interpreted the First Testament materials through Jesus (1 Cor 2:2; 2 Cor 3:14), and Goldingay would serve himself and the church if he did the same.

I agree with Longman that knowing a character's thoughts or

feelings is impossible (219) *unless* Scripture discloses them. Jesus said that Abraham "saw" his day "and was glad" (John 8:56), so we can expect to find textual clues of this. Longman claims that my conviction that Abraham understood the predictive significance of Isaac's sacrifice is "far from certain" (218). One hundred percent agreement is not expected in a *five views* book, and we assess valid interpretation on the basis of arguments, not certainty. Nevertheless, Longman is correct that "the story of the binding of Isaac has a typological significance to Christ's sacrifice" regardless of "whether or not Abraham had a sense" of this (219). As for Proverbs 8:22–31, Longman confronts my "daring" assertion that "the first-person speech . . . mutes the feminine portrayal" of Wisdom in the passage (220). My point here was *not* to deny that the text portrays Wisdom as a lady but instead to stress (1) that it does so as a rhetorical move to effect godliness, and (2) that 30:4 portrays *this same Wisdom* as God's *Son*. If I am correct that God's "son" in 30:4 is Wisdom, then I am on solid ground to see the final editor associating Wisdom with God's Son in Proverbs 8. The link is made even more explicit if the plural "Holy One[s]" in 30:3 and in the thesis of 9:10 indeed refer to God and Wisdom. Significantly, Jesus occasionally used feminine imagery of himself (e.g., Matt 23:37), and he even associates his own ministry with Lady Wisdom, who is "proved right by her deeds" (11:19). Whether the whole book seeks to train royal sons is secondary to my main argument regarding the link between Proverbs 30:4 and 8:22–31. Longman never addresses this argument! As for Isaiah 42:1–4, Longman asserts that "no one was reading Isaiah 42 . . . at the time of Jesus" in the way I have. He fails to account for Simeon who was "waiting for the consolation of Israel" and who identified Jesus as fulfilling *Isaiah's* hope for a global Savior (Luke 2:25, 32). Simeon grasped what Jesus's disciples failed to get but should have from the prophets' clear testimony (Luke 24:25–26).

Dharamraj asserts that my messianic readings are often "beyond the scope of the Common Reader" (224). True! But they are not beyond the scope of Christians who interpret Scripture in light of itself and like Jesus and the apostles did. These Christians are the Ideal Readers (1 Cor 2:13–14; 2 Cor 3:14) who agree with Jesus that Moses wrote of him (John 5:46). Against Dharamraj, I never stated that Jesus is the only fish in the Old Testament sea. Other themes, characters, and motifs exist. Nevertheless, we must affirm that Jesus is in the Old Testament and that he came to fulfill it all (Matt 5:17; Luke 24:44). Lastly, I do not separate Genesis 22:1–19 from its immediate context, but I do claim that this text significantly develops the book's messianic "seed" theme. My interpretations may be "esoteric" due more to present scholarly bias than to unfaithfulness, for my method results in a highly textually based interpretation with conclusions that align with those of the biblical authors themselves.

I agree with Carter that Scripture's "primary and literal sense" is God's authorial intent as gleaned from the close, continuing, and complete contexts (232). Regarding Proverbs 8:22–31, I see no reason why David, Solomon, and Agur could not first have rightly spoken of the divine Son and why Proverbs' editor(s) could not have identified such and then brought the varied God-guided perspectives together to form a more composite picture. This is how progressive revelation works. I am suggesting that the final editor saw complementary intentions in the varied sources and drew them together in a way that allowed all those sources to enjoy enhanced meaning in the book's final form. Now that God has closed the canon, however, the only meaning of the various passages is the divine author's composite one.

Jesus said that his Bible testifies about him (John 5:39). My Redemptive-Historical, Christocentric approach reads the Old Testament through and for Christ, considering every passage in the light of its close, continuing, and complete contexts. The approach distinguishes itself from the others by claiming that Christians can rightly understand how the Old Testament *itself* anticipates Christ and the world's saving hope (Rom 16:25–26; cf. Luke 24:45–47). This is made possible only through Christ (2 Cor 3:14), the aid of the Spirit (1 Cor 2:13–14), and careful exegesis and theology (2 Tim 2:15). But Jesus is part of the Old Testament's meaning (against Goldingay), seen in the first reading (against Longman), linked with the Old Testament authors' intention (against Dharamraj), and evident apart from a deeper meaning dependent on the New Testament itself (against Carter).

Rather than wiping out sinners after Adam's fall, God mercifully revealed himself and his will in a book. From one perspective, every word of the Old Testament testifies to Christ because every word is blood bought. With this, we can see and celebrate Jesus at least through

(1) direct messianic predictions, (2) salvation-historical trajectories, (3) similarities and contrasts, (4) typology, (5) Yahweh's identity and activity, (6) ethical ideals, and (7) living out the law of love. The Old Testament's human authors searched intently to learn about the Christ and his time, and God revealed to them that their Spirit-led interpretations would serve Christians even more than themselves (1 Pet 1:10–12).

PREMODERN APPROACH

CRAIG A. CARTER

The purpose of this essay is to defend the premodern approach to the christological interpretation of the Old Testament and to explain why it is necessary for us to retrieve it today. All Christians believe that the Hebrew Bible testifies to Jesus Christ and is fulfilled by him. The question that causes disagreement is *how* we find him in the Old Testament.

Prior to the modern period, interpreters in the mainstream of Christian theology saw Christ in the Old Testament in a wide variety of ways, for example:

- Christ fulfills Old Testament prophecy. This means that he is the subject of certain messianic prophecies, which constitute a relatively small number of texts.[1]
- Many persons, things, and events in the Old Testament are types of Christ. This means that he is the antitype and that his significance is elucidated by the types. That makes Jesus the subject of a lot more of the Old Testament.[2]

---

1. These include texts such as Exod 12:46, cf. John 19:36; Ps 16:8–11, cf. Acts 2:25–33; Ps 22:18, cf. Matt 27:35; Isa 7:14, cf. Matt 1:23; Micah 5:2, cf. Matt 2:5–6; Zech 9:9, cf. Matt 21:5.
2. For a good recent work that introduces typology, see Mitchell L. Chase, *40 Questions about Typology and Allegory* (Grand Rapids: Kregel, 2020).

- We can interpret the Old Testament according to the fourfold sense, as containing a christological or spiritual sense that is an extension or expansion of the literal sense. This means that Jesus is spoken of in even more passages of the Old Testament.[3]
- In his life and ministry, Jesus recapitulates Israel's history, and he does for God's people what they had failed to do for themselves, thus re-creating in his own person the renewed Israel of God. This means that even more of the Old Testament points to Jesus and that much of the New Testament relates to the Old Testament.
- The Son himself speaks in the Old Testament, which we can see by using prosopological exegesis to understand texts where the Father speaks to the Son and the Son replies or where the Messiah speaks. This means that the Old Testament is not only about Jesus; in a very real sense, it is *by* Jesus, the Son and Messiah![4]

The premodern approach is open to seeing Christ in the Old Testament in all these ways, which means that Christ is seen in almost every part of the Old Testament. Ignatius of Antioch, in the early second century, went so far as to assert that the Old Testament *is* Jesus Christ.[5]

Introduction to the Approach

Since the rise of materialism, mechanism, and atheism in the European Enlightenment, however, there has been a tendency in Western biblical studies to downplay the clarity with which Christ is seen in the Old Testament. What is often called "historical criticism" began as early as Spinoza, but it became central to theology in the nineteenth century. The narrow, naturalistic definition of history that animated this approach

---

3. For a discussion of this complex topic, see my *Interpreting Scripture with the Great Tradition: Recovering the Genius of Premodern Exegesis* (Grand Rapids: Baker Academic, 2018), chap. 6, "Letting the Literal Sense Control All Meaning."

4. For a good treatment of prosopological exegesis, see Matthew W. Bates, *The Birth of the Trinity: Jesus, God, and the Spirit in the New Testament and Early Christian Interpretation of the Old Testament* (Oxford: Oxford University Press, 2015).

5. John Behr, in his introduction to Irenaeus, *The Apostolic Demonstration of the Cross*, Popular Patristics 17 (Crestwood, NY: St. Vladimir's Seminary Press, 1997), quotes Ignatius's *Letter to the Philadelphians* 8–9, where Ignatius speaks of how the Old Testament contains the revelation of Christ. Referring to the Hebrew Scriptures as "the archives," he writes: "For me the archives are Jesus Christ, the inviolable archives are his cross and death and His resurrection and the faith which is through him."

led to the rejection of miracles and to extensive doctrinal revisionism, which ended up splitting Protestantism in the early twentieth century. Whatever benefits or gains historical criticism may have brought to the study of the Bible, one negative effect has been that it has weakened confidence in the central conviction of the historic church that Jesus is the true fulfillment of the Old Testament.

Conservative biblical scholars have tried to work as much as possible within the narrow parameters of the naturalism of historical criticism, while also attempting to preserve the truth of as much of the biblical teaching as possible. Many conservatives replace what is often called the "historical-critical method" with what they call the "grammatical-historical method," which can be understood as a conservative version of the former approach that seeks to avoid the radical implications of philosophical naturalism to the greatest extent possible. Liberal historical critics, however, frequently see this as inconsistent and dishonest.[6]

After nearly two centuries of historical criticism, many modern scholars—including some conservative ones—have come to accept the claim that the New Testament writers read Jesus into the Old Testament. This is a seismic shift in the church's theology. Some would draw the logical conclusion that we should completely reject the christological message of the New Testament, but others would say that the doctrine of inspiration justifies taking the apostles' "reading in" as in some sense "true." But how the Old Testament can both not refer to Jesus and also refer to Jesus, if human authorial intent is decisive for the meaning of the text, has never been clearly worked out. Therefore, I agree with those who see this as an untenable position. The idea that the apostles read Jesus into the Hebrew Bible is tantamount to saying that the rabbinic Jews who opposed the first-century apostles were right all along and the fledgling Christian church should never have gotten off the ground. Their view was that Christianity was built on a false premise, and so we should either give it up altogether or, at least, give up belief in Jesus as the Christ, which seems to me like pretty much the same thing.

The premodern approach, therefore, needs to be recovered for the sake of the integrity of the church's confession of Jesus as the Christ.

---

6. For example, see John Barton, *The Nature of Biblical Criticism* (Louisville: Westminster John Knox, 2007), 171–72.

If the Trinitarian and christological orthodoxy of the creedal tradition was developed using the premodern approach, which I believe is the case, then to reject the premodern approach is to place a question mark beside historic orthodoxy itself. It has never been demonstrated that Nicene and Chalcedonian orthodoxy can be derived from exegesis that strictly employs only the historical-critical approach. Coincidentally or not, we see concurrent with the rise of historical criticism over the past two hundred years the parallel rise of extensive doctrinal revisionism and the sharp decline of creedal orthodoxy. Until it has been demonstrated that it is possible to reject the premodern approach to exegesis while simultaneously retaining adequate exegetical foundations for Trinitarian and christological orthodoxy as the meaning of the Bible as a whole, I believe it is reasonable to assume that they stand or fall together. Thus, the stakes could not be higher in this discussion.

Part 1: The Nature of Scripture

The premodern approach is not a single neat and tidy method for reading the text that can easily be summarized. It takes various forms in different historical situations. As we saw above, it includes reading techniques as varied as messianic prophecy, typology, allegory, prosopological exegesis, and theological readings of history. It would be a mistake, therefore, to call it a "method" in the modern sense. It is more accurately termed a spiritual discipline. Premodern exegesis involves a certain kind of reader who stands in a certain kind of relation to a certain kind of God. The reader is a believer who sincerely seeks God and is open to believing what Scripture teaches and to doing what God wills. The God of Scripture is the transcendent Creator of the cosmos, the sovereign Lord of history, and the one who alone is to be worshiped. The reader is finite; God is infinite. Yet God stoops down to our level in Scripture to speak in ways that we, created in his image, are capable of understanding. The relationship initially is one of Lord and servant, and yet in his grace God increasingly transforms it into a relationship of friendship (John 15:15). Reading Scripture is a means by which God sanctifies us.

Rather than seeing the premodern approach as a mechanical method guaranteed to produce the correct interpretation if executed properly, it is better to understand it as pressing various preexisting reading techniques and hermeneutical methods into the service of exegesis, which is viewed as wrestling with what God is saying to his people through the text. The question "What does this text mean?" is answered by prayerfully contemplating all aspects of the text until one is able to put what it says into one's own words. Stating the meaning of the text in one's own words is the essence of all good interpretation. Both the premodern and the modern approaches utilize all the available scholarly resources for interpretation, including philology, history, archaeology, textual criticism, literary theory, comparative religion, and so forth. But they use these resources for different purposes, which are determined by different theological understandings of the nature of the task of biblical interpretation. The modern approach seeks to identify the intended meaning of the original human author, which it equates with the literal sense; the premodern approach seeks to hear God speak through the literal sense of the text. In the premodern approach, the literal sense is the divine author's intended meaning as communicated through the human author's words.

We could say that the premodern approach is faith seeking understanding and a spiritual discipline for sanctification oriented to the goal of worship, while the modern approach attempts to be a neutral, objective method by which the reader gains mastery over the text and reconstructs its meaning in terms of what the original human author meant to say. This is why modern commentary series such as the International Critical Commentary or the Old Testament Library employ a wide variety of contributors, including Roman Catholic, conservative and liberal Protestant, Jewish, and agnostic scholars. The rationale is that the employment of a modern, scientific method should be possible no matter what the faith commitments of the interpreter might be. Faith is bracketed out in so-called "scientific exegesis." I would argue that this method would be appropriate only if we knew in advance that we were dealing with a merely human book. But if the Bible is the inspired word of God, then bracketing out faith in God may prevent us from understanding what it actually means. For this reason, it can be argued that the premodern approach actually is more scientific than the modern approach, if one is prepared to grant that the Bible is special revelation from God. In the Aristotelian concept of a science, the method used must be appropriate to the subject matter being studied.

Since the scriptural texts are complex entities stemming from different centuries, written in different genres, and with different purposes, no one-size-fits-all method will suffice. In some situations, philology is crucial, while in other cases translation is hardly a problem at all. Sometimes the historical context is critical to understanding the text, while at other times it is practically irrelevant except in the most general terms. Sometimes the literal sense is clear, but what it means to us today is unclear; other times the literal sense itself is disputed. And when it comes to poetry, the literal sense is conveyed nonliterally, which adds to the complexity of interpretation. The distinct roles of the human authors and divine author add to the complexity of the task; Scripture itself informs us that the Old Testament prophets did not understand fully everything they were inspired to write (1 Pet 1:10–12). The meaning cannot be limited *only* to what the original human author meant to say to the intended audience at the time, but the meaning cannot contradict or ignore that meaning. We must strive to know what the divine author means to say *through* the inspired human author. The human author is dead, but the divine author is alive, and this is why Scripture never goes stale or becomes irrelevant as the generations pass. At times exegetes take a good thing too far and fall into subjectivism and idiosyncratic interpretations. In such cases, the tradition usually corrects itself and shifts back to the center. Interpretations that lead to contradictions in Scripture have always been viewed as unacceptable, at least until the advent of modern historical criticism.

In sum, it should be understood that defending something called "the premodern approach" means neither defending every single interpretation by every single premodern interpreter nor assuming that there is one monolithic method of exegesis called "the premodern approach." The variety of reading techniques mentioned above is not exhaustive of the many different forms taken in premodern interpretation. However, I would argue that to ignore the premodern approach and to use only modern methods is to miss out on the riches of the best interpretive practices in Christian history. In fact, it would mean ignoring the exegesis that led to the creedal deposit of Trinitarian and christological orthodoxy, which has been the foundation of the faith of the church for more than fifteen hundred years.

In my opinion, the nature of Scripture should be more determinative for interpretation than any methodology that someone might bring to the interpretation of Scripture, because the nature of Scripture itself dictates how it must be interpreted. In the rest of this section, I will attempt to describe the Bible's uniqueness as a witness to Jesus Christ and the theological implications of the nature of the Bible for biblical hermeneutics.

The Nature of Scripture as Apostolic Proclamation of Christ

In Luke's description of Paul's first missionary journey, we are told that Barnabas and Saul sailed to Cyprus, and when they arrived at Salamis "they proclaimed the Word of God in the synagogues of the Jews" (Acts 13:5 ESV). This became the normal pattern for Paul's missionary work. He made a point of visiting the synagogue on his first Sabbath day in a new city to "reason with" the Jews there (Acts 17:1–2). Hence, Paul states programmatically, the gospel is for everyone who believes, for the Jew first and also the Greek (Rom 1:16).

The obvious question is, what was he discussing in these synagogue meetings? What was in dispute? Of what was he trying to convince the Jews? Central to the synagogue service was the reading of the Scriptures, and so the discussion undoubtedly centered on the proper interpretation of the Scriptures. We can safely assume that the central interpretive issue at stake between Paul and his opponents was whether Jesus of Nazareth was, in fact, the Messiah prophesied in the Scriptures. Is Jesus the fulfillment of the Law, the Prophets, and the Writings? This comprehensive question can be broken down into a number of more specific questions, such as "Does the Messiah come once or twice?" "Does not Elijah have to come first?" "What does the Messiah actually do, according to the Scriptures?" and "How does the Davidic king relate to other scriptural figures such as the suffering servant of Isaiah 53, the Son of Man of Daniel 7, and the prophet like Moses spoken of in Deuteronomy 18?"

We know from Paul's letters and the rest of the New Testament that the apostles saw Jesus as related to the Hebrew Scriptures in ways that go far beyond merely fulfilling a few specific prophecies, such as being born in Bethlehem (Mic 5:2) or being born of a virgin (Isa 7:14).

They did not downplay such specific prophecies, but the way in which they understood the Scriptures to speak of Jesus went far deeper than simply him fulfilling certain, specific prophecies, any one of which would have been insufficient in and of itself to prove his messiahship. For example, it is seen as significant by Matthew that Psalm 22:18 was fulfilled by the soldiers casting lots for his garment (Matt 27:35). But someone who was not the messiah could have died without having his garments torn, and even if one piles up a heap of such fulfillments, one would not thereby have gotten to the heart of why the apostles saw Jesus as the Messiah.

Jesus fulfilled the Scriptures in such a way that much in them that had been mysterious and opaque suddenly became comprehensible and clear. He is the Reality; the law, the temple, and the sacrifices were the shadows. On the road to Emmaus, he stressed the comprehensiveness of the scriptural witness to him: "And beginning with Moses and *all* the Prophets, he interpreted to them in *all* the Scriptures the things concerning himself" (Luke 24:27 ESV, emphasis added). Note the stress on *all* the Scriptures. In the next story, Jesus appears to the disciples and says, "These are my words that I spoke to you while I was still with you, that *everything* written about me in the Law of Moses and the Prophets and the Psalms must be fulfilled" (Luke 24:44 ESV, emphasis added). Once again, note the comprehensiveness of the fulfillment. Let us consider briefly how the apostles saw Jesus as fulfilling the Law, the Prophets, and the Writings.

First, we take the epistle to the Hebrews, which presents Jesus as fulfilling the law of Moses. The law was but a shadow of things to come, and the sacrifices could never make those who offer them perfect (Heb 10:1). "For it is impossible for the blood of bulls and goats to take away sins" (Heb 10:4 ESV). But "we have been sanctified through the offering of the body of Jesus Christ once for all" (Heb 10:10 ESV). The Mosaic tabernacle, that is, the earthly sanctuary and sacrificial ritual, are called "copies of the heavenly things" (Heb 9:23). Jesus Christ is presented as the reality to which the law pointed.

Second, in the Gospel of Mark, we see how Jesus is the fulfillment of the book of Isaiah in numerous ways. Rikki E. Watts demonstrates that Mark goes far beyond citing a few Isaianic proof texts to prove that Jesus is the fulfillment of Isaiah's vision. Watts shows that the deep structure of Isaiah's eschatology shapes the Gospel of Mark extensively.[7] Jesus is presented as the solution to Israel's sin problem that was at the heart of the book of Isaiah.

Third, in the Acts of the Apostles, we see how Jesus fulfills the Psalms. We have already noted Luke's conviction that the prophetic, messianic, and eschatological interpretation of the Psalms is rooted in the teaching of our Lord himself (Luke 24:44). On the day of Pentecost, Peter called David a prophet and asserted that David "foresaw and spoke about the resurrection of the Christ, that he was not abandoned to Hades, nor did his flesh see corruption" (Acts 2:30–31 ESV). Peter quoted both Psalm 16:8–11 and Psalm 110:1 (Acts 2:25–35) and interpreted the death and resurrection of Jesus as fulfilling the Psalms.

The New Testament Gospels, history, and epistles all present Jesus as fulfilling the Law, the Prophets, and the Writings. Predictions made in the Scriptures were fulfilled in Jesus's life and ministry. Jesus performed characteristic signs of the messianic age, such as the blind being made to see, the lame being made to walk, those possessed by demons being delivered, and the dead being raised. Numerous types like Jonah in the belly of the fish, the manna in the wilderness, and the scapegoat bearing the sins of the nation found their antitype in Jesus. The central problem of the history of Israel was how a holy God could be bound in an eternal covenant to an unholy people. The solution was a sin-bearing, suffering servant named Jesus who is revealed to be Yahweh come to save his people from their sins and make them holy. Jesus is the seed of the woman promised in Genesis 3:15 who would crush Satan's head. He is the seed of Abraham through whom would come blessing to the nations as predicted in Genesis 12:1–3. He is the son of David who would sit on the throne of his father David forever, thus fulfilling the Davidic covenant of 2 Samuel 7. Jesus came the first time as the suffering servant of Isaiah 53, but he will come again in power and glory as the anointed world conqueror of Isaiah 63. As he said to the high priest at his trial, he is the heavenly Son of Man who will be "seated at the right hand of Power and coming on the clouds of heaven" (Matt 26:64 ESV; cf. Dan 7:13–14).

---

7. Rikki E. Watts, *Isaiah's New Exodus in Mark*, Biblical Studies Library (Grand Rapids: Baker Academic, 2000).

Approximately a third of the New Testament consists of citations, quotations, or allusions to Scripture.[8] It is no exaggeration to say that the New Testament simply *is* an interpretation of the true meaning of what Christians refer to as the Old Testament. It is also clear that at the heart of that interpretation stands the life, ministry, death, resurrection, ascension, and future second coming of the Lord Jesus Christ. Rabbinic Judaism presents an alternative interpretation of the Hebrew Bible, one that rejects Jesus as the Messiah and leaves the Hebrew Scriptures as a giant question with no answer. To be a believer in Jesus makes a Jew a messianic Jew, and it causes a gentile to be grafted into the Israel of God by grace (Rom 11:17–24). The heart of Christian faith is faith in Jesus as the Messiah of the Hebrew Scriptures.

The most important thing is not what methods or techniques we use in interpreting Scripture or what metaphysical presuppositions we happen to bring to the reading of Scripture from our own culture and era. We are inevitably children of our own age and culture, and some of our presuppositions and methods will undoubtedly be wrong and/or in need of revision as we go along. What is crucial is that we allow whatever assumptions and techniques we bring to our reading of Scripture to be challenged by the biblical texts themselves as we ask what believing the apostolic proclamation of Jesus as the Messiah entails. God's word is alive and active and sharper than any two-edged sword (Heb 4:12), so it is fully capable of breaking through to us as we read no matter where we are coming from—if we are open to the Spirit (1 Cor 2:10–14). It is crucial to see that only if our docility meets the activity of God's Spirit can our believing response to the gospel itself—our belief that Jesus is the Christ—become foundational to our hermeneutics. This is the self-involving logic of Christian theology.

Biblical interpretation cannot be pursued in a completely neutral, objective manner, because as we read the Scriptures, we are forced to consider their claims on us. Only the response of faith will impel us to allow the apostolic proclamation to correct our thinking and open our minds to the correct meaning. Why would I adopt for myself the theological assumptions derived from the text by exegesis if I reject the

---

8. Andrew E. Hill and John H. Walton, *A Survey of the Old Testament*, 3rd ed. (Grand Rapids: Zondervan, 2009), 744.

message contained in the text? But what if adopting those theological assumptions is a prerequisite for a deeper insight into the meaning of the text? This is why Augustine and Anselm speak for the orthodox tradition in teaching that we must believe in order to understand. So, the question we must address is how our faith in Jesus as the Messiah should shape our hermeneutics.

The Theology of Hermeneutics

To do this, we need to ask, "What assumptions about God and the nature of biblical inspiration underlie the apostolic proclamation of Jesus as the Messiah?" In other words, what would one have to believe in order for the message of Paul, Peter, and the other apostles to make sense? I believe this is the most fruitful way into theological hermeneutics.[9]

We believe in the transcendent Creator who is the sovereign Lord of history and the one who alone is to be worshiped. Such a one can tell the future, inspire prophets to speak truly about the future, and bring to pass what is predicted. This concept of God is found in one of the theological high points of the Old Testament, Isaiah 40–48. Here Isaiah sums up the nature of the God who has revealed himself to Israel and who is described in Genesis, Exodus, and the Psalms. The historical exodus is taken by Isaiah to be a prototype for the great eschatological event at the end of history in which God will be revealed in glory and power as all the promises to Abraham and David are fulfilled. The return of the Jews from Babylon to Jerusalem is a beginning of that eschatological event (Isa 40:1–5).

The transcendence of God means he is not part of, or continuous in being with, the cosmos. God is high and exalted and does not exist as a being among beings, but as the Creator and sovereign Lord of all. Such a God is capable of speaking and acting in history to judge and to save without constraints or limitations. Such a God is able to predict what is still future to us because he is not in time like we are. This God is real but not materially or temporally limited, which is to say he is transcendent of space and time. Since a cause must be greater than its effect, God is greater than the creation. Although it is possible for human beings to

---

9. For a fuller development of the ideas in this section, see my *Interpreting Scripture with the Great Tradition*, chap. 2, "Theological Hermeneutics."

know God, it is not possible to comprehend God completely. We have true, but not exhaustive, knowledge of God.

Since God is the transcendent Creator and sovereign Lord of history, he is capable of creating creatures in his image to whom he can communicate his will. It is because he has created us in the image of the Logos, with language and logic, that we are able to hear and understand his speech. And since he is Lord in both creation and history, he is capable of inspiring biblical texts by a combination of miracle and providence in such a way that they become fit vessels for his use. The Bible as a whole is a document that no human community could have produced by immanent material processes alone. Only such a God could have inspired a text that contains divine revelation and thus requires an approach to interpretation that is not presuming a framework of naturalism.

The Scriptures do, however, contain truth that humans are capable of discovering on their own by the usual processes of observation and analysis. For example, in the Wisdom Literature we find true teaching on parent-child relationships that could be (and likely were) derived from observing family life. In Luke 1:1–4 the evangelist describes doing research similar to what anyone does in writing a biography: reading other accounts, collecting eyewitness testimony, and arranging material in orderly fashion. If these books of Scripture seem to emerge by natural processes, then why are they considered to be inspired Scripture? They are inspired through divine providence. Other parts of the Bible could only be known to the human author by direct, special revelation from God. For example, John sees into the throne room of heaven (Rev 4:1), and Isaiah receives the name of Cyrus (Isa 44:28), the emperor who will allow the return from exile, by miraculous means. Such revelation cannot be reduced to natural processes (2 Pet 1:21). It comes by means of a miracle. But Scripture that comes about through providence is no less inspired than that which comes through miracle because both providence and miracle are acts of the transcendent Creator. Neither providence nor miracle are merely natural in the sense of being generated by immanent causes unrelated to God, who is the First Cause of all.

The crucial point to note here is that inspiration through providence and miracle is possible because of the nature of God, and belief in the former depends on belief in the latter. If one does not believe in God, or if one believes in a very different kind of God (say a pantheistic conception, for example), then it is not going to be possible to believe in the traditional, Christian understanding of inspiration. So, belief in God turns out to be the basis for belief in the inspiration of Scripture and the foundational element of hermeneutics.

Part 2: Interpretive Steps for Readers

On the basis of this theological description of hermeneutics, we can identify some practical principles to guide the reading of Holy Scripture. These principles are developed in more depth in part 2 of my book *Interpreting Scripture with the Great Tradition*. What follows is a brief summary and not an exhaustive discussion of hermeneutical principles. The goal of exegesis is to restate the meaning of the text in other words, which sounds simple but is not simple in practice. The four principles below should guide the interpreter in exegesis.

The usual steps of exegesis, such as establishing the text from the original languages, translating, analyzing the type of literature, examining the historical context, identifying figures of speech, and so forth are well-known to all who take a basic hermeneutics course, and I will not take time to rehearse them here. Instead, it will be more beneficial to lay out the principles guiding the interpreter at each step along the way.

Principle 1: The Unity of Scripture

Since the Bible has numerous human authors but only one divine author, the apparent diversity cannot negate the deep unity of the Bible as a single book. Jesus Christ is the central theme of the Bible from Genesis to Revelation, and both Testaments testify to him. As Augustine put it, "The New is hidden in the Old and the Old is revealed in the New."[10]

The unity of Scripture has three major implications for how we interpret it. The first is that Scripture does not contradict Scripture. Since there is only one divine author and that author is infallible, the Bible, when rightly interpreted, is inerrant. Thus, it will not contradict itself any more than God would contradict himself. This principle functions as a major check on uncontrolled speculation as to the meaning of the text.

10. Augustine, *Questions on the Heptateuch* 2.73, in *Writings on the Old Testament*, The Works of Saint Augustine: A Translation for the 21st Century, trans. Joseph T. Lienhard and Sean Doyle (New York: New City Press, 2016), 125 (Exodus, 73).

The second implication is that the relationship between the Testaments must have a principle of unity, and that principle of unity is Jesus the Christ. He holds the Scripture together as a single, coherent revelation. Because of Christ, we can understand the relation between the Testaments as one of promise and fulfillment. This provides a basis for the possibility of predictive prophecy, and it also places limits on how major themes of Scripture should be articulated. To make something else the central theme of Scripture would be to fail to do justice to the material principle of unity, which is the person and work of Jesus Christ.

The third implication is that intertextual interpretation is legitimate. By this I mean that similar texts in different parts of the canon may be supposed to shed light on one another because of the unity of Scripture resulting from divine authorship and divine inspiration. If the Bible as a whole is one book by one author with one theme, then it is reasonable to think that one part of it will be able to shed light on another part. This has been the conviction of interpreters throughout the history of the church, although modern historical critics often find it bizarre and incomprehensible when they observe premodern theologians using apparently unrelated texts from different parts of the Bible to shed light on one another.

Principle 2: The Priority of the Literal Sense

The literal sense is the basis of all good interpretation. It is like the foundation of a house. Of course a good foundation does not eliminate the need for a roof and walls, yet a house is not a house without one. Many texts have a *sensus plenior*, but any additional sense must meet two minimal conditions to be acceptable: (1) it cannot contradict the literal sense, and (2) it must be related to it in some logical manner. Meeting these two conditions does not necessarily mean that a given interpretation is correct, but only that it is not automatically ruled out *a priori*.

The fuller sense can be an extension or expansion of the literal sense, and it can be a specification or clarification of the literal sense. But it cannot be something that has no basis in or relationship to the literal sense whatsoever. In the providence of God, he has ensured that any fuller sense he intends to become clear to later generations is supported by the foundation of what he inspired the original author to write. For example, the act of crucifixion per se was probably not known by Isaiah, and he did not articulate a fully developed doctrine of substitutionary atonement. Yet God inspired the prophet to write chapter 53 in such a way that the death of Christ on a cross, and the meaning of that death, is depicted there. This is clear in hindsight.[11] Nothing in Isaiah 53 is contradicted either in the account of the crucifixion in the Gospels or in the doctrine of substitutionary atonement developed in the Epistles as the theological meaning of that act of crucifixion. The doctrine of substitutionary atonement certainly is more fully developed in Paul's epistles than it is in Isaiah 53, but it is reasonable to say that Paul's doctrine is an expansion of ideas and themes contained in Isaiah 53:4–6, not a repudiation of them or a doctrine that is entirely unrelated to Isaiah 53. So, to read Isaiah 53 as being about substitutionary atonement does not violate the principle of the priority of the literal sense any more than understanding it as a prediction of a crucifixion contradicts the vision Isaiah saw. We are talking about layers of meaning in a text, not about conflicting meanings being attributed to the same text.

Principle 3: The Reality of the Spiritual Sense

Thomas Aquinas offered a concise and clear account of the medieval understanding of the fourfold sense of Scripture.[12] He quoted Augustine and Gregory the Great and explained that because the ultimate author of Scripture is God, the words of the Bible reveal a mystery. This means that reading Scripture involves encountering mystery, that is, truth too high and profound for the human mind to grasp fully. So the words themselves are signs by which things are signified, and the things signified also have significations as well. This is the basis for a theory of multiple layers of meaning within the text.

Thomas identified the literal sense with the historical sense and said it was the first signification. However, he said there is also a further signification by which the things signified in the literal sense signify other things, which he understood to be the spiritual sense. The spiritual sense of Old Testament texts has a threefold division in which there

---

11. This is why Isaiah 53 is cited about thirty-eight times by most of the writers of the New Testament. Andrew E. Hill and John H. Walton, *A Survey of the Old Testament*, 3rd ed. (Grand Rapids: Zondervan, 2009), 745.

12. Thomas Aquinas, *Summa Theologica*, trans. Fathers of the Dominican Province, 5 vols. (Notre Dame: Ave Maria Press, 1948), 1.1.10.

is an allegorical sense that signifies Christ, a moral sense that relates to what we ought to do, and the anagogical sense, which relates to eschatology. The spiritual sense thus relates to what we must believe (faith), what we should do (love), and what we can expect (hope). The basis for our faith, hope, and love is the literal sense as expanded in the threefold spiritual sense.

Does the existence of a spiritual sense introduce an intolerable level of indeterminacy into the text? Some theologians in the post-liberal school, such as Stephen Fowl, argue that by connecting the New Testament interpretation of the Old Testament text so closely to the literal sense, Thomas Aquinas initiated a trajectory leading to increasing indeterminacy in meaning. Insofar as the literal sense is stretched by seeing Jesus Christ as part of it, the stability of meaning is undermined. This indeterminacy of the text means that the reading community becomes the true source of meaning. Fowl says that the literal sense becomes a matter for the community to debate; it must be "hashed out" and is known by "communal assent."[13] If this interpretation of what Thomas was doing was correct, then postmodernism would have begun rather earlier than most people have assumed! But it is not correct. As Brevard Childs points out, to read Thomas this way is to miss Thomas's "careful attention to the ontological force exerted by the subject matter itself (its *res*)."[14] As I argued above, the content of the apostolic proclamation is Jesus Christ as the ontological reality made known in revelation. Indeterminacy is controlled by the centrality of Jesus Christ in the Bible.

Jesus Christ is the reality to which the things signified in the words of Scripture refer. He thus determines the true interpretation of Scripture; the role of the reading community is to believe in him and to recognize him as what Scripture reveals. Jesus Christ is the *res* of Scripture. To believe that Jesus Christ is the Promised One of the Hebrew Scriptures is precisely what it means to say that the New Testament interpretation of the Old Testament is true. The ontological reality of Jesus Christ, as he is proclaimed in the New Testament and as he is contained in the Old

---

13. Stephen E. Fowl, *Engaging Scripture: A Model for Theological Interpretation* (Eugene, OR: Wipf and Stock, 2008), 39.

14. Brevard S. Childs, *The Struggle to Understand Isaiah as Christian Scripture* (Grand Rapids: Eerdmans, 2004), 164.

Testament, is (1) the basis of the unity of the Testaments, (2) the basis of the unity of the literal and spiritual senses, and (3) the basis of the objectivity of the spiritual sense.

Principle 4: The Christological Control on Meaning

It should be clear by now that this fourth principle flows inevitably and naturally out of all that has been said so far. The ontological reality of Jesus Christ as the Word of God, who was God and was with God in the beginning (John 1:1–3), and as the one who is spoken of in the Law, the Prophets, and the Writings, is the basis for truly theological hermeneutics and also the basis for determining what is and is not the true meaning of the text. All interpretations of Old Testament texts are subject to the control that is placed on the interpreter by the ontological reality to which those texts witness. The meaning does not "belong" to the individual interpreter, to the academic guild, or even to the ecclesial community. It belongs to the triune God—Father, Son, and Holy Spirit—who speaks the word through his prophets and is himself the content of that word. The same Holy Spirit both inspired the Scriptures and continuously illumines their meaning to readers throughout history. Jesus tells us that all that the Father has belongs to him (John 16:15). The role of the Spirit is to testify to Jesus, to take what is Christ's and declare it to us (John 15:26; 16:13–14). The Holy Trinity reveals truth to us through the proper interpretation of Scripture.

What this means is that the correct interpretation of the meaning of any text is just the opposite of indeterminate; it is determined by the triune God. We can think of it this way: Jesus Christ is the word who speaks, the word which is spoken, and the reality (*res*) of which the word speaks. All interpretations of the text must cohere with and arise out of the Trinitarian reality that is the cause of the text. Any interpretation that fails to cohere with and arise out of Jesus Christ, therefore, is inadequate. This is the christological control on meaning that enables a coherent system of doctrine to emerge from exegesis. To be sure, paradox will characterize true interpretation of Scripture, but not contradiction.

Is it not strange that historical criticism, in the name of neutrality and scientific objectivity, has resulted in the introduction of endless contradictions into biblical interpretation and the atomization of Scripture into unrelated fragments, while the supposedly subjective exegesis of the fathers resulted in the orthodox, Trinitarian, and christological consensus of Nicaea and Chalcedon that has endured for over fifteen hundred years? Why does the approach that has been derided as subjective lead to a coherent system of theology while the supposedly objective approach leads to the fragmentation of the Bible into a jumble of incompatible human opinions? Why is it that the premodern approach can be preached authoritatively as the word of God while the modern one cannot? Perhaps David Steinmetz identified the answer to such questions in the title of his classic essay "The Superiority of Pre-Critical Exegesis."[15]

Part 3: Case Studies

Given the nature of the Bible as a two Testament book with Jesus Christ as its central theme and the four principles described above, how might we go about interpreting particular passages of Scripture? In this section we will look at three Old Testament passages—one from the Law, one from the Prophets, and one from the Writings—to illustrate how the principles can be put into practice while bearing in mind the unique, inspired nature of Scripture.

Genesis 22:1-19

The sacrifice of Isaac in Genesis 22 has a clear literal meaning, which John Calvin identifies as the test of Abraham's faith in God and God's promise to bring salvation to the world through Abraham's descendants. Calvin emphasized the significance of the event for the history of redemption and does not treat it as if it were about the ethics of a man offering his son as a sacrifice in obedience to a divine command. Genesis 22 focuses on the action in the story rather than the inner psychological state of the characters. The emotions of Abraham and the question of Isaac's obedience and submission remain under the surface of the narrative and do not seem to be the point so far as the narrator is concerned. Calvin did not assign a typological meaning to the various elements of

---

15. David C. Steinmetz, "The Superiority of Pre-Critical Exegesis," *Theology Today* 37 (1980): 27–38; reprinted as chapter 1 of David C. Steinmetz, *Taking the Long View: Christian Theology in Historical Perspective* (Oxford: Oxford University Press, 2009), 1–14.

the story, but he acknowledged that Isaac was "the mirror of eternal life, and the pledge of all good things."[16]

This passage also has a spiritual meaning, which expands the literal sense. The fathers of the church interpret Genesis 22 as full of typologies of Christ and his resurrection. Most are awed by this passage and overwhelmed with the aura of mystery that surrounds it. Even John Chrysostom, who did not go as far with allegory as his Alexandrian counterparts, said of this text, "All this, however, happened as a type of the cross. Hence Christ too said to the Jews, 'Your father Abraham rejoiced in anticipation of seeing my day; he saw it and was delighted.'"[17]

Mark Sheridan comments, "Even Chrysostom abandons his customary moralizing and employs a typological interpretation."[18] It is no exaggeration to say that all the fathers saw the passage as pointing to Christ in various ways. Caesarius of Arles said that Abraham is a type of God the Father and Isaac is a type of Christ.[19] He and many others called attention to the fact that verse 4 tells us that the near sacrifice occurred on "the third day." Origen commented that the third day "is always applied to mysteries."[20] Isaac carrying the wood prefigures Christ carrying his cross, and the ram stuck in the briars by its horns foreshadows Christ wearing the crown of thorns.[21]

Those who would make a hard and fast distinction between typology and allegory have a problem with this passage because the sheer number of types clustered together in one story cause it to be practically indistinguishable from an allegory. For premodern interpreters like Origen, however, the text itself must be permitted to determine which reading technique is appropriate in each interpretive situation. Origen took Abraham's words in response to Isaac's question ("Where is the sacrifice?") as prophecy: "He does not speak about the present but about the future. . . . God himself will provide himself a sheep."[22] So we have

---

16. John Calvin, *Genesis*, trans. John King, repr. ed., Calvin's Commentaries 1 (Grand Rapids: Baker, 2005), 565.

17. Chrysostom, cited in Mark Sheridan, ed., *Genesis 12–50*, ACCSOT 2 (Downers Grove, IL: IVP Academic), 110.

18. Sheridan, 106.

19. Caesarius of Arles, cited in Sheridan, 102.

20. Origen, cited in Sheridan, 103.

21. Caesarius of Arles, cited in Sheridan, 104.

22. Origen, cited in Sheridan, 105.

here a predictive prophecy similar to the ironic saying of Caiaphas: "It is better for you that one man should die for the people, not that the whole nation should perish" (John 11:50 ESV). Both Abraham and Caiaphas spoke more truly than they knew, which is a pattern in the prophets according to Peter (1 Pet 1:10–12).

How should we interpret this passage? I would suggest that a premodern approach should be guided by two main principles: the canonical context is decisive, and the spiritual sense must be shown to emerge from the literal sense. The literal sense of the passage is canonically expanded and christologically bounded.

First, let us consider the canonical expansion of the literal sense. Two key New Testament passages are of decisive importance for establishing the expanded literal sense of Genesis 22. First, note Hebrews 11:17–19: "By faith Abraham, when he was tested, offered up Isaac, and he who had received the promises was in the act of offering up his only son, of whom it was said, 'Through Isaac shall your offspring be named.' He considered that God was able even to raise him from the dead, from which figuratively speaking, he did receive him back" (ESV).

Here the author of Hebrews offers an interpretation of Abraham's faith. Abraham's faith was not merely blind obedience; he "considered" (*logisamenos*) that God was able even to raise him from the dead." Why did Abraham reason this way? In a second key New Testament text, Paul explains that Abraham understood the miraculous nature of Isaac's birth as evidence of God's power. He notes what God said to Abraham:

> "I have made you the father of many nations"—in the presence of the God in whom he believed, who gives life to the dead and calls into existence the things that do not exist. In hope he believed against hope, that he should become the father of many nations, as he had been told, "So shall your offspring be." He did not weaken in faith when he considered his own body, which was as good as dead (since he was about a hundred years old) or when he considered the barrenness of Sarah's womb. (Rom 4:17–19 ESV)

We see here a link between the doctrine of *creatio ex nihilo* and the miraculous birth of Isaac, both of which are similar to resurrection in that they entail creating life out of nonlife. Abraham's faith is in God as the Creator who is able to raise the dead and give a child to a couple in old age precisely because he is the God who brings the cosmos into being out of nothing.

Second, we are given the crucial clue to the interpretation of Genesis 22 in Hebrews 11:18 when it alludes to God's words in Genesis 21:12: "Through Isaac shall your offspring be named" (ESV). This clue, reinforced by the mention of resurrection in Hebrews 11:19 and topped off by the use of the Greek word *parabolē* (parable or archetype), shows that Hebrews is interpreting Genesis 22 christologically. We do not have time to go into detail here about the use of the term "offspring" (or "seed," *zeraʿ*) in Genesis 22:18, 2 Samuel 7:12, and various other texts. Suffice it to say that the trajectory of Scripture narrows the identity of the Redeemer from the seed of the woman to the seed of Abraham to the seed of David to the singular messianic figure who sits on the throne of David forever. We are dealing in Genesis 22 with a christological text that fits snugly into an unfolding narrative of redemption extending across the canon of the Christian two Testament Bible.

The passage must be interpreted in its canonical context, which means that we are justified in expanding the literal sense to include the spiritual sense referring to Christ. We are not justified in reading any spiritual sense whatsoever into the text; but only one that terminates on Jesus Christ as understood through the lens of the Abrahamic covenant. We thus have a christological control on a canonical expansion of the literal sense.

However, if we assume that Isaac is a type of Christ, should we also accept the allegorizing of the wood as the cross, the three days as prefiguring the resurrection of Christ on the third day, and the ram as Christ? I would accept these three examples as types and be open to seeing the Genesis 22 narrative as an allegory because there are so many types and not just one. However, in a very important sense there is only one main christological type (Isaac the only, beloved son corresponds to Christ the only, beloved Son; cf. Luke 3:22; 20:13) and all the others are subsumed under it. Debate over this point can easily degenerate into semantics. The key issue, from my perspective, is not whether we call it allegory or not, but whether the passage has an expanded literal christological sense. If we can agree that it does, then we can surely work out the details as to the best terminology to use to describe it. Our hermeneutical theory should be developed as we figure out the best way to describe the reality found in the text, which is just the opposite of fitting the meaning of the text into our preexisting hermeneutical categories.

Proverbs 8:22-31

Does Proverbs 8 speak of Christ when it speaks of Wisdom as existing prior to creation and as active in creation? Verse 22 of this passage was a key "proof text" for the Arian side in the fourth-century debates over the ontological status of the eternal Son of God. The ESV renders it, "The Lord possessed me at the beginning of his work." But the ESV includes a footnote indicating that the Septuagint has "created." This is because, although the Hebrew verb used here is *qanah* ("possess"), the Septuagint translates using the verb *ktizō* ("create"). The fourth-century fathers worked from the Septuagint translation and assumed the meaning "to create." All sides in the fourth-century controversies followed the New Testament apostles in reading the Old Testament references to Wisdom as having a christological reference (John 1:1–3; Col 1:16–17; Heb 1:3, 10–12). So, both sides in the Arian debate agreed that Proverbs 8:22–31 speaks of Christ.

Athanasius dealt with this passage extensively in his *Second Oration against the Arians*, and he employed his Trinitarian hermeneutics to argue that verse 22 is speaking of the creation of the human nature of the incarnate Son and not the creation of the preexistent Son. What principle did he employ? He pointed out that throughout Scripture we see references to both the humanity and the divinity of Christ, so we can apply a christological hermeneutic to each text in order to discern whether it is speaking of his humanity or his divinity. Athanasius argued that the divine, preexistent Son is eternally generated by the Father, and so the Father and Son are mutually constitutive and coeternal. Athanasius saw verse 22 as referring to the humanity of Christ, which is created.[23] As Khaled Anatolios shows, this Trinitarian approach to hermeneutics became central to the way the pro-Nicene fathers read

---

23. Athanasius of Alexandria, *Four Discourses against the Arians* 2.51, in *Nicene and Post-Nicene Fathers, Second Series*, ed. Philip Schaff and Henry Wace, repr. ed. (Peabody, MA: Hendrickson, 1994), 4:376.

Scripture.[24] Since they regarded divine authorial intent as primary and the Bible as a unity, they assumed coherence throughout.

The Hebrew verb *qanah* in Proverbs 8:22 does not usually have the sense of "created" in the Hebrew Bible. Derek Kidner says that only six or seven out of eighty-four uses allow for the sense of "create," and none require it.[25] So it would seem that either the Septuagint rendering is misleading or the verb *ktizō* did not mean only "create" in the minds of the translators of the Septuagint. In any case, *qanah* can mean "begotten" in the sense of "get." Eve said in Genesis 4:1, for example, "I have gotten [*qanah*] a man with the help of the Lord" (ESV). So the idea in Proverbs 8:22 would seem to be best translated by a verb that refers to generation rather than by one that refers to creation. If that is the case, then Athanasius's interpretation would be changed in the sense that Proverbs 8:22 would refer to the divine nature of the preexistent Son, not to the creation of the human nature of the God-man. But Arius would still be wrong. John Gill, another premodern exegete, interpreted Proverbs 8:22 as "The Lord possessed me" and rejected the Septuagint translation, which he associates with the error of Arius.[26]

In my view, Proverbs 8 is speaking about the preexistent Son as the agent by which God created the cosmos (vv. 22–29). By Wisdom (which in the minds of the New Testament writers is closely associated with the Logos) God brings forth the creation, and so it reflects the rationality of the Logos in the way it functions and holds everything together. Wisdom delights in its order and structure (vv. 30–31). Athanasius's Trinitarian hermeneutics is valid, but reading verse 22 as referring to the incarnation and the creation of the human nature of Jesus Christ is unnecessary here, since the text does not speak about Wisdom being created but as already being "possessed" by the Lord even at the very beginning of creation. The text teaches eternal generation and so is speaking of the eternal Son of God. The christological interpretation

---

24. Khaled Anatolios, *Retrieving Nicaea: The Development and Meaning of Trinitarian Doctrine* (Grand Rapids: Baker Academic, 2011), 108–26.

25. Derek Kidner, *Proverbs: An Introduction and Commentary*, TOTC 17 (Downers Grove, IL: InterVarsity Press, 1964), 79.

26. John Gill, *An Exposition of the Old Testament*, Baptist Commentary Series (London: Matthews and Leigh, 1810), 4:382.

of the fathers, as modified by Gill, stands as a legitimate extension of the literal sense.

Isaiah 42:1-4

The key issue in the interpretation of Isaiah 42 is the identity of the Lord's servant and the nature of his mission. It is crucial to see this passage in its proper context in the book of Isaiah and the Bible as a whole. To anticipate the conclusion, the servant is the mysterious suffering servant spoken of climactically in chapter 53, who is revealed in the New Testament to be Jesus Christ. We only have space here to sketch a rough outline of a proper exegesis of this passage.

This passage has been known as the first Servant Song since the work of Bernhard Duhm in the late nineteenth century. He identified the four "Servant Songs" (42:1–9; 49:1–13; 50:4–9; 52:13–53:12) and suggested that they were independent compositions incorporated into the book of Isaiah. In modern historical-critical studies, this suggestion invites a form-critical approach that I regard as mostly unhelpful. Much better, in my opinion, and in keeping with a premodern approach, is a literary-theological treatment in which the figure of the "servant" is seen as the theme of chapters 41–53. We have the introduction of "Israel, my servant," in Isaiah 41:8, and the term occurs all through these chapters, not just in the Servant Songs.

The premodern approach to the interpretation of this passage presupposes the unity of Isaiah as a book. The main theme of Isaiah is "the Holy One of Israel," a phrase that occurs twenty-six times, scattered throughout all the major sections of the book. The phrase encapsulates the problem of the book: how can a holy God fulfill the eternal covenant promises made to Abraham and David when Israel is so persistently unholy and God must punish sin? The problem is that it seems that the Lord must either go against his own word and leave sin unpunished or else fail to keep his covenant promises to bless all the nations through the seed of Abraham. If the nation is allowed to stand, the Lord is tolerating sin, but if the nation is destroyed, a descendent of David will not sit on David's throne forever.

Isaiah sees two problems: a political problem, which is minor, and a sin problem, which is major. The Lord is the sovereign ruler of the cosmos and in full control of history. The pagan empires (Assyrian,

Babylonian, and Persian) are putty in his hands. Delivering Israel or allowing judgment to fall on the nation is simple for him. But how can the sinful inclinations of the human heart be changed? How can sin be atoned for? How can sin be punished without destroying Israel?

Isaiah actually speaks of various servants in these chapters, three of which are significant for our purposes here. First, we see the originally chosen servant, Israel. But Israel has failed in their task. Isaiah knows this from the start of his ministry; his commission was to preach exile and judgment (Isa 6:9–12). Israel is a blind and deaf servant (Isa 42:18–19). Second, we see Cyrus, who (shockingly) is portrayed as God's "anointed" (Isa 45:1) and God's "shepherd" (Isa 44:28). He is the "lesser servant" who solves the smaller problem, namely, the political problem of exile. Third, we see the mysterious figure who is identified with Israel yet seems to be an individual within Israel who is addressed by the Lord:

> It is too light a thing that you should be my servant
> > to raise up the tribes of Jacob
> > and to bring back the preserved of Israel;
> I will make you a light for the nations,
> > that my salvation may reach to the end of the earth.
> > (Isa 49:6 ESV)

This one is the "greater servant" who, in the climax of this section in chapter 53, deals with the sin problem by making atonement through his suffering, death, and resurrection. To add to the sense of mystery that pervades these oracles in chapters 40–53, the Lord himself declares at various points that he himself will be "your Redeemer, the Holy One of Israel" (Isa 48:17).

The debate between rabbinic Judaism and messianic Judaism is not actually over whether or not the suffering servant is Israel. Both would agree that the servant is Israel *in some sense*. The difference is that the streams of rabbinic Judaism that hold to a collective interpretation would say that the servant is *only* Israel, whereas messianic Judaism and premodern Christian interpretation would say he is *both*.[27] Only when

---

27. The Targum of Jonathan teaches a messianic interpretation of Isaiah 53. Some of the rabbis of the Christian era saw it as referring to Messiah ben Joseph. Many others, however, taught a collective interpretation in which the servant is the righteous remnant of Israel,

this fact is appreciated can we make headway in exegeting Isaiah 42:1–4. Since the servant arises out of Israel, he in a sense *is* Israel. This is why the New Testament opens by presenting Jesus Christ as the descendent of Abraham and David in Matthew 1:1. This is why he recapitulates the history of Israel in his person going down to Egypt, returning out of Egypt, going through the Red Sea in baptism, dealing with temptation in the wilderness for forty days, feeding the multitudes in the wilderness, conquering the enemies of God's people by overcoming demons, instituting the messianic kingdom by healing the blind, making the lame to walk and the deaf to hear, and raising the dead. He is the temple—he is Israel! All who take refuge in him, who believe in his name and put their faith in him, are incorporated into him and thus become part of the redeemed people of God. The Christian church is not a replacement for Israel; it is gentiles grafted into the remnant of Israel to create the redeemed people of God promised in the Abrahamic covenant.

The rejection of "God's chosen servant" is expected and seen clearly in the ministry of Jesus. Matthew calls attention to it repeatedly. All four Gospels and Acts quote Isaiah 6:9–10, which speaks of the pattern by which the majority of Israel repeatedly rejects the prophets and Yahweh himself. And in Matthew 12:18–21, we have Isaiah 42:1–3 quoted as the explanation for the rejection of Jesus. Jesus, in Luke 24:25–27, stresses that his suffering and death should have been expected. Why? Because it was foretold in Isaiah very clearly. Yet, the apostles are convinced that just as Isaiah said, "He will not grow faint or be discouraged till he has established justice in the earth; the coastlands wait for his law" (Isa 42:4 ESV). The "coastlands" here refer to the spread of the saving effects of the servant's work over the whole earth as Christ's witnesses carry out the Great Commission.

The one described in Isaiah 42:1–4 is the "greater servant" of Isaiah 49–53, who emerges out of Israel to do for Israel what Israel had failed to do for themselves. He is able to do this because, in some undefined

---

including such famous names as Rashi. See C. R. North, *The Suffering Servant in Deutero-Isaiah: An Historical and Critical Study*, 2nd ed. (Oxford: Oxford University Press, 1956), 9–22. Also, see Stefan Schreiner, "Isaiah 53 in the Sefer Hizzuk Emunah ("Faith Strengthened") of Rabbi Isaac ben Abraham of Troki," in *The Suffering Servant: Isaiah 53 in Jewish and Christian Sources*, ed. Bernd Janowski and Peter Stuhlmacher, trans. Daniel P. Bailey (Grand Rapids: Eerdmans, 2004), 418–61. For Rabbi Isaac ben Abraham, the servant is Israel suffering in exile.

and mysterious way, he actually is the Lord himself, acting in Israel's history to redeem Israel and, in so doing, bring blessing to the whole earth. It is little wonder that the New Testament apostles, writing under the inspiration of the Holy Spirit, were able to see that in Jesus Christ the Isaianic text was fulfilled.

Conclusion

The premodern approach to the interpretation of Christ in the Old Testament itself arises out of the Bible's own account of the metaphysical situation in which interpretation occurs. This is why it is superior to all approaches that are rooted in other metaphysical accounts of reality (such as philosophical naturalism). The ontological reality to which the text bears witness exerts control on the process of interpretation by requiring a focus on God's self-revelation through his Word. Since God is the transcendent Creator and sovereign Lord of history who alone is worthy of worship, the true interpretation of Scripture depends on recognizing it as a unified book centered on Jesus Christ. The Bible is *literally* about Jesus Christ. This is why the expanded literal sense of the Old Testament text, under the hermeneutical control of New Testament Christology, bears witness to him. Like the disciples on the road to Emmaus, we come to the Scriptures and expect that he will open them up and interpret to us "in all the Scriptures the things concerning himself" (Luke 24:27 ESV).

JOHN GOLDINGAY

I'm glad Dr. Carter urged the importance of premodern interpretation of the Scriptures. I have found commentators such as Jerome, Calvin, and Trapp at least as illuminating as the average modern commentator. A major reason is that they don't divide articulating the text's inherent meaning, in its context, from its significance for God's relationship with us. On the other hand, I also see a positive theological significance in approaches of a grammatical-historical kind, whereas Dr. Carter sets himself over against them. So that difference will be a focus of my response to this chapter.

Premodern and Grammatical-Historical

Dr. Carter contrasts a premodern and a naturalistic historical-critical approach. Here's my attempt to take up the wording he uses when he sets these approaches over against one another, but to reformulate it so that it might describe something more grammatical-historical:

> The grammatical-historical approach seeks to identify the intended meaning of the original human author, which it equates with the literal sense and with the divine author's intended meaning communicated through the human author's words, and thereby to hear God speak through the literal sense of the text. The grammatical-historical approach is faith seeking understanding and a spiritual discipline for sanctification oriented to the goal of worship, a method by which the reader seeks to be

mastered by the text in light of what the divine author was saying through the original, human author.

I don't think the grammatical-historical method developed simply as an attempt to clean up the historical-critical method. Rather, scholars such as Carl Friedrich Keil and Franz Delitzsch wisely declined to take the development of a "historical approach" to the Scriptures to its logical conclusion. Perhaps they would accept the definition I just reformulated, but they didn't build it into the way they wrote their commentaries because they were working in the shadow of that developing stress on history. And conservative commentators have continued to accept that framework, at least until the rise of attempts to write theological commentaries over recent decades (as if there really could be a properly non-theological commentary on the Scriptures!).

A large part of the problem lies with the word *historical*. The kind of interpretation that Dr. Carter critiques separates the historical and the theological. Nebuchadnezzar's destruction of Jerusalem became simply a historical question. What that event signified about God and his relationship to Israel and to the world became a separate question that could be left on one side because it was not historical. One might expect that Christians and Jews, atheists and agnostics, would be able to agree on the answer to the first question, though not on the second. But in between those two questions is another. The documents recording Israelite history don't confine themselves to the empirical historical facts. They express the facts' theological significance. And that is actually part of the texts' historical meaning. Yet modern commentaries of any religious persuasion pay little attention to the inbuilt theological significance of the story they tell. And it means they fail as exegesis. The text's historical meaning includes its religious and theological message. Commentators don't have to agree with this message, but they fall short of their task if they don't exegete it. It doesn't make any difference whether they are Jews or Christians, agnostics or atheists: their task is to enter empathetically into the text and elucidate it. In principle and in theory, it's as possible for unbelieving as for believing commentators to do this work of elucidation. And they often do, sometimes because they are less worried when there are things in the text that disagree with their own theological position.

Anyone who recognizes the authority of the Scriptures should surely want to be grammatical-historical in the sense of seeking to listen in on what God gave the prophets to say to their people in their time, because understanding what the scriptural authors wrote for their audience helps modern readers hear what God might be saying to us. But when premodern commentators read Jesus into the Scriptures, they imperil the possibility of our being able to understand and hear that message.

Grammatical-Historical and Historical-Critical

Dr. Carter refers to the suggestion that a grammatical-historical approach is dishonest. John Barton's specific point in the passage he references is that reading any text involves first discovering what it means, then deciding whether it is true, and that this is how we should read the Scriptures. I'm not sure he's right about texts in general, but I plead guilty with regard to the Scriptures: I assume they are true before I start reading. I'm not clear that this makes my study dishonest, though in a sense it does make it noncritical in that I decline to start from what I might, as a modern person, think is obviously true and make that the principle for criticizing things. As Dr. Carter notes, "critical" can come to mean rationalistic or naturalistic: in reading a text, one lets one's own experience provide the critical principle for deciding whether the thing could have happened. Jesus couldn't have risen from the dead because resurrections don't happen. But even scholars who work with a historical-critical paradigm may not operate in that rationalistic way.

Biblical criticism started off as the implementing of an attitude to the teaching of tradition or of the church regarding the meaning of the Scriptures, not of an attitude to the Scriptures themselves. In this sense, historical-critical interpretation is quite possible for someone who recognizes the authority of the Scriptures—indeed, it is a requirement. Anyone who recognizes the Scriptures' authority will surely want to be critical in the way Jesus was. The devil quoted Psalm 91 to him in a Christ-centered way, and Jesus questioned his interpretation (Matt 4:5–7). We don't simply assume that the meaning of the Scriptures is what Christian tradition says it is, or what scholars say it is, or what the preacher says it is (Acts 17:11). We are critical, not in the sense of being judgmental but in the sense that we are prepared to ask questions. And the basis for deciding the answer to the questions lies in the text itself.

Generally, I don't think that scholars who take a grammatical-historical approach are more constrained by their presuppositions than scholars who take a historical-critical approach. Admittedly, there is another sense in which conservative scholarship can be critiqued as inconsistent and dishonest. Commentators may seem to accept the conclusions of a historical-critical approach where the conclusions fit their presuppositions, but not where they don't. A classic example would be accepting the results of archaeological discoveries when they support the story told in Joshua (e.g., concerning the destruction of Hazor, at least as interpreted by its excavator) but not when they don't (e.g., concerning the destruction of Jericho and Ai, about which the usual view is that they had been destroyed long before Joshua's time).

As my opening sentences hinted, being naturalistic isn't the only problem with the historical-critical method. At least as deleterious is its inclination to focus so predominantly on the historical development of texts and on the historical events to which they refer. There is nothing theologically wrong with these two forms of inquiry. But the damaging result of that focus is a neglect of the text in favor of continuing a conversation among scholars about what the process might have been and what might have happened. Over the past two or three centuries, this focus has taken attention away from study of the text itself, both by people who accept the Scriptures' authority and by people who don't. In theory, at least, the strength and importance of the grammatical-historical method is that it focuses on the text itself (not the history behind it, in either sense) and on its meaning as an act of communication with "our ancestors."

Comments Regarding the Three Case Studies

In Genesis 22 Dr. Carter describes typological interpretation as concerned with the text's spiritual meaning. But he has already shown that the text's literal meaning is spiritual: the story is about the spiritual relationship between God and Abraham. Does an interpretation of the passage in light of the New Testament exclude God's continuing to speak to us on the basis of the text's original spiritual meaning?

Whereas I will note that Dr. Carter discusses Isaiah 42:1–4 in light of its context in the book, he seems to disregard the context with Proverbs 8:22–31. In reading Colossians back into Proverbs, he ignores

Proverbs' own point about the challenge to heed wisdom. The discussion also illustrates a problem about every attempt to read Christ into the First Testament. On the one hand, we then learn only what we knew already from the New Testament; it must be so if our reading is to be canonical. And on the other hand, we lose the text's own meaning in its original context when God was speaking to his people.

With Isaiah 42, I'm glad Dr. Carter doesn't fall for the idea of Servant Songs, and instead he does see Isaiah 42 in the context of Isaiah 41–53. But then he says that "the central problem of the history of Israel was how a holy God could be bound in an eternal covenant to an unholy people" (247). Isaiah gives no indication of sensing that this is a problem; nor does the First Testament elsewhere. And only a part of one sentence in the New Testament refers to it as a problem (Rom 3:25–26). Wasn't it premodern theologians (!) who turned it into the central problem as they focused on God as Judge? The First Testament thinks more of God's relationship with his people as personal and familial and doesn't have a problem with God "carrying" our sin (the literal meaning of the verb translated "forgive")—which is what he was doing on the cross. Is Dr. Carter not reading the Scriptures in light of a human tradition of interpretation of which he should be critical for the sake of the Scriptures themselves?

I might append a broader point. Dr. Carter says that "Jesus fulfilled the Scriptures in such a way that much in them that had been mysterious and opaque suddenly became comprehensible and clear. He is the Reality; the law, the temple, and the sacrifices were the shadows" (246). While the New Testament does use the word "shadow" (Col 2:17; Heb 8:5; 10:1), it doesn't say that the Scriptures were mysterious or opaque. Indeed, Paul notes Moses's comment that "the word is near you, on your lips and in your heart" (Rom 10:8 NRSV; cf. Deut 30:11–14). The problem was not opaqueness but unwillingness. The First Testament doesn't think law, temple, or sacrifices are mysterious, though the New Testament does see new significance in them when they help us understand Jesus.

There is a kind of converse point. Jesus encouraged John the Baptizer's disciples to believe in him because of things they had seen and heard—the blind receiving their sight, the lepers being cleansed, and so on (Luke 7:18–23). Some irony attaches to Dr. Carter's comment that "characteristic signs of the messianic age, such as the blind being made to see, the lame being made to walk, those possessed by demons being delivered, and the dead being raised were performed by Jesus," because the First Testament does not associate any of these actions with the Messiah. Isaiah 35 does mention the first two, but they are aspects of what will happen when God brings people back from the exile; the chapter doesn't refer to the Messiah. Thus, when Jesus points out that he has been doing those things, he doesn't invite those disciples to link them with the Scriptures. And when his own disciples come to reaffirm their faith in him after his crucifixion, it is on the basis of God raising him from among the dead, not on the basis of a link with the Scriptures. The scriptural link follows, but it's not the foundation.

TREMPER LONGMAN III

Dr. Carter suggests a recovery of "the premodern approach to the christological interpretation of the Old Testament" (239). He rightly points out that there was a period of time when premodern interpreters were ignored because Enlightenment-influenced (modernist) scholars thought that interpretation prior to the rise of historical criticism was not worth knowing. Such a view is still held by some, maybe many, but the emergence of postmodern thinking has challenged the idea that one can actually achieve a neutral, objective, value-free interpretation to which modernist scholars aspired. Indeed, thanks to work by scholars like Carter, most theologically oriented Old Testament interpreters do take advantage of premodern insights into the text as a matter of reception history.

The idea that we can learn from premodern thinkers like Augustine, Aquinas, and Calvin is certainly valid and profitable, as evidenced by Carter's appropriation of their insights in his article. But I found his criticism of modernist interpretive strategies confusing and wrong-minded.

Let me begin, though, by affirming his critique of the historical-critical method, which arguably is the most consistent form of Enlightenment hermeneutics in that, as Carter rightly says, it operates with a "narrow, naturalistic definition of history" (240).[1] In the first place, it asserts the principle of autonomy, which insists that the

---

1. For a fuller account and critique of historical criticism, see Tremper Longman III, "History and the Old Testament," in *Hearing the Old Testament: Listening for God's Address*, ed. Craig G. Bartholomew and David J. H. Beldman (Grand Rapids: Eerdmans, 2012), 96–121.

interpreter break with tradition and assume an attitude of skepticism. Second, historical criticism, as the name implies, takes a critical stance toward the text, treating any interpretation as provisional and open to change. As practiced by historical critics, these first two principles lead to what has been called a hermeneutic of suspicion, as opposed to a hermeneutic of trust, the former of which Carter would rightly warn us.

However, rather than a pure hermeneutic of suspicion on the one hand, or an out-and-out rejection of the first two principles on the other, I would say that interpreters should exercise a certain humility and self-criticism in their interpretations—after all, it is the Bible and not our interpretations that are inerrant.[2] However, from what Carter says about historical criticism, I imagine he rightly has historical criticism's third principle primarily in his mind, the principle of analogy, which asserts that the historian cannot accept as historically true anything that is not part and parcel of their own present experience. So much for the sea splitting or Lazarus coming back from the dead or the resurrection of Jesus. Carter is right to disavow this kind of interpretation as undermining not only a Christian reading of the Old Testament but Christianity itself.

But problems arise when Carter brings historical-grammatical interpretation into the discussion, which he correctly understands as the practice of more conservative biblical scholars like myself. Historical-grammatical exegesis is indeed a form of modernist interpretation, but it does not necessarily bracket the supernatural. Rather, it presumes that God was speaking through Scripture most immediately and directly to the original audience, which is not those of us who live in the twenty-first century. The final form of Samuel-Kings, for instance, was addressed to an exilic audience, and Chronicles was written to a postexilic audience. In other words, the human authors clearly (as the text itself reveals) had a specific audience in mind when they wrote.[3]

The historical-grammatical method seeks to understand biblical books in their original setting. Such study involves translation (text

---

2. Of course, in accordance with the Westminster Confession of Faith's statement on perspicuity, I would affirm that those matters that are essential to salvation are so clearly taught in so many ways that no reasonable doubt can be cast on them.
3. This is true of the books of the New Testament as well. We don't call the book of Romans "Romans" for nothing.

criticism, philology), genre analysis, ancient Near Eastern comparisons, and literary analysis (based on the conventions of Hebrew storytelling and poetry). Later Carter does say that "both the premodern and the modern approaches utilize all the available scholarly resources for interpretation, including philology, history, archaeology, textual criticism, literary theory, comparative religion, and so forth" (243). Wonderful! Carter thus reveals himself as a historical-grammatical modernist interpreter. Indeed, the premoderns did some of this work at times themselves. Jerome was something of a text critic and philologist (though we have a lot more resources today, including his work). Augustine used literary theory as he studied (though he applied Greco-Roman standards to Hebrew poetry rather than asking how the Hebrews wrote poetry).

So again, maybe Carter and I are closer than his essay suggests, since he seems to throw historical-grammatical exegesis under the bus.[4] Perhaps he is writing with rhetorical flourish when he does so. Indeed, Carter, like the premoderns, does care about the literal sense, at least most of the time (see below on the premodern interpretation of the Song of Songs). He claims that modernist readers use the literal meaning (defined as the intended meaning of the human author) for a different purpose than premodern readers. The latter want to hear the voice of God speaking through the literal sense to get to an expansion of the literal sense that points to Christ. And I can agree with that, but if that is the case, let's study the text with historical-grammatical exegesis to get to that "literal meaning" as a first step.

Again, I am confused about Carter's views on this matter, but I do worry that his approach doesn't give enough credence to the literal sense before moving beyond it. And besides his critique of historical-grammatical exegesis in this chapter, there are two other reasons that lead me to worry that he actually does want to dissuade us from historical-grammatical interpretation.

First, Carter sounds very similar to Rusty Reno, the editor of the Brazos Theological Commentary, who in the preface to that series also rails against historical studies. Reno rejects historical study in

---

4. He cites John Barton as an example of his impression that "liberal historical critics, however, frequently see this [historical-grammatical exegesis] as inconsistent and dishonest" (241). I'm not sure why Carter, who has no great love for historical critics, thinks this statement is somehow a telling blow against historical-grammatical exegesis. I certainly don't.

favor of reading the biblical books through the "rule of faith." There are some very fine commentaries in that series (e.g., Telford Work on Deuteronomy, Daniel Treier on Proverbs and Ecclesiastes), but then there are those like Francesca Murphy's on 1 Samuel, about which I comment: "All I can say is that I don't know what Murphy is talking about, but it's not the text of Samuel."[5]

It's a little unfair to cite Reno and Murphy in a critique of Carter's approach, but these three scholars are similar in their disparagement of historical studies. It's true that Carter seems to make room for historical studies in his second principle of interpretation ("the priority of the literal sense" [252]), though what I believe is a necessary historical-grammatical approach is only hinted at there at best. This is the second reason why I think that Carter is actually critical of the historical-grammatical approach. When it comes to his case studies, he does give us a paragraph of what seems to be a summary of the meaning of Genesis 22 in its original context, but there is nothing comparable in his other two case studies.

In short, my concern about Carter's presentation of premodern interpretation is similar to the worry expressed by Mark Boda concerning Reno's approach. In a review of theological commentary in the Reno style, Boda charges that Reno wrongly makes us choose between "the historical-theological approach of modernity and the ahistorical-theological approach of premodernity."[6] There is a third way. One can have a robust theological/christological reading of the text that is also understood in the context of its original setting. In other words, our interpretation can be and actually must be historical and theological, not one or the other.

Let me conclude with what I think is an example of premodern exegesis gone awry because of a lack of consideration of the original historical context determined by historical-grammatical exegesis—namely, the premodern interpretation of the Song of Songs.[7]

---

5. Tremper Longman III, *Old Testament Commentary Survey*, 5th ed. (Grand Rapids: Baker Academic, 2013), 55.

6. Mark J. Boda, "Theological Commentary: A Review and Reflective Essay," *McMaster Journal of Theology and Ministry* 11 (2009–10): 144.

7. For more detail about the history of interpretation of the Song, see Tremper Longman III, *Song of Songs*, NICOT (Grand Rapids: Eerdmans, 2001), 20–47.

We start getting commentary on the Song of Songs starting around AD 100 from both Jewish and Christian scholars. Both interpret the book as an allegory. For Jewish readers, the man of the Song represents God while the woman stands for Israel. For Christian readers, the man stands for God or Christ while the woman stands for the church or the individual Christian. Even the details of the Song are pressed into service for this allegorical reading. For instance, to Hippolytus, in an interpretation of 1:13 that is passed down through the centuries up to the modern period, the sack of myrrh that is lodged between the woman's breasts is Christ, while the breasts are the Old and New Testaments.

This type of interpretation was passed down through the premodern period uncritically as far as I can see. But matters changed when the premodern period transitioned to the modern period. Though not at the start of the modern period, the nineteenth century was pivotal for our understanding of the Song. For one thing, premodern interpretations that were passed down were not subjected to critical analysis. But with the rise of modernism, interpreters were encouraged to question their interpretation (see above how this can indeed devolve into an unhealthy skepticism but does not have to). One might imagine the last premodern teacher passing on Hippolytus's interpretation of 1:13 to the first modernist student. The teacher says, "Son (because at that time he would be male), the breasts are the Old and New Testaments." Rather than simply accepting the tradition, the student says, "What? Why? Why would I understand the breasts as representing the Old and New Testaments?" And the teacher would have no good reason since the Song of Songs is not an allegory. There is nothing within the book that would lead one to think it is an allegory (no such genre signals). In the nineteenth century, the modernist interpreter would appeal to Egyptian love songs that are similar in many ways to the Song. He would appeal to contemporary Arab wedding songs and on and on. Thus, a modernist historical-grammatical interpretation helps us read the Song better.

The problem with the premoderns' allegorical interpretation of the Song is that they miss all the wonderful insight about God's gift of sexuality and physical intimacy that the Song offers.[8] They miss how

8. See Dan B. Allender and Tremper Longman III, *God Loves Sex: An Honest Conversation about Sexual Desire and Holiness* (Grand Rapids: Baker, 2014).

the Song is the story of the redemption of sexuality that was broken at the fall.

Now, it would be wrong to stop at this point. There is indeed a theological and Christotelic interpretation of the Song as it is read within the context of the canon, based on the pervasive use of the marriage metaphor to refer to the relationship between God and his people. Then, of course, that metaphor is appropriated by New Testament authors to speak about our relationship with Christ (Eph 5:21–33). Thus, after our first reading of the Song to get its rich teaching about sexuality, we then can read it canonically to see that indeed it does point to Christ by way of the marriage metaphor.

In closing, though, I want to reaffirm Carter's project of learning from premodern interpreters, and I also applaud for the most part the Christocentric insights that he draws from them in regard to our three case studies. However, we lose way too much if we ignore the insights of modernist historical-grammatical exegesis while we do so.[9]

---

9. The occasion does not call on me to affirm that we get positive insights from postmodern interpretation too, but see Tremper Longman III, "Reading the Bible Postmodernly," *Mars Hill Review* 12 (1998): 23–30.

RESPONSE TO CRAIG A. CARTER
(THE RECEPTION-CENTERED, INTERTEXTUAL APPROACH)

HAVILAH DHARAMRAJ

I smiled when reading the opening line of this chapter: "The purpose of this essay is to defend the premodern approach to the christological interpretation of the Old Testament and to explain why it is necessary for us to retrieve it today" (239). Premodern exegesis probably sees itself as forcing its way into present-day academic discourse after Steinmetz's sterling publication in 1980 gave it a foot in the door.[1] However, in the fast-growing church of South Asia, and probably other parts of the world, the premodern approach needs no defense. In my experience, it enjoys a hearty welcome at pulpits across the Protestant denominations. If anything, other methods of exposition have to fight for their place at the table—or more specifically, at the pulpit. Since this book (and series) is largely church-facing and meant as a resource for both those who preach and those who hear the Bible preached, the premodern approach well deserves attention.

To some Christians, the Old Testament is a jumble of obsolete rituals and archaic customs—from animal sacrifices to the levirate practice. Here are stories following stories in a dizzying pileup of names we can barely pronounce, let alone remember—from Ahithophel to Zelophehad. Here is a deity who is not easy to figure or to relate to—unapproachable, rather scary, and someone who gives his blessing to burning whole cities to the ground. Like Aslan, he is not safe. Unlike Aslan, he may not be good. Even seminary students have often set foot into the Introduction

---

1. David C. Steinmetz, "The Superiority of Pre-Critical Exegesis," *Theology Today* 37 (1980): 27–38.

to the Old Testament class with a marked indifference to the first thirty-nine books of the Bible. So, while the church fathers used their mix of exegetical methods to teach their flock the relevance of the Old Testament to their faith in Jesus, many a present-day preacher uses them to quickly move their congregation from the unknown into the known. It might even be the case that the preachers themselves are in wild, unfamiliar territory and are looking anxiously for a passage into the New Testament. That passage is, nearly always, through finding Jesus in the text—using much the same array of methods as the premodern approach: "messianic prophecy, typology, allegory, prosopological exegesis, and theological readings of history" (242).

Given that this (panicked) flight from the Old Testament can result in (hermeneutically) unorthodox exits, it would have helped if Dr. Carter had allowed some space for the following.

First: *defining and describing the methods* listed would have helped immensely—even if briefly, and even if only limited to the ones deployed in the case studies. (The term *prosopological exegesis* was new to me, and I would have welcomed being educated with a description and a quick example.) This would have helped the reader understand that the premodern approach is not a case of "anything goes." Looking to identify the interpretative moves made in the case studies, I found this central to the approach: "The literal sense of the passage is canonically expanded and christologically bounded" (258).

Applying this to the three cases, we see that for Genesis 22, the canonical expansion was made through two New Testament texts that comment on Abraham (Heb 11:17–19; Rom 4:17–19). A third New Testament text (Heb 11:18) was used to demonstrate the reading as christologically bounded. In the case of Proverbs 8, the canonical expansion cited several New Testament texts (John 1:1–3; Col 1:16–17; Heb 1:3, 10–12), and these provided the necessary christological boundaries. How exactly to understand the Wisdom poem christologically required an assessment and modification of Athanasius's reading. In the case of Isaiah 42, the canonical expansion is first extended to a thematic reading over Isaiah 41–53 to identify the "greater servant" of chapters 49–53 as Jesus. A further canonical expansion is made by tracking the theme of the rejection of this "greater servant" across the Gospels and Acts, which provide the christological boundaries.

Carter makes clear that his interest is not to identify the method(s) used: "Our hermeneutical theory should be developed as we figure out the best way to describe the reality found in the text, which is just the opposite of fitting the meaning of the text into our preexisting hermeneutical categories" (260). But, if armed only with the exhortation to look for christological expansion across the canon—via the New Testament's reference to the Old Testament, via a premodern exegete, or via a thematic investigation—the intended reader of this chapter might go away no further enlightened than before they read the chapter. Rather, since they are encouraged that "Scriptures do, however, contain truth that humans are capable of discovering on their own by the usual processes of observation and analysis" (250), they would carry on as before, beating hasty exits from the Old Testament to the New, any which way they can.

Second: *balancing rather than polarizing*. In this chapter we have an "us" and "them" separated by clearly drawn battle lines: the modern versus the premodern. For example, "The modern approach seeks to identify the intended meaning of the original human author, which it equates with the literal sense; the premodern approach seeks to hear God speak through the literal sense of the text" (243). I assume that "modern approach" here refers to both the historical and literary. If that is so, finding a middle ground rather than forcing a choice between approaches might work better, especially given that we know both approaches have their share of embarrassing excesses. That is why Carter includes the disclaimer that defense of the premodern approach does not include "defending every single interpretation by every single premodern interpreter" (244). Rather than set one approach against another, I find the commonly used triple analogy of window-picture-mirror approach to Bible interpretation to be more productive. The text is a window into the world in which it is set; the text is a painting to be admired in both its big picture and its intricate detail; the text is a mirror in which readers can see themselves. The window analogy has a production-centered emphasis, the mirror analogy has a reception-centered emphasis, and the painting analogy is somewhere in between.

I am persuaded that a balance between the three is what best leads to—to use Walter Moberly's phrase—a "careful and prayerful" reading of the text. The keen Common Reader buys a *Cultural Backgrounds Study*

Bible precisely to balance their prayerful reading with a careful reading, one which includes all the kinds of historical information they would bring to bear on the text if they were reading, say, Arthur Miller's *The Crucible*. The reader wouldn't make much sense of the play unless they knew something about the Salem witch hunts and McCarthyism. The same applies for the befuddled Common Reader who comes across, say, the story of Tamar tricking her father-in-law, Judah, into impregnating her, and then being commended as "more righteous" than he (Gen 38). One would be hard put to launch from that story into a christologically bounded canonical expansion without totally ignoring the startling story line, its feisty heroine, and its cleverly constructed plot. Certainly, ignoring the characters and the plot is what happens with Calvin's reading of Genesis 22, summarized in the chapter as an example of premodern reading: "The emotions of Abraham and the question of Isaac's obedience and submission remain under the surface of the narrative and do not seem to be the point so far as the narrator is concerned" (256).

Early in his chapter, Carter helpfully affirms, "Both the premodern and the modern approaches utilize all the available scholarly resources for interpretation, including philology, history, archaeology, textual criticism, literary theory, comparative religion, and so forth" (243). Showing how, say, history or archaeology or literary theory work for the case studies would have mitigated the sharp divide between the premodern and the modern approaches. There is a certain value in "both-and" which gets diminished when one has to pick sides.

Third: *finding Jesus* through *rather than* in *the Old Testament*. My good friend and mentor Christopher Wright cautions against a "Where's Waldo" approach to Old Testament texts. One of his early books was titled, pointedly, *Knowing Jesus through the Old Testament*. I think he makes a point by using the preposition *through*. In my region, sermons are intent on extracting—even, wrenching—a set of (supposedly christologically bounded) propositions from Old Testament texts. To watch exquisitely crafted poems and oracles—and worse, narratives— being rapidly reduced to propositions is distressing. At the very least, it neglects to pay a carefully constructed piece of literature the attention it deserves. Of the three case studies in the chapter, I wondered if the Wisdom poem had not been rapidly reduced to such a proposition: "Proverbs 8 is speaking about the preexistent Son as the agent by which

God created the cosmos (vv. 22–29)" (261). This is the pitfall of reading the Old Testament, looking to find Jesus *in* it. If our interest was to understand or know Jesus *through* the Old Testament, we might linger much longer on the text and be well rewarded by its contribution to our faith and practice.

One reason the approach is eager to find Jesus in the Old Testament is stated like this: "The premodern approach is faith seeking understanding" (243). I propose that an alternative route for "faith seeking understanding" is to study each genre of the Old Testament alongside its contemporaneous counterparts, whether it be historiography or the legal canon or poetry or proverbial wisdom or speculative wisdom. We might even study them alongside parallel sacred texts of religions in the region. In my experience, reading the creation account in Genesis alongside its Mesopotamian and Egyptian cosmogonies, and alongside the Hindu and Islamic cosmogonies, has helped many students understand God the Creator in a unique light. In a multireligious environment, we better understand our Creator God when we read him against gods ancient and current. Having understood the attributes and nature of God as Genesis 1–2 lays it out, we move on to the New Testament's celebration of Jesus's role and function in creation. On the other hand, if our interest in Genesis 1 was limited to, say, identifying the Trinity *in* 1:1–2 and 1:26 ("let us make"), we would miss out on the very point of the creation stories—to teach us who God is through his act of creating the world. For starters, here is a "bachelor" God, who does not need a consort, who creates the universe rather than procreating it. Here is a God who creates all humankind—not just kings—in his image. For many a seminary student, this is Christian faith seeking to understand and appreciate God in an ancient text. It is *through* this understanding and appreciation of the God of Genesis 1–2 that many seekers are set on the road to meeting Jesus.

The premodern method, it seems to me, scans the Old Testament for Jesus, highlighter in hand. When it thinks it has found him, it marks him in neon and assumes that its task of reading the text for "meaning" has been well executed. And we know how difficult it is to read a text—as it is meant to be read—once someone has gone over it with a highlighter. Rather, if we could set out interpretative moves by which to work out canonical expansion, and if we could deploy the premodern and modern approaches in cooperation with each other, we postmoderns would know Jesus better through the Old Testament. And it would be a richer and deeper knowing, achieving what the premodern approach so nobly makes its pursuit: "a spiritual discipline for sanctification oriented to the goal of worship" (243).

JASON S. DEROUCHIE

I am grateful to Dr. Carter for clearly synthesizing the hermeneutics and practice of an orthodox approach to theological interpretation of Scripture. As with my first reading of his *Interpreting Scripture with the Great Tradition*,[1] I found myself affirming many of his claims, appreciating most of his critiques and cautions, and aligning with many of his conclusions. This is especially true regarding his comments about Scripture's nature. Carter and I agree that "the nature of Scripture itself [as God's revealed word] dictates how it must be interpreted" (245) and that the spiritual truths that shape the whole of Scripture require spiritual people (i.e., believers) to spiritually discern the text's meaning (see esp. 1 Cor 2:14). These convictions ground why I assert that we must read the Old Testament *through* Christ, as regenerated believers, in order to properly grasp the fulness of all God intended in the Old Testament. I further affirm that the Old Testament testifies to Christ, that Jesus fulfills the Old Testament, that the New Testament authors were not reading Jesus into the Old Testament text, and that the text's "literal sense is the divine author's intended meaning as communicated through the human author's words" (243). Despite this substantial agreement, our approaches differ concerning the proper interpretive steps a reader should employ for rightly seeing Christ in the Old Testament.

---

1. Craig A. Carter, *Interpreting Scripture with the Great Tradition: Recovering the Genius of Premodern Exegesis* (Grand Rapids: Baker Academic, 2018).

Evaluating Carter's Interpretive Steps for Readers

Carter opens his essay by affirming five ways that he believes premodern interpreters faithfully saw Christ in the Old Testament. Of these five, I can immediately affirm in whole propositions 1, 2, and 4: (1) that Christ fulfills direct Old Testament prophecy, (2) that numerous Old Testament types elucidate Christ, and (4) that Jesus is the renewed Israel of God whose life and ministry recapitulate much of the nation's history, succeeding where they had failed. I must qualify, however, propositions 3 and 5.

Proposition 3 asserts, "We can interpret the Old Testament according to the fourfold sense, as containing a christological or spiritual sense that is an extension or expansion of the literal sense" (240). By "the fourfold sense," Carter refers to the patristic hermeneutic of seeing four levels of meaning in every biblical text. Alongside a text's "literal sense" (level 1), the text also bears a "spiritual or christological sense" that God intends us to grasp through the text's figures (the "allegorical sense," level 2), ethical implications (the "tropological sense," level 3), and future trajectories (the "anagogical sense," level 4). We are thus "talking about layers of meaning in a text, not about conflicting meanings being attributed to the same text" (253).

Among other things, I appreciate that the Great Tradition stresses that a Christian approach to Scripture must be christological and that all Scripture is unified around a redemptive movement from promise to fulfillment in Jesus Christ. I also agree with Carter that Scripture's unity demands that it be noncontradictory, that it interpret itself, and that Jesus's role at its center should guide and limit how we interpret major themes.

Nevertheless, I question whether one could faithfully identify a fourfold sense within every Old Testament text. Moreover, and more to the point of this response, I am concerned that Carter consistently treats the "spiritual sense" as something foreign to the Old Testament text itself. For example, he claims that this spiritual sense is only "clear in hindsight" as part of the deeper christological meaning, that it stands as "the expanded literal sense of the Old Testament," and that one can only identify it "under the hermeneutical control of New Testament Christology" (265). Hence, we need *not* justify through Old Testament exegetical and theological wrestling the "spiritual sense" we identify.

All three case studies are representative of Carter's claims. For Carter, Genesis 22:1–19 anticipates Christ only as "a *canonical expansion* of the literal sense" (259, emphasis added). Similarly, Carter lets the New Testament govern his interpretation of Proverbs 8:22–31 and regards "the christological interpretation of the fathers . . . as a legitimate *extension* of the literal sense" (261, emphasis added). Finally, Carter affirms that only "the New Testament apostles, writing under the inspiration of the Holy Spirit, were able to see that in Jesus Christ the Isaianic text was fulfilled" (265). In contrast, I assert that Old Testament authors intentionally wrote of messianic realities, which frequently makes the "spiritual" and "literal" senses one and the same.

Much of Carter's basis for distinguishing the "literal" and the "spiritual" senses appears to derive from his interpretation of 1 Peter 1:10–12, a text he believes stresses that "the Old Testament prophets did not understand fully everything they were inspired to write" (244). He further lumps Abraham with Caiaphas (John 11:50–52) as those who "spoke more truly than they knew, which is a pattern in the prophets according to Peter" (258). But Peter never claimed that the Old Testament prophets were ignorant of the full meaning when he wrote,

Concerning this salvation, the prophets who prophesied about the grace that was to be yours searched and inquired carefully, inquiring what person or time[2] the Spirit of Christ in them was indicating when he predicted the sufferings of Christ and the subsequent glories. It was revealed to them that they were serving not themselves but you. (1 Pet 1:10–12 ESV)

The text emphasizes that the Old Testament prophets were those who "searched and inquired carefully" about the messiah and his coming, apparently *from the biblical text.* Yes, "they were carried along by the Holy Spirit" (2 Pet 1:21), but their prophecies were Spirit-led *interpretations*

---

2. In contrast to the NIV and CSB, I believe the ESV is correct in identifying that the Old Testament prophets inquired about both "what person or time" (similarly, see NRSV, NET, NASB). Peter always uses the Greek *tis* as a pronoun and *poios* as an adjective, which would result in a translation like "what-person or what circumstances." See G. D. Kilpatrick, "Peter 1.11: ΤΙΝΑ Ἡ ΠΟΙΟΝ ΚΑΙΡΟΝ," *NovT* 28 (1986): 91–92; Mark Dubis, *1 Peter: A Handbook on the Greek Text*, Baylor Handbook on the Greek New Testament (Waco, TX: Baylor University Press, 2010), 19.

(v. 20), such that they viewed the meaning of their texts as organically connected to the previous ones. The biblical writers were "taught by the Spirit," but this happened as they were rightly "explaining spiritual realities" gained both from the Old Testament and the Spirit's recollection of Jesus's teaching (1 Cor 2:13; cf. Luke 24:27).[3] We should, therefore, expect that often the "literal sense" *is* the "spiritual" or "christological sense." A deep wrestling with the Old Testament text itself will reveal what the New Testament authors themselves saw *in their biblical text*.

Carter writes as though God spoke at various levels but that the human authors never intentionally did this. In contrast, I propose that "the human authors regularly wrote at two or more different levels at the same time and on purpose."[4] This is the whole essence of typology, which I believe is always divinely predictive and usually intentionally so on the part of the human author. What this means is that I can faithfully speak God's word (1 Pet 4:11) and guard against error (2 Pet 3:16; cf. Jas 3:1) only when I rightly handle Scripture (2 Tim 2:15), proving my christological reading by reasoned argument from the Old Testament itself (Acts 17:11; 19:8; 28:23) and not by simply finding deeper levels of meaning verified by New Testament claims. The New Testament provides both the answer key and the algorithm to our Old Testament interpretation, but the interpreter must still work the problem (i.e., interpret the OT text in context and through Christ's resurrection) in order to see how they arrive where they do. Carter's failure to seek Old Testament warrant for Scripture's "spiritual sense" runs at least two risks: (1) treating the New Testament authors as those who interpret Old Testament texts by the Spirit in ways divorced from their original contexts, and (2) affirming any orthodox christological interpretation of Scripture, regardless of whether right doctrine is drawn from wrong texts.

Additionally, I have reservations about Carter's proposition 5: "The Son himself speaks in the Old Testament, which we can see by using

---

3. Jesus promised that the Spirit of truth would teach the apostles by bearing witness to Christ, recalling his teaching, and guiding them to truth (John 14:26; 15:26; 16:13–15); they would in turn bear witness to Jesus and relay this message to the masses as the true word of God (John 15:27; 17:17; cf. 1 Cor 14:37; Titus 1:3). The result is the New Testament, which captures "the faith that was once for all entrusted to God's holy people" (Jude 3). As with Yahweh's old covenant prophets through whom God spoke (Heb 1:1; 2 Pet 1:21), Paul's words were nothing less than the interpretation of "spiritual realities with Spirit-taught words" (1 Cor 2:13).

4. Using the wording of my doctoral research fellow Brian Verrett.

prosopological exegesis to understand texts where the Father speaks to the Son and the Son replies or where the Messiah speaks" (240). I affirm that "the Son himself speaks in the Old Testament," but I am not convinced that our awareness of this comes through what Matthew Bates tags "a reading technique whereby an interpreter seeks to overcome a real or perceived ambiguity regarding the identity of the speakers or addressees (or both) . . . by assigning nontrivial *proposa* (i.e., nontrivial vis-à-vis the 'plain sense' of the text) to the speakers or addressees (or both) in order to make sense of the text."[5] I question this claim not only because the pattern of Palestinian Jewish interpretation of the Hebrew Scripture prior to AD 70 appears to have been highly governed by the biblical context[6] but also, and more importantly, because I see strong evidence in the Old Testament itself for the claims the New Testament authors are making. One is almost always able to recognize the messianic thrust of an Old Testament passage by reading it in the light of the whole book, by accounting for informing theology in antecedent Scripture and in the flow of redemptive history, and by affirming the reality of predictive prophecy. Rather than requiring a special "reading technique," what one needs is to observe carefully, understand rightly, and evaluate fairly what is there, reading every passage in light of the close, continuing, and canonical contexts.[7]

Conclusion

Carter affirms that "the Bible is *literally* about Jesus Christ" (265, emphasis original). However, he appears to see "the expanded literal sense of the Old Testament text" that "bears witness" to Christ as only possible

---

5. Matthew W. Bates, *The Birth of the Trinity: Jesus, God, and Spirit in New Testament and Early Christian Interpretations of the Old Testament* (Oxford: Oxford University Press, 2016), 218. Carter points to Bates's work as "a good treatment of prosopological exegesis" (240n4), and Carter builds off Bates's definition in *Interpreting Scripture with the Great Tradition*, 192–201.

6. David Instone-Brewer, *Techniques and Assumptions in Jewish Exegesis before 70 CE*, TSAJ 30 (Tübingen: Mohr Siebeck, 1992).

7. For a helpful evaluation of prosopological exegesis with similar conclusions, see Peter J. Gentry, "A Preliminary Evaluation and Critique of Prosopological Exegesis," *SBJT* 23.2 (2019): 105–22. For a helpful critique of Theological Interpretation of Scripture as a movement with conclusions that Carter mostly affirms, see D. A. Carson, "Theological Interpretation of Scripture: Yes, but . . . ," in *Theological Commentary: Evangelical Perspectives*, ed. R. Michael Allen (London: T&T Clark, 2011), 187–207; cf. Carter, *Interpreting Scripture with the Great Tradition*, 248–51.

"under the hermeneutical control of New Testament Christology" (265). I see Jesus more organically in the Old Testament itself than Carter does, making his view more open to critique than mine that one is forcing the Old Testament text to say certain things. "Through Christ" I am now able to read the old covenant materials as a pointer to the glories of the new covenant (2 Cor 3:14 ESV). Through Jesus's resurrection, the Old Testament's message now becomes more fully understood (Rom 11:25–26). But what this usually means is that I am now empowered, as a spiritual man, to read the spiritual text as both God *and* the human author intended. That is, my reading of the Old Testament itself within its close and continuing contexts allows me to rightly grasp what the Old Testament prophets themselves saw and meant, and the canonical context confirms this reading and adds greater clarity to the person and time of the Messiah's work.

REJOINDER

CRAIG A. CARTER

Interacting with my coauthors has been a privilege, and I thank them all for their thoughtful responses to my chapter.

Dr. Dharamraj correctly perceives that I decenter method in favor of the ontological meaning of the text controlling all methods. I remain unpersuaded, however, that good interpretation will balance a reception-centered approach with a historical approach. The rule that we find Jesus through but not in the Old Testament seems inadequate to explain why the apostles were correct to interpret Christ as the fulfillment of the Old Testament. If one is not convinced that the Old Testament is all about Christ, one is forced to choose between reading him in or interpreting the Old Testament nonchristologically, which I would see as a false dilemma.

Dr. Goldingay recognizes the weakness of the modern idea that we can separate the historical and the theological meaning of texts. For example, Jews, Christians, and atheists may read a passage depicting the destruction of Jerusalem and agree on the history, but they will radically disagree on the theological significance of the historical event. He notes that the text's historical meaning includes the theological significance of the story it tells, and therefore exegesis must attend to the theological meaning of the text's use of history. I could not agree more! Where we differ, however, is that I argue that the meaning intended by the Old Testament text includes the christological meaning. The reason we differ seems to be that I do not limit the literal sense to what the human author consciously intended to say. Because of inspiration, I think we must (with the entire premodern church) take into account the Divine Author's intent in inspiring the human writer to write what is written.

Dr. Longman expresses appreciation for highlighting premodern interpretation and suggests that there is a new openness to it today because of the rise of postmodern thinking. The danger here is that we misunderstand premodern interpretation as inherently subjective and therefore compatible with postmodern hermeneutics. In fact, premodern interpretation claims that Christ objectively is the true meaning of the Old Testament, which is something postmodern approaches would not do. Dr. Longman fears that I "throw historical-grammatical exegesis under the bus," and this fear appears to be based on his assumption that objectivity in interpretation depends entirely on sticking to the conscious intention of the human author as the total meaning of the literal sense. Much of my response to Dr. DeRouchie below applies to Dr. Longman as well.

It is disappointing that Dr. DeRouchie appears unwilling to accept that inspiration requires the discernment of a divine authorial intent in Old Testament passages that goes beyond what the human author consciously understood and intended. I say "understood" because one cannot coherently *intend* something one does not *understand*. So, to cite one of many possible examples of how this is problematic, this means the writer of Leviticus must have understood and consciously intended to present the laws of sacrifice as types of the coming divine messiah who would offer himself as the atonement for sins by the shedding of his blood. The writer of Hebrews 8–10 clearly sees Old Testament sacrifice as the basis for understanding the meaning of Christ's death. If Hebrews is right, then Leviticus has a christological meaning. And if it has a christological meaning, the human author of Leviticus must have consciously intended it. But did he?

I believe that meaning is there in the Old Testament text and is correctly discerned by Hebrews because the divine author of Leviticus intended that meaning when he inspired Moses to write Leviticus. But I do not see why it is necessary to assume that the meaning of Leviticus must be restricted to that which Moses consciously understood as he wrote it. I would argue that the human author consciously did intend a messianic meaning in *some* Old Testament texts but not in *all* the Old Testament texts cited by the New Testament apostles as having a christological meaning. In the case of Leviticus, if the human author had consciously intended the sacrificial system to be a description of the work of the messiah, then we would expect the messiah to be mentioned explicitly. But this is not the case. Most interpreters do not see the types in Leviticus as consciously intended by their human author to reveal Christ. As a result, many deny the christological meaning of Leviticus and leave the fact that Hebrews asserts it as a problem for the New Testament scholars to sort out.

Dr. DeRouchie stands in the mainstream of conservative evangelical hermeneutics throughout the period of post-Enlightenment higher criticism, but evangelicals make too big a concession to modernity when we agree to limit the meaning of the Old Testament text to nothing more than what the human author consciously intended to say. History shows that once that concession is made, it is often followed by a gradual shrinking of the christological content of the Old Testament through a relentless historicizing of its meaning. We see this process at work in Dr. Goldingay's work. He is by no means as liberal as most higher critics, but starting from the same point as Dr. DeRouchie, namely, by limiting the meaning of the text to what the human author consciously intended, he has arrived at the conclusion that the premodern commentators "read Jesus into the Scriptures" (268). In his chapter, he claims that Christ is not in any of the three passages we consider in this book. That is where I fear Dr. DeRouchie's restriction of the meaning of the Old Testament text to conscious, human, authorial intent alone ends up.

Dr. DeRouchie seems to misunderstand the point of the fourfold sense when he says that the spiritual sense is "something foreign to the Old Testament text" (285). That is exactly the opposite of what the fourfold sense means. The point of saying that Scripture has a spiritual sense in addition to the literal sense is that the spiritual sense does not have to be "read into" the Old Testament texts since it is already there by inspiration. It only has to be *perceived* by the illumination of the Spirit because it has been there ontologically all along.

CONCLUSION

BRIAN J. TABB AND ANDREW M. KING

Is Christ in the Old Testament? In many ways, this question gets to the heart of what it means to read the Old Testament as *Christian* Scripture. The complexity of the matter is evident in the fact that there are five representative views in this book! Each contributor, within the limited scope and parameters of the volume, offers different ways forward. Our hope is that this book will equip believers to read the whole of the Bible more faithfully as God's word to his global church. Doubtlessly, readers will resonate more or less with aspects of each view. The goal, however, is not to adopt a particular label, but rather, to develop a faithful and robust approach to Scripture that is self-aware of our presuppositions and methodology. One of the fruits of a faithful approach to this important question is its capacity to move us from the meaning of the inspired text toward worship and mission. For, as Scripture, the Old Testament is able both to make one wise for salvation through faith in Christ Jesus and to equip Christians for every good work (2 Tim 3:15–17). We trust that as readers continue to sit under the Scriptures, including the Old Testament, they will find much to fuel their love for our triune God and for their neighbor.

As we bring this book to a close, we can reflect briefly on each view and the respective responses engendered by it. This conclusion gives particular attention to the orienting questions related to the nature of Scripture, authorial intent, criteria for identification, and specific steps for readers. We examine areas of agreement and disagreement along the way, as well as a few open questions for readers to consider.

First Testament Priority Approach

The First Testament priority approach presented by John Goldingay maintains that Scripture is unified in its theology, ethic, and spirituality, with Jesus as the climax of the scriptural story. This does not, however, give interpreters a license to read Jesus back into the First Testament. As progressive revelation, Scripture requires interpreters to respect the discrete witness of the Old Testament. To aid this reading, Goldingay distinguishes "meaning," which is inherent in the Old Testament context itself, from "significance," which involves later applications of a text to a new context. To understand the meaning of an Old Testament text is to comprehend what the human author was saying to his original audience. To read a later New Testament appropriation of an Old Testament text (its "significance") as though it were the original "meaning" is to misunderstand the Holy Spirit's intention. Thus, both Testaments should be read on their own terms. While some contributors, especially Longman and Dharamraj, appreciate Goldingay's concern for the discrete witness of the Old Testament, all contributors express concerns about the distinction between meaning and significance, albeit for different reasons. Carter, for example, says that this bifurcation puts the emphasis far too much on the human author of Scripture over against the divine author. Carter says that the nature of inspiration subsumes human authorial intent as but one level of divine authorial intention. Yet for Goldingay, the meaning we can discern from a First Testament text should accord with the human author's purpose, though he also acknowledges that the Spirit can use texts in the lives of believers in unintended ways. Goldingay affirms that there are typological aspects to God's actions in the biblical story. He argues that typology is not prospective, prefiguring future people or events; rather, it represents later authors' appropriation of the First Testament's significance, not meaning.

Thus, Goldingay answers the question, "Is Christ in the Old Testament?" with an unequivocal no. Goldingay does acknowledge in his rejoinder that he may have overstated his case at points. Nevertheless, he says that rather than mining for Christ in the Old Testament, God's purposes for the Old Testament in the life of the church lay elsewhere. Dharamraj is largely sympathetic with Goldingay. She agrees that reading Jesus back into the Old Testament sabotages the capacity for the Old Testament to teach, correct, and train in right living (2 Tim 3:16). The problem is exacerbated, she says, by the reality of global Bible illiteracy. Jumping straight to Jesus deprives readers of the richness of the Old Testament. Dharamraj says that rather than seeing Christ *in* the Old

Testament, readers can know Christ *through* the Old Testament. Her disagreements with Goldingay lay primarily in the way he articulates his view, rather than in the view itself. The strongest opposition comes from Carter and DeRouchie, who both appeal (among other arguments) to the New Testament's claims that Jesus's contemporaries should have expected him (e.g., Luke 24:25). While Goldingay does not provide specific interpretive steps, he presents ten illuminating questions interpreters should consider as they read a First Testament text. These questions help readers move from the original context to show that the passage may shed light on Jesus.

Christotelic Approach

The Christotelic approach outlined by Tremper Longman III encourages readers to adopt a two-stage reading strategy of Old Testament texts. The first reading involves assuming the posture of the original audience. What did this passage mean in its original context? Discovering meaning here comes through the work of historical-grammatical exegesis. Like Goldingay's chapter, Longman's first reading respects the discrete witness of the Old Testament as it promotes an author-centered understanding of meaning. This level of reading draws criticism from some contributors as limiting the meaning to what was in the mind of the human authors. Longman, however, rejects this charge, stating that he is concerned with what is written, not with what else may be in the mind of the author.

Yet beyond the first reading, the claims of the New Testament lead Longman to follow with an additional reading. This second reading aims to understand the Old Testament's fuller divine meaning, likely unknown to the human author, by asking how Christ's redemptive work impacts our interpretation of the text. Goldingay resonates with Longman's goal but questions the validity of Longman's two-stage reading, especially in light of the way the New Testament authors use the Old Testament. Rather than dividing these readings into two stages, Goldingay asserts that these two readings interweave, as the New Testament authors describe the significance of an Old Testament text. He also questions Longman's view of progressive revelation. Goldingay is concerned that the concept of progressive revelation will legitimate ignoring parts of the Old Testament as irrelevant, in favor of what is considered more relevant in the New Testament. Dharamraj shares Goldingay's concern. She says that she would prefer to take Longman's first reading further toward Christian application. Carter appreciates Longman's desire to hold traditional Christian conclusions but says that his first reading, utilizing the historical-critical method, is at odds with the conclusions drawn in the second reading. In Carter's view, the two readings cannot coexist in the long run. Longman, however, strongly rejects the characterization of his view as historical-critical and invites readers to judge for themselves.

The question whether Christ is in the Old Testament receives both a no and a yes in Longman's view. The first reading would lead to the negative conclusion, while the second reading allows the text to speak of Christ. The notion of *sensus plenior* ("fuller sense") undergirds this second reading. While the second reading connects the text to Christ, Longman says this would have been a surprise to the human author. He notes that he takes seriously Jesus's chastisement of the disciples in Luke 24:25 as "foolish" and "slow to believe all that the prophets have spoken." Some readers may find that he does justice to this element, while those more sympathetic to the views of Carter and DeRouchie may be less convinced. Longman acknowledges that the two-reading strategy is more of an art than a science, a point appreciated by some other contributors.

Reception-Centered, Intertextual Approach

The Reception-Centered, Intertextual Approach presented by Havilah Dharamraj begins with the assumption that the sixty-six books of the Protestant canon are in conversation with one another. With an abundance of potential intertexts across the canon, the reader can find meaningful and productive associations between Old Testament passages with christological resonance and New Testament texts. Important to this view is the notion of the Common Reader. This phrase is a technical term emerging from the field of comparative literature that appreciates the social location and experiences of the interpreter. In her chapter, Dharamraj assumes a Common Reader with a degree of familiarity with the Old Testament text and various inputs, what she calls public meaning, that inform a rich christological linkage of two passages. While the choice of intertexts is reader-centered, she utilizes text-centered and author-centered methods of interpretation in each case. This, she says, acknowledges the sophisticated relationship between the text and the reader, a tension well-known from the history of hermeneutics. Some contributors, such as Carter, question whether this method can rightly be considered exegesis, which extracts the meaning of the text, rather than reading meaning into the text. Since the reception-centered approach is focused on how the texts are received by the Common Reader, in contrast to a production-centered intertextuality (i.e., connections intended by the author), authorial intention is not a primary concern for her method. Several contributors express concern about the subjective nature of this approach. Dharamraj responds that this is often how the church has read Scripture, connecting intertexts that were beyond the minds of the original authors. Carter concurs but questions the metaphysical framework that undergirds her method. If the modern naturalism contained in the historical-critical method is used with this approach, it can lead to unorthodox conclusions.

Are there limits to the intertexts that may be paired? Dharamraj states that for a meaningful conversation between texts, they must share a dominant theme—an *icon*, such as "the kingly protagonist" in Isaiah 42 and Revelation 19. Overall, while this view probes christological resonance in the Old Testament, whether Christ is *in* the Old Testament is not the real question Scripture wants us to ask. The nature of Scripture allows the Common Reader to detect correspondences that would be unknown to the human author. Dharamraj sets forth five clearly defined methodological steps, including an evaluative component. This, she maintains, provides checks and balances against an overly creative reading. DeRouchie, however, is not satisfied with what he sees as subjective and minimal criteria for evaluation (intuition, public meaning, and orthodoxy). Dharamraj acknowledges the potential for misuse, but she reasons that both reader-centered and author-centered approaches require care and self-reflection to illuminate God's word.

Redemptive-Historical, Christocentric Approach

Jason S. DeRouchie outlines the redemptive-historical, Christocentric approach, "a multifaceted approach that accounts for the central role Jesus plays in redemptive history" (181). The Old and New Testaments are unified in their unfolding of five covenants, with the divine Son as the key to the whole. DeRouchie says that to properly interpret an Old Testament passage, the reader must attend to three levels of context (close, continuing, and complete). Appreciating these contexts allows for a careful reading of a passage in its immediate context, as well as its purpose in the progress of revelation. Yet unlike Longman's two-stage reading strategy, DeRouchie combines both readings. Rather than first bracketing out Christ for a close reading of the Old Testament text, he claims that Christ provides both the "answer key and the algorithm" for interpreting the Old Testament (186). Grasping the message of the Old Testament is not merely a literary or historical endeavor but is fundamentally a Christian one. Thus, alongside Carter, he affirms that Christ is indeed in the Old Testament, although Carter's approach has a more explicit metaphysical framework. A difference emerges between DeRouchie and Carter on the degree to which the Old Testament authors were conscious of the christological sense. DeRouchie understands the Old Testament authors to have consciously discerned patterns and trajectories that climax in Christ, while Carter puts greater emphasis on the role of the divine author in discerning the christological sense.

While he does not provide specific interpretive steps, DeRouchie lists seven ways the Old Testament magnifies Jesus. Other contributors object to DeRouchie's view on the grounds that it is overly clever and idiosyncratic. Dharamraj retorts that though DeRouchie says that the mystery hidden in the Old Testament is revealed in the New Testament, there remains a substantial amount of mystery in the interpretation of Old Testament passages, as evident from the five views represented here. She says that even on this side of the cross and resurrection, Old Testament passages such as DeRouchie's three case studies need to be decoded. She likens this to a dot-connecting exercise across biblical books that overlooks the immediate context (e.g., DeRouchie associates Prov 8 with Prov 30:1–6). Goldingay and Longman join Dharamraj to challenge what they consider contested exegetical decisions. Dharamraj says that DeRouchie's method for seeing Christ in the Old Testament is more of a large fishing net than a key for exegesis. When he casts the net over a passage, he is always able to catch something. DeRouchie responds that though his method may be esoteric from a modern scholarly perspective, it is not out of step with the hermeneutics of the New Testament authors. Our goal as interpreters, he says, is to take our hermeneutical cues from Jesus and the apostles on how to interpret the Old Testament.

Premodern Approach

Craig Carter introduces the premodern approach. This view, which draws on the theological resources of the early church, understands biblical interpretation as a spiritual discipline. This stands in contrast to what Carter identifies as a shift in the modern period wrought by historical criticism. Carter maintains that Scripture is not just any book that allows for any kind of interpretive method. The nature of the Old and New Testaments as the word of the living God dictates the way it should be understood, a point echoed by DeRouchie. In other words, readers cannot attain a proper interpretation of the Bible if they have not submitted to the lordship of Christ. Or, stated differently, hermeneutics without Trinitarian faith is dead. Scripture thus requires a certain kind of reader: a Spirit-filled Christian who does the task of interpretation from a posture of faith. Goldingay responds that it is the meaning of the text itself, not the theological persuasion of the interpreter, that matters, asserting that it is possible for both Christians and non-Christians to arrive at a proper understanding of the original meaning of an Old Testament passage. Where Christians and non-Christian interpreters part ways, says Goldingay, is with respect to the theological significance of the text. Proper grammatical-historical method should arrive at the same meaning that was intended for the original audience. This again highlights Goldingay's distinction between meaning and significance. From a different angle, Longman challenges Carter's description of grammatical-historical exegesis. Although skeptical forms of this method are common, the method itself need not require opposition to the supernatural, for interpreters such as Jerome and Augustine employed aspects of grammatical-historical interpretation. Longman rejects an either/or dichotomy between a historical and theological interpretation, believing both are necessary.

A key issue for Carter's view is whether a spiritual sense should be included in the "literal meaning" of a text. DeRouchie, who is most closely aligned with Carter's approach, critiques Carter for distinguishing between the Old Testament text's "literal" and "spiritual" senses. DeRouchie expresses concern that Carter treats the spiritual as something foreign to the Old Testament text itself, as DeRouchie's own view allows for more conscious understanding on the part of the human author. The other contributors, in one way or another, all raise the question of biblical warrant for identifying a christological sense. Carter is more comfortable saying that even when the Old Testament authors may have been unaware of a particular meaning, the divine author can include this spiritual meaning in the literal sense. This is not reading Jesus back into the Old Testament, he says, but merely recognizing that Jesus is its ultimate referent.

As a spiritual discipline, Carter says that biblical interpretation cannot be reduced to a singular method. To aid readers, he provides four principles that should guide interpretation. Regarding authorial intent, Carter states that the triune God spoke through human authors. While all the contributors would affirm this in a general sense, the premodern view understands the literal sense of an Old Testament text to be the revelation of the triune God through, but not limited to, the intention of the human authors. The accent rests on the divine in divine-human authorship. In this way, Carter gives a resounding yes to seeing Christ in the Old Testament. Various responses to the premodern view note caution regarding its potential subjectivity. Is the premodern approach simply an older rendition of a postmodern hermeneutic? Carter rejects this claim, stating that the divine author, not the interpreter, is the source of meaning. As such, Old Testament interpretation is canonically and christologically bound. As Carter advocates for the fourfold sense of Scripture, he makes clear that these senses are already there in the text by inspiration and are not a foreign grid imposed upon it.

Wrapping Up

We hope this brief summary reveals some of the key points of commonality and tension between the views represented. Each view arises organically from each contributor's understanding of Scripture and authorial intent, addressing several key interpretive questions. How does the nature of Scripture affect how we interpret it? Does progressive revelation work for or against seeing Christ in the Old Testament? Does the Divine Author intend more than the human author recorded? Is the intention of the divine author coterminous with that of the human author? How do we reconcile the New Testament's claims about

Christ's fulfillment of Scripture with a contextually faithful reading of the Old Testament? Similarly, how should we understand the role of later Scripture in interpreting the meaning of earlier Scripture? Does the interpreter's social location come into play in the process of reading? These questions all touch on our understanding of the nature and authorship of Scripture and how these pertain to the interpreter. Another question to consider is whether any Christian interpreter can actually apply the method of each of the five views independently. Do these five views require specialized or technical knowledge that is out of reach for the ordinary Christian? Is the methodology presented by any of the views accessible to interpreters more generally?

Our hope is that readers will discover methods of addressing the question of Christ in the Old Testament that will impact their personal Bible reading and their engagement with Scripture in the life of the church. We desire for this volume to be a conversation starter rather than a conversation ender. If the reader is driven back to the text of Scripture with fresh eyes and a humble heart, we will have accomplished part of the goal for which we set out. Yet we also desire readers to escape Christ's rebuke on the Emmaus road of being "foolish" and "slow of heart to believe all that the prophets have spoken" (Luke 24:25).[1] Christian interpreters are entrusted with a great and glorious task of hearing and proclaiming the word of Christ as they ought, and our hope is that believers will not throw away their shot.

---

1. See, for example, Brian J. Tabb, *After Emmaus: How the Church Fulfills the Mission of Christ* (Wheaton, IL: Crossway, 2021).

WORKS CITED ▐███████████████████

Abernethy, Andrew T., and Gregory Goswell. *God's Messiah in the Old Testament: Expectations of a Coming King*. Grand Rapids: Baker Academic, 2020.

Alexander, T. Desmond. "Further Observations on the Term 'Seed' in Genesis." *TynB* 48 (1997): 363–67.

Allender, Dan B., and Tremper Longman III. *God Loves Sex: An Honest Conversation about Sexual Desire and Holiness*. Grand Rapids: Baker, 2014.

Anatolios, Khaled. *Retrieving Nicaea: The Development and Meaning of Trinitarian Doctrine*. Grand Rapids: Baker Academic, 2011.

Anderson, Francis, and David Noel Freedman. *Micah: A New Translation with Introduction and Commentary*. AB 24E. New York Doubleday, 2000.

Aquinas, Thomas. *Summa Theologica*. Translated by Fathers of the Dominican Province. 5 vols. Notre Dame: Ave Maria, 1948.

Athanasius. *The Orations of St Athanasius against the Arians*. Edited by W. Bright. Reprint ed. Cambridge: Cambridge University Press, 2014.

Augustine. *Writings on the Old Testament*. Translated by Joseph T. Lienhard and Sean Doyle. Works of Saint Augustine 1/14. Hyde Park, NY: New City Press, 2016.

Aune, David E. *Revelation 17–22*. WBC 52C. Nashville: Thomas Nelson, 1998.

Baker, D. L. *Two Testaments, One Bible*. Leicester: Inter-Varsity Press, 1976.

Barr, James. *Old and New in Interpretation*. London: SCM, 1966.

Barton, John. "Déjà Lu: Intertextuality, Method or Theory?" Pages 1–16 in *Reading Job Intertextually*. Edited by Katharine Dell and Will Kynes. LHBOTS 574. New York: Bloomsbury, 2013.

———. *The Nature of Biblical Criticism*. Louisville: Westminster John Knox, 2007.

Bates, Matthew W. *The Birth of the Trinity: Jesus, God, and the Spirit in the New Testament and Early Christian Interpretation of the Old Testament*. Oxford: Oxford University Press, 2015.

Beale, G. K. "The Cognitive Peripheral Vision of Biblical Authors." *WTJ* 76 (2014): 263–93.

———. "Finding Christ in the Old Testament." *JETS* 63 (2020): 25–50.

———. *Handbook on the New Testament Use of the Old Testament: Exegesis and Interpretation*. Grand Rapids: Baker Academic, 2012.

———. "The Origin of the Title 'King of Kings and Lord of Lords' in Revelation 17.14." *NTS* 31 (1985): 618–20.

Beckwith, Roger T. *The Old Testament Canon of the New Testament Church*. London: SPCK, 1985.

Beetham, Christopher A. *Echoes of Scripture in the Letter of Paul to the Colossians*. BibInt 96. Leiden: Brill, 2008.

Bernard, J. H. *A Critical and Exegetical Commentary on the Gospel according to St. John*. Edited by A. H. McNeile. 2 vols. ICC. Edinburgh: T&T Clark, 1929.

Beuken, W. A. M. "Mišpāṭ: The First Servant Song and its Content." *VT* 22 (1972): 1–30.

Blenkinsopp, Joseph. *Isaiah 40–55*. AB 19A. New York: Doubleday, 2002.

Blomberg, Craig. "Matthew." Pages 1–110 in *Commentary on the New Testament Use of the Old Testament*. Edited by G. K. Beale and D. A. Carson. Grand Rapids: Baker Academic, 2007.

Bockmuehl, Markus N. A. *Seeing the Word: Refocusing New Testament Study*. Studies in Theological Interpretation. Grand Rapids: Baker Academic, 2006.

Boda, Mark J. "Theological Commentary: A Review and Reflective Essay." *McMaster Journal of Theology and Ministry* 11 (2009–2010): 139–50.

Brown, Jeannine K. *Scripture as Communication: Introducing Biblical Hermeneutics*. 2nd ed. Grand Rapids: Baker Academic, 2021.

Brown, Raymond E. *The Gospel according to John (I–XII)*. AB 29. New Haven: Yale University Press, 1966.

Brueggemann, Walter. *Theology of the Old Testament: Testimony, Dispute, Advocacy*. Minneapolis: Fortress, 1997.

Calvin, John. *Genesis*. Translated by John King. Reprint ed. Calvin's Commentaries 1. Grand Rapids: Baker, 2005.

Caneday, Ardel. "The Word Made Flesh as Mystery Incarnate: Revealing and Concealing Dramatized by Jesus as Portrayed in John's Gospel." *JETS* 60 (2017): 751–65.

Carson, D. A. *The Gospel according to John*. PNTC. Grand Rapids: Eerdmans, 1991.

———. "Theological Interpretation of Scripture: Yes, But . . . ." Pages 187–207 in *Theological Commentary: Evangelical Perspectives*. Edited by R. Michael Allen. London: T&T Clark, 2011.

———. "Understanding Misunderstandings in the Fourth Gospel." *TynBul* 33 (1982): 59–91.

Carter, Craig A. *Contemplating God with the Great Tradition: Recovering Trinitarian Classical Theism*. Grand Rapids: Baker Academic, 2021.

———. *Interpreting Scripture with the Great Tradition: Recovering the Genius of Premodern Exegesis*. Grand Rapids: Baker Academic, 2018.

Charlesworth, James H., ed. *The Old Testament Pseudepigrapha*. 2 vols. Garden City, NY: Doubleday, 1983, 1985.

Chase, Mitchell L. *40 Questions about Typology and Allegory*. Grand Rapids: Kregel, 2020.

Childs, Brevard S. *Biblical Theology of the Old and New Testaments: Theological Reflections on the Christian Bible*. Minneapolis: Fortress, 1993.

———. *The Struggle to Understand Isaiah as Christian Scripture*. Grand Rapids: Eerdmans, 2004.

Collins, C. John. "A Syntactical Note (Genesis 3:15): Is the Woman's Seed Singular or Plural?" *TynB* 48 (1997): 139–48.

Collins, John J. *The Scepter and the Star: Messianism in Light of the Dead Sea Scrolls*. 2nd ed. Grand Rapids: Eerdmans, 2010.

Dell, Katherine, and Will Kynes. "Introduction." Pages xv–xxiii in *Reading Job Intertextually*. Edited by Katharine Dell and Will Kynes. LHBOTS 574. New York: Bloomsbury, 2013.

DeRouchie, Jason S. "The Blessing-Commission, the Promised Offspring, and the Toledot Structure of Genesis." *JETS* 56 (2013): 219–47.

———. *How to Understand and Apply the Old Testament: Twelve Steps from Exegesis to Theology*. Phillipsburg, NJ: P&R, 2017.

———. "Lifting the Veil: Reading and Preaching Jesus' Bible through Christ and for Christ." *SBJT* 22.3 (2018): 157–79.

———. "The Mystery Revealed: A Biblical Case for Christ-Centered Old Testament Interpretation." *Them* 44 (2019): 226–48.

———, ed. *What the Old Testament Authors Really Cared About: A Survey of Jesus' Bible*. Grand Rapids: Kregel, 2013.

———. "Why the Third Day? The Promise of Resurrection in All of Scripture." *Midwestern Journal of Theology* 20.1 (2021): 19–34.

———, Oren R. Martin, and Andrew David Naselli. *40 Questions about Biblical Theology.* Grand Rapids: Kregel, 2020.

Dharamraj, Havilah. *Altogether Lovely: A Thematic and Intertextual Reading of the Song of Songs.* Minneapolis: Fortress, 2018.

———. "The Curious Case of Hagar: Biblical Studies and the Interdisciplinary Approach of Comparative Literature." *Journal of Asian Evangelical Theology* 23.2 (2019): 49–71.

———. *Ruth.* Asia Bible Commentary. Cumbria, UK: Langham Global Library, 2019.

Dodd, C. H. *According to the Scriptures: The Sub-Structure of New Testament Theology.* London: Nisbet, 1952.

Dubis, Mark. *1 Peter: A Handbook on the Greek Text.* Baylor Handbook on the Greek New Testament. Waco, TX: Baylor University Press, 2010.

Enns, Peter. *Inspiration and Incarnation: Evangelicals and the Problem of the Old Testament.* 2nd ed. Grand Rapids: Baker Academic, 2015.

Fairbairn, Patrick. *The Typology of Scripture.* Reprint ed. Grand Rapids: Zondervan, 1952.

Fee, Gordon D. *Philippians.* IVP New Testament Commentary Series 11. Downers Grove, IL: IVP Academic, 1999.

Fishbane, Michael. "Types of Biblical Intertextuality." Pages 39–44 in *Congress Volume: Oslo 1998.* Edited by André Lemaire and Magne Sæbø. VTSup 80. Leiden: Brill, 2000.

Fitzmyer, Joseph A. *The One Who Is to Come.* Grand Rapids: Eerdmans, 2007.

Fowl, Stephen E. *Engaging Scripture: A Model for Theological Interpretation.* Reprint ed. Eugene, OR: Wipf and Stock, 2008.

Fox, Michael V. *Proverbs 1–9: A New Translation with Introduction and Commentary.* AB 18A. New York: Doubleday, 2000.

France, R. T. *The Gospel of Matthew.* NICNT. Grand Rapids: Eerdmans, 2007.

Freedman, H., and M. Simon, eds. *Midrash Rabbah.* London: Soncino, 1939.

Garcia Martinez, Florentino, and Eibert J. C. Tigchelaar, eds. *The Dead Sea Scrolls Study Edition.* Grand Rapids: Eerdmans, 2000.

Gentry, Peter J. "A Preliminary Evaluation and Critique of Prosopological Exegesis." *SBJT* 23.2 (2019): 105–22.

———, and Stephen J. Wellum. *Kingdom through Covenant: A Biblical-Theological Understanding of the Covenants.* 2nd ed. Wheaton, IL: Crossway, 2018.

George, Geoman K. "Early 20th Century British Missionaries and Fulfilment Theology: Comparison of the Approaches of William Temple Gairdner to Islam in Egypt, and John Nichol Farquhar to Hinduism in India." Pages 11–22 in *Christian Witness between Continuity and New Beginnings: Modern Historical Missions in the Middle East.* Edited by Martin Tamcke and Michael Martens. Studien zur Orientalischen Kirchengeschichte 39. Berlin: LIT Verlag, 2006.

Gese, Hartmut. "Wisdom, Son of Man, and the Origins of Christology: The Consistent Development of Biblical Theology." *HBT* 3 (1981): 23–57.

Gill, John. *An Exposition of the Old Testament.* The Baptist Commentary Series. London: Matthews and Leigh, 1810.

Goldingay, John. *Approaches to Old Testament Interpretation.* Updated ed. Leicester: Apollos, 1990.

———. *Biblical Theology: The God of the Christian Scriptures.* Downers Grove, IL: InterVarsity Press, 2016.

———. *Do We Need the New Testament? Letting the Old Testament Speak for Itself.* Downers Grove, IL: InterVarsity Press, 2015.

———. *Genesis.* Baker Commentary on the Old Testament Pentateuch. Grand Rapids: Baker Academic, 2020.

———. *The Message of Isaiah 40–55: A Literary-Theological Commentary.* London: T&T Clark, 2005.

———. *Proverbs, Ecclesiastes and the Song of Songs for Everyone.* Louisville: Westminster John Knox, 2014.

———. *Reading Jesus's Bible: How the New Testament Helps Us Understand the Old Testament.* Grand Rapids: Eerdmans, 2017.

———. "Servant of Yahweh." Pages 700–707 in *Dictionary of the Old Testament Prophets.* Edited by M. J. Boda and J. G. McConville. Downers Grove, IL: InterVarsity Press, 2012.

Goldsworthy, Graeme. *Preaching the Whole Bible as Christian Scripture: The Application of Biblical Theology to Expository Preaching.* Grand Rapids: Eerdmans, 2000.

Goppelt, Leonhard. *Typos: The Typological Interpretation of the Old Testament in the New.* Translated by Donald H. Madvig. Grand Rapids: Eerdmans, 1982.

Graham, Billy. "Jesus, the Hope of the World." YouTube. www.youtube.com/watch?v=duJdk-rrl40.

Grogan, Geoffrey W. "Isaiah." Pages 435–863 in *Proverbs–Isaiah.* Edited by Tremper Longman III and David E. Garland. Revised ed. EBC 6. Grand Rapids: Zondervan, 2008.

Hamilton, Victor P. *The Book of Genesis, Chapters 18–50.* NICOT. Grand Rapids: Eerdmans, 1995.

Harshav, Benjamin. *Explorations in Poetics.* Stanford, CA: Stanford University Press, 2007.

Hawthorne, Gerald F. *Philippians.* WBC 43. Waco, TX: Word, 1983.

Hays, Richard B. *Echoes of Scripture in the Gospels.* Waco, TX: Baylor University Press, 2016.

Hays, Richard B. *Echoes of Scripture in the Letters of Paul.* New Haven: Yale University Press, 1989.

———. *Reading Backwards: Figural Christology and the Fourfold Gospel Witness.* Waco, TX: Baylor University Press, 2014.

Hill, Andrew E., and John H. Walton. *A Survey of the Old Testament.* 3rd ed. Grand Rapids: Zondervan, 2009.

Hirsch, E. D. *Validity in Interpretation.* New Haven: Yale University Press, 1967.

Hooker, Morna D. "Philippians." Pages 467–549 in *The New Interpreter's Bible, Volume 11.* Edited by Leander E. Keck. Nashville: Abingdon, 2000.

Hugenberger, G. P. "The Servant of the Lord in the 'Servant Songs' of Isaiah: A Second Moses Figure." Pages 105–40 in *The Lord's Anointed: Interpretation of Old Testament Messianic Texts.* Edited by Philip E. Satterthwaite et al. Grand Rapids: Baker Academic, 1995.

Huizenga, Leroy A. "The Old Testament in the New, Intertextuality and Allegory." *JSNT* 38 (2015): 17–35.

Hunter, Trent, and Stephen J. Wellum. *Christ from Beginning to End: How the Full Story of Scripture Reveals the Full Glory of Christ.* Grand Rapids: Zondervan, 2018.

Instone-Brewer, David. *Techniques and Assumptions in Jewish Exegesis before 70 CE.* TSAJ 30. Tübingen: Mohr Siebeck, 1992.

Irenaeus. *On the Apostolic Preaching.* Edited by John Behr. Popular Patristics Series 17. Crestwood, NY: St. Vladimir's Seminary Press, 1997.

Johnston, S. I. "Riders in the Sky: Cavalier Gods and Theurgic Salvation in the Second Century A.D." *CP* 87 (1992): 307–16.

Kaiser Jr., Walter C. "Genesis 22:2: Sacrifice Your Son?" Pages 126–27 in *Hard Sayings of the Bible*. Edited by Walter C. Kaiser Jr. et al. Downers Grove, IL: InterVarsity Press, 1996.

———. "The Identity and Mission of the 'Servant of the Lord.'" Pages 87–108 in *The Gospel according to Isaiah 53: Encountering the Suffering Servant in Jewish and Christian Theology*. Edited by Darrell L. Bock and Mitch Glaser. Grand Rapids: Kregel, 2012.

———. *Towards an Exegetical Theology: Biblical Theology for Preaching and Teaching*. Grand Rapids: Baker, 1981.

Kendrick, Graham. "The Servant-King." Thankyou Music, 1983.

Kidner, Derek. *Proverbs: An Introduction and Commentary*. TOTC 17. Downers Grove, IL: InterVarsity Press, 1964.

Kilpatrick, G. D. "1 Peter 1.11: TINA 'H POION KAIRON." *NovT* 28 (1986): 91–92.

Kline, Meredith G. *By Oath Consigned: A Reinterpretation of the Covenant Signs of Circumcision and Baptism*. Grand Rapids: Eerdmans, 1968.

Köstenberger, Andreas J. "John." Pages 415–512 in *Commentary on the New Testament Use of the Old Testament*. Edited by G. K. Beale and D. A. Carson. Grand Rapids: Baker Academic, 2007.

Kruse, Colin G. *John: An Introduction and Commentary*. 2nd ed. TNTC 4. Downers Grove, IL: InterVarsity Press, 2017.

Leeuwen, Raymond C. Van. "Proverbs." Pages 17–264 in *The New Interpreter's Bible, Volume 5*. Edited by Leander E. Keck. Nashville: Abingdon, 1997.

Leveen, Adriane. "Reading the Seams." *JSOT* 29 (2005): 259–87.

Levenson, Jon D. *The Hebrew Bible, the Old Testament, and Historical Criticism: Jews and Christians in Biblical Studies*. Louisville: Westminster John Knox, 1993.

Leventhal, Barry R. "Messianism in Proverbs." Pages 639–46 in *The Moody Handbook of Messianic Prophecy: Studies and Expositions of the Messiah in the Old Testament*. Edited by Michael A. Rydelnik and Edwin Blum. Chicago: Moody, 2019.

Levine, Baruch. *Leviticus*. JPS Torah Commentary. Philadelphia: Jewish Publication Society, 1989.

Lincoln, Andrew T. "Colossians." Pages 553–669 in *The New Interpreter's Bible, Volume 11*. Edited by Leander E. Keck. Nashville: Abingdon, 2000.

Lints, Richard. *The Fabric of Theology: A Prolegomenon to Evangelical Theology*. Grand Rapids: Eerdmans, 1993.

Lloyd-Jones, Sally. *The Jesus Storybook Bible*. Grand Rapids: Zondervan, 2007.

Logan, Alice. "Rehabilitating Jephthah." *JBL* 128 (2009): 665–85.

Longenecker, Richard N. "'Who is the Prophet Talking About?' Some Reflections on the New Testament's Use of the Old." *Them* 13 (1987): 4–8.

Longman III, Tremper. *The Fear of the Lord Is Wisdom: A Theological Introduction to Wisdom in Israel*. Grand Rapids: Baker Academic, 2017.

———. "History and the Old Testament." Pages 96–121 in *Hearing the Old Testament: Listening for God's Address*. Edited by Craig G. Bartholomew and David J. H. Beldman. Grand Rapids: Eerdmans, 2012.

———. *Immanuel in Our Place: Seeing Christ in Israel's Worship*. Phillipsburg, NJ: P&R, 2001.

———. *Old Testament Commentary Survey*. 5th ed. Grand Rapids: Baker Academic, 2013.

———. *Proverbs*. BCOTWP. Grand Rapids: Baker Academic, 2006.

————. *Psalms: An Introduction and Commentary*. TOTC 15–16. Downers Grove, IL: InterVarsity Press, 2014.

————. "Reading the Bible Postmodernly." *Mars Hill Review* 12 (1998): 23–30.

————. *Song of Songs*. NICOT. Grand Rapids: Eerdmans, 2001.

————, and Raymond B. Dillard. *An Introduction to the Old Testament*. 2nd ed. Grand Rapids: Zondervan, 2006.

Louth, Andrew. *Discerning the Mystery: An Essay on the Nature of Theology*. Oxford: Oxford University Press, 1983.

Lucey, Michael. "A Literary Object's Contextual Life." Pages 120–35 in *A Companion to Comparative Literature*. Edited by Ali Behdad and Dominic Thomas. Chichester: Wiley-Blackwell, 2011.

Margalit, Baruch. "Why King Mesha of Moab Sacrificed his Oldest Son." *BAR* 12.6 (1986): 62–63.

Martin, Ralph P. *Colossians and Philemon*. New Century Bible Commentary. Grand Rapids: Eerdmans, 1973.

McKenzie, Tracy J., and Jonathan Shelton. "From Proverb to Prophecy: Textual Production and Theology in Proverbs 30:1–6." *Southeastern Theological Review* 11.1 (2020): 3–30.

Melito of Sardis. *On Pascha: With the Fragments of Melito and Other Material Related to Quartodecimans*. Translated by Alistair Stewart-Sykes. Crestwood, NY: Saint Vladimir's Seminary, 2001.

Merkle, Benjamin L. *Discontinuity to Continuity: A Survey of Dispensational and Covenantal Theologies*. Bellingham, WA: Lexham, 2020.

Michaels, J. Ramsey. *Revelation*. IVP New Testament Commentary 20. Downers Grove, IL: IVP Academic, 1997.

Milgrom, Jacob. *Leviticus 1–16: A New Translation with Introduction and Commentary*. AB 3. New York: Doubleday, 1991.

Morris, Leon. *The Gospel according to John*. Revised ed. NICNT. Grand Rapids: Eerdmans, 1995.

Motyer, J. Alec. *The Prophecy of Isaiah: An Introduction and Commentary*. Downers Grove, IL: InterVarsity Press, 1993.

North, C. R. *The Suffering Servant in Deutero-Isaiah: An Historical and Critical Study*. 2nd ed. Oxford: Oxford University Press, 1956.

O'Brien, Peter T. *Colossians, Philemon*. WBC 44. Waco, TX Word, 1982.

Oropeza, B. J. "Intertextuality." Pages 453–63 in vol. 1 of *The Oxford Encyclopedia of Biblical Interpretation*. Edited by Steven L. McKenzie. 2 vols. Oxford: Oxford University Press, 2013.

————, and Steve Moyise, eds. *Exploring Intertextuality: Diverse Strategies for New Testament Interpretation of Texts*. Eugene, OR: Cascade, 2016.

Osborne, Grant R. *The Hermeneutical Spiral: A Comprehensive Introduction to Biblical Interpretation*. Downers Grove, IL: InterVarsity Press, 1991.

Oswalt, John N. *The Book of Isaiah, Chapters 40–66*. NICOT. Grand Rapids: Eerdmans, 1998.

Owen, John. *The Works of John Owen*. Edited by William Goold. 23 vols. Edinburgh: Banner of Truth Trust, 1965.

Pelikan, Jaroslav, and Valerie Hotchkiss, eds. *Creeds and Confessions of Faith in the Christian Tradition: Volume I: Early, Eastern and Medieval*. New Haven: Yale University Press, 2003.

Pellegrino, Cardinal Michele. "General Introduction." Pages 13–137 in *Sermons*. Works of Saint Augustine III/1. Hyde Park, NY: New City, 1990.

Petter, Thomas D. "The Meaning of Substitutionary Righteousness in Isa 53:11: A Summary of the Evidence." *TJ* 32 (2011): 165–89.

Porter, Stanley E., ed. *The Messiah in the Old and New Testaments*. Grand Rapids: Eerdmans, 2007.

Postell, Seth D. "Proverbs 8—The Messiah: Personification of Divine Wisdom." Pages 647–53 in *The Moody Handbook of Messianic Prophecy: Studies and Expositions of the Messiah in the Old Testament*. Edited by Michael A. Rydelnik and Edwin Blum. Chicago: Moody, 2019.

Rydelnik, Michael A. "The Messiah and His Titles." Pages 29–38 in *The Moody Handbook of Messianic Prophecy: Studies and Expositions of the Messiah in the Old Testament*. Edited by Michael A. Rydelnik and Edwin Blum. Chicago: Moody, 2019.

Sailhamer, John. *NIV Compact Bible Commentary*. Grand Rapids: Zondervan, 1994.

Saussure, Ferdinand de. *Course in General Linguistics*. Chicago: Open Court, 1983.

Schaff, Philip, and Henry Wace, eds. *Nicene and Post-Nicene Fathers, Second Series*. Reprint ed. 14 vols. Peabody, MA: Hendrickson, 1994.

Schreiner, Stefan. "Isaiah 53 in the Sefer Hizzuk Emunah ("Faith Strengthened") of Rabbi Isaac ben Abraham of Troki." Pages 418–61 in *The Suffering Servant: Isaiah 53 in Jewish and Christian Sources*. Edited by Bernd Janowski and Peter Stuhlmacher. Translated by Daniel P. Bailey. Grand Rapids: Eerdmans, 2004.

Schreiner, Thomas R. *The King in His Beauty: A Biblical Theology of the Old and New Testaments*. Grand Rapids: Baker, 2013.

———. *Romans*. 2nd ed. BECNT. Grand Rapids: Baker Academic, 2018.

Scott, R. B. Y. *Proverbs-Ecclesiastes*. AB 18. Garden City, NY: Doubleday, 1965.

———. "Wisdom in Creation: The 'Āmôn of Proverbs viii.30." *VT* 10 (1960): 213–23.

Scrivener, Glen. "Psalm 88: Worship, Lament and the Hope of Christ." YouTube. www.youtube.com/watch?v=HvOR-Zgz7o&t=167s.

Segal, Alan F. "'He Who Did Not Spare His Own Son . . .': Jesus, Paul, and the Aqedah." Pages 169–84 in *From Jesus to Paul: Studies in Honour of Francis Wright Beare*. Edited by Peter Richardson and John C. Hurd. Waterloo, ON: Wilfrid Laurier University Press, 1984.

Seifrid, Mark. "Romans." Pages 607–94 in *Commentary on the New Testament Use of the Old Testament*. Edited by G. K. Beale and D. A. Carson. Grand Rapids: Baker Academic, 2007.

Seitz, Christopher R. "The Book of Isaiah 40–66." Pages 307–552 in *The New Interpreter's Bible, Volume 6*. Edited by Leander E. Keck. Nashville: Abingdon, 2001.

Shepherd, Michael B. *The Text in the Middle*. StBibLit 162. New York: Lang, 2014.

Sheridan, Mark, ed. *Genesis 12–50*. ACCSOT 2. Downers Grove, IL: InterVarsity Press, 2002.

Smothers, Colin James. "In Your Mouth and in Your Heart: A Study of Deuteronomy 30:12–14 in Paul's Letter to the Romans in Canonical Context." PhD diss., The Southern Baptist Theological Seminary, 2018.

Snodgrass, Klyne. "The Use of the Old Testament in the New." Pages 29–51 in *The Right Doctrine from the Wrong Texts? Essays on the Use of the Old Testament in the New*. Edited by G. K. Beale. Grand Rapids: Baker Academic, 1994.

Spalinger, Anthony. "A Canaanite Ritual Found in Egyptian Reliefs." *JSSEA* 8 (1978): 47–60.

Spellman, Ched. "The Scribe Who Has Become a Disciple: Identifying and Becoming the Ideal Reader of the Biblical Canon." *Themelios* 41 (2016): 37–51.

———. *Toward a Canon-Conscious Reading of the Bible: Exploring the History and Hermeneutics of the Canon.* New Testament Monographs 34. Sheffield: Sheffield Phoenix Press, 2014.

Starling, David I. "Justifying Allegory: Scripture, Rhetoric, and Reason in Gal 4:21–5:1." *Journal for Theological Interpretation* 9 (2015): 227–46.

Steinmann, Andrew E. "Jesus and Possessing the Enemies' Gate (Genesis 22:17–18; 24:60)." *BSac* 174 (2017): 13–21.

Steinmetz, David C. "The Superiority of Pre-Critical Exegesis." *Theology Today* 37 (1980): 27–38.

———. *Taking the Long View: Christian Theology in Historical Perspective.* Oxford: Oxford University Press, 2009.

Stokes, Ryan E. *The Satan: How God's Executioner Became the Enemy.* Grand Rapids: Eerdmans, 2019.

Strickland, Geoffrey. *Structuralism or Criticism? Thoughts on How We Read.* Cambridge: Cambridge University Press, 1981.

Stuckenbruck, Loren T. "Messianic Ideas in Apocalyptic and Related Literature of Early Judaism." Pages 90–116 in *The Messiah in the Old and New Testaments.* Edited by Stanley E. Porter. Grand Rapids: Eerdmans, 2007.

Tabb, Brian J. *After Emmaus: How the Church Fulfills the Mission of Christ.* Wheaton, IL: Crossway, 2021.

Townend, Stuart. "How Deep the Father's Love for Us." Thankyou Music, 1995.

Vanhoozer, Kevin J. *Is There a Meaning in This Text? The Bible, the Reader, and the Morality of Literary Knowledge.* Grand Rapids: Zondervan, 1998.

Vawter, Bruce. "Prov 8:22: Wisdom and Creation." *JBL* 99 (1980): 205–16.

Wall, Robert W. *Colossians and Philemon.* IVP New Testament Commentary 10. Downers Grove, IL: IVP Academic, 1993.

Waltke, Bruce. *The Book of Proverbs, Chapters 1–15.* NICOT. Grand Rapids Eerdmans, 2004.

Walton, John H. "Genesis." in *Genesis, Exodus, Leviticus, Numbers, Deuteronomy.* Edited by John H. Walton. ZIBBCOT 1. Grand Rapids: Zondervan, 2007.

Watts, Rikk E. *Isaiah's New Exodus in Mark.* Biblical Studies Library. Grand Rapids: Baker Academic, 2000.

Westermann, Claus. *Isaiah 40–66.* Translated by David Stalker. OTL. Philadelphia: Westminster John Knox, 1969.

Wimsatt, W. K., and M. Beardsley. "The Intentional Fallacy." Pages 3–18 in *The Verbal Icon: Studies in the Meaning of Poetry.* Lexington: University Press of Kentucky, 1954.

Wolde, Ellen van. "Texts in Dialogue with Texts: Intertextuality in the Ruth and Tamar Narratives." *BibInt* 5 (1997): 1–28.

Woolf, Virginia. *The Common Reader.* New York: Harcourt, 1953.

Wright, Christopher J. H. *How to Preach and Teach the Old Testament for All Its Worth.* Grand Rapids: Zondervan Academic, 2016.

———. *Knowing Jesus through the Old Testament.* Downers Grove, IL: InterVarsity Press, 1992.

Yurco, Frank J. "3,200-Year-Old Picture of Israelites Found in Egypt." *BAR* 16.5 (1990): 20–38.

SCRIPTURE INDEX

SUBJECT INDEX